Core Data by Tutorials

iOS 8 AND SWIFT EDITION

By the raywenderlich.com Tutorial Team

Aaron Douglas, Saul Mora, Matthew Morey, Pietro Rea

Core Data by Tutorials (iOS 8 and Swift Edition)

Aaron Douglas, Saul Mora, Matthey Morey, and Pietro Rea

Notice of Rights

Notice of Liability

Trademarks

ISBN: 978-0-9896751-9-2

Table of Contents:

Dedications

"To my partner, Mike, who supports all of the weirdness that is me."

–Aaron Douglas

"To my Wife – without your tireless support behind the scenes, all my work the world enjoys would not be possible."

–Saul Mora

"To my amazing wife Tricia and my parents - Thanks for always supporting me."

–Matthew Morey

"To my Core Data mentors Otto, Ron, Ahmed and Siva."

–Pietro Rea

Introduction

By Greg Heo

What is Core Data? You'll hear a variety of answers to this question: It's a database! It's SQLite! It's *not* a database! And so forth.

Here's the technical answer: Core Data is an **object graph management** and **persistence** framework in the OS X and iOS SDKs.

That means Core Data can store and retrieve data, but it is *not* a relational database like MySQL or SQLite. Although it can use SQLite as the data store behind the scenes, you don't think about Core Data in terms of tables and rows and primary keys.

Imagine you're writing an app to keep track of dining habits. You have a varied set of objects: restaurant objects, each with properties such as name and address; categories, to organize the restaurants; and visits, to log each visit to a restaurant. The object graph in memory might look something like this:

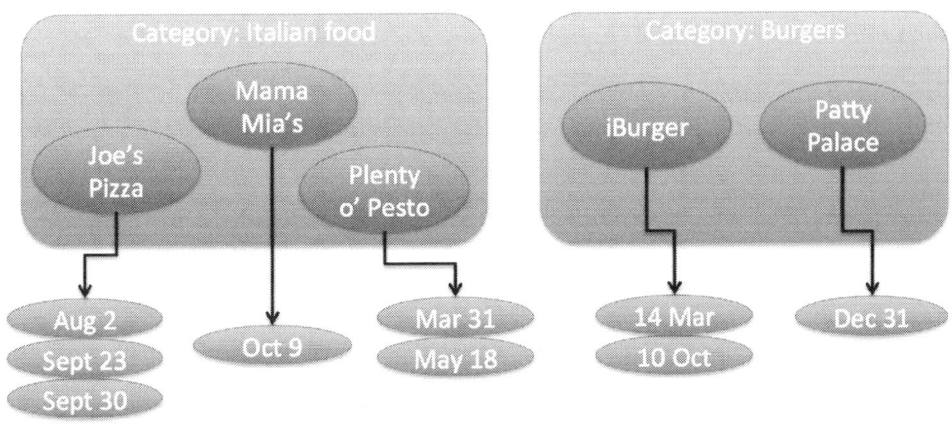

Object graph management means Core Data works with objects that you define, such as the ones in the diagram above. For example, each restaurant (represented by a red bubble) would have a property pointing back to the category object. It would also have a property holding the list of visits.

Since Cocoa is an object-oriented framework, you're probably storing data in objects already. Core Data builds on this to keep track of the objects and their relationships to each other. You can imagine expanding the graph to include what the user ordered, ratings and so on.

Persistence means the data is stored somewhere durable such as the device's flash memory or "the cloud." You point to the entire graph and just say "save." When your app launches, you just say "load" and the entire object graph pops up in memory again, ready for use. That's Core Data at work!

Maybe your users eat out a lot and have thousands of restaurant visits—rest assured Core Data is smart about lazily loading objects and caching to optimize both memory usage and speed.

Core Data has many other features aside from simply storing and fetching data: You can perform custom filtering with predicates, sort the data and synchronize a data store with iCloud, among other things. You'll learn all about these features and more in this book.

What you need

To follow along with the tutorials in this book, you'll need the following:

- **A Mac running OS X Mavericks (10.9.5) or later**. You'll need this to be able to install the latest version of Xcode.
- **Xcode 6.1 or later**. Xcode is the main development tool for iOS. You can download the latest version of Xcode for free from the Mac app store here: https://itunes.apple.com/app/xcode/id497799835?mt=12
- **One or more devices (iPhone, iPad or iPod Touch) running iOS 8 or later, and a paid membership to the iOS development program [optional]**. You'll only need a paid membership and a physical iOS device for Chapter 7, "Syncing with iCloud." For the rest of the book, you can get by with the iOS 8 Simulator that comes with Xcode.

Once you have these items in place, you'll be able to follow along with every chapter in this book.

Who this book is for

This book is for iOS developers who already know the basics of iOS and Swift, and want to learn Core Data.

If you're a complete beginner to iOS, we suggest you read through *The iOS Apprentice, 3rd Edition* first. That will give you a solid foundation in building iOS apps from the ground-up.

If you know the basics of iOS development but are new to Swift, we suggest you read *Swift by Tutorials* first. That book has a similar hands-on approach and takes you on a comprehensive tour through the Swift language.

You can find both of these prerequisite books at our store: http://www.raywenderlich.com/store

How to use this book

This book will teach you the fundamentals of Core Data by means of hands-on tutorials. You'll jump right into building a Core Data app in Chapter 1, as we think most people learn best by doing. We encourage you to type along with the instructions in the book.

If you're new to Core Data or want to review the basics, we suggest you start with Chapters 1–3. These chapters cover the fundamentals of Core Data and you'll need the knowledge in them to understand the rest of the book.

Otherwise, we suggest a pragmatic approach. Each chapter stands on its own, so you can pick and choose the chapters that interest you the most.

What's in store

Here's a quick summary of what you'll find in each chapter:

1. **Chapter 1, Your First Core Data App**: You'll click **File\New Project** and write a Core Data app from scratch! This chapter covers the basics of setting up your data model and then adding and fetching records.

2. **Chapter 2, NSManagedObject Subclasses**: `NSManagedObject` is the base data storage class of your Core Data object graphs. This chapter will teach you how you customize your own managed object subclasses to store and validate data.
3. **Chapter 3, The Core Data Stack**: Under the hood, Core Data is made up of many parts working together. In this chapter, you'll learn about how these parts fit together, and move away from the starter Xcode template to build your own customizable system.
4. **Chapter 4, Intermediate Fetching**: Your apps will fetch data all the time, and Core Data offers many options for getting the data to you efficiently. This chapter covers more advanced fetch requests, predicates, sorting and asynchronous fetching.
5. **Chapter 5, NSFetchedResultsController**: Table views are at the core of many iOS apps, and Apple wants to make Core Data play nicely with them! In this chapter, you'll learn how `NSFetchedResultsController` can save you time and code when your table views are backed by data from Core Data.
6. **Chapter 6, Versioning and Migration**: As you update and enhance your app, its data model will almost certainly need to change. In this chapter, you'll learn how to create multiple versions of your data model and then migrate your users forward so they can keep their existing data as they upgrade.
7. **Chapter 7, Syncing with iCloud**: Move beyond storing data locally on a single device, to cloud storage and synchronizing across all the user's devices. This chapter covers how to extend an existing Core Data app to use iCloud.
8. **Chapter 8, Unit Tests**: Testing is an important part of the development process, and you shouldn't leave Core Data out of those tests! In this chapter, you'll learn how to set up a separate test environment for Core Data and see examples of how to test your models.
9. **Chapter 9, Measuring and Boosting Performance**: No one ever complained that an app was too fast, so it's important to be vigilant about tracking performance. In this chapter, you'll learn how to measure your app's performance with various Xcode tools and then pick up some tips for dealing with slow spots in your code.
10. **Chapter 10, Multiple Managed Object Contexts**: In this final chapter, you'll expand the usual Core Data stack to include multiple managed object contexts. You'll learn how this can improve perceived performance and help make your app architecture less monolithic and more compartmentalized.

Source code and forums

You can get the source code for the book here:

- http://www.raywenderlich.com/store/core-data-by-tutorials/source-code

Some of the chapters also include starter projects or other required resources, and you'll definitely want to have these on hand as you go through the book.

We've set up an official forum for the book at http://www.raywenderlich.com/forums. This is a great place to ask questions you have about the book or about developing Core Data apps, or to submit any errors or suggested updates.

PDF Version

We also have a PDF version of this book available, which can be handy if you ever want to copy/paste code or search for a specific term through the book as you're developing.

And speaking of the PDF version, we have some good news!

Since you purchased the physical copy of this book, you are eligible to buy the PDF version at a significant discount if you would like (if you don't have it already). For more details, see this page:

- http://www.raywenderlich.com/store/core-data-by-tutorials/upgrade

License

By purchasing *Core Data by Tutorials*, you have the following license:

- You are allowed to use and/or modify the source code in *Core Data by Tutorials* in as many apps as you want, with no attribution required.
- You are allowed to use and/or modify all art, images and designs that are included in *Core Data by Tutorials* in as many apps as you want, but must include this attribution line somewhere inside your app: "Artwork/images/designs: from *Core Data by Tutorials* book, available at http://www.raywenderlich.com."

- The source code included in *Core Data by Tutorials* is for your personal use only. You are NOT allowed to distribute or sell the source code in *Core Data by Tutorials* without prior authorization.

About the authors

Pietro Rea is an iOS developer based in Hoboken, NJ. He started writing code in high school and currently specializes in Objective-C, Swift and iOS. These days, he develops mobile applications for Quidsi, an Amazon company. You can follow him on Twitter as @pietrorea or on his blog at www.pietrorea.com

Saul Mora is an engineer at Coursera, in Mountain View, California. He enjoys writing apps, riding bicycles and traveling the world. Saul is a frequent speaker at many iOS and Mac developer conferences and also produces a podcast for developers called NSBrief (nsbrief.com). Occasionally, you can find Saul teaching the wonders of programming to the next generation of developers.

Aaron Douglas was that kid taking apart the home appliances at five years of age to see how they worked. Today he's a full-time iOS developer with a passion for doing things right the first time. He enjoys camping during the summer and pretending to be a storm chaser while sitting at home. Find him on the Interwebs as @astralbodies.

Matthew Morey is an engineer, developer, hacker, creator, and tinkerer. As an active member of the iOS community and a Lead Developer at ChaiOne he has led numerous successful mobile projects worldwide.

When not developing apps he enjoys traveling, snowboarding, and surfing. He blogs about technology and business at matthewmorey.com.

About the editors

Richard Turton was the technical editor for this book. He is an iOS developer for a leading UK mobile agency, a prolific Stack Overflow participant and the author of a development blog, commandshift.co.uk.

When he's not in front of a computer, he is underneath one or both of his daughters as a horse, monkey or cushion.

Bradley C. Phillips was the editor for this book, and was the first editor to come aboard at raywenderlich.com. He has worked as a journalist and previously directed the intelligence department of an investigative firm in New York City.

Right now, Bradley works freelance and pursues his own projects. Contact him if you need a skilled and experienced editor for your blog, books or anything else.

Greg Heo was the final pass editor for this book, and has been part of the editorial team at raywenderlich.com since 2012.

He has been nerding out with computers since the Commodore 64 era in the 80s and continues to this day on the web and on iOS. He likes caffeine, codes with two-space tabs and writes with semicolons.

Chapter 1: Your First Core Data App

By Pietro Rea

Welcome to Core Data! In this chapter, you'll write your very first Core Data app. You'll see how easy it is to get started with all the resources provided in Xcode, from the starter code templates to the data model editor.

You're going to hit the ground running right from the first chapter in this book; by the end of the chapter you'll know how to:

- model data you want to store in Core Data using Xcode's model editor;
- add new records to Core Data;
- fetch a set of records from Core Data; and
- display the fetched results to the user in a table view.

You'll also get a sense of what Core Data is doing behind the scenes, and how you can interact with the various moving pieces there. This will put you well on your way to understanding the next two chapters, which continue the introduction to Core Data with more advanced models and data validation, amongst other things.

We're getting ahead of ourselves though – it's time to build an app!

Getting started

Open Xcode and create a new iPhone project based on the **Single View Application** template. Call the app **HitList** and make sure **Use Core Data** is checked:

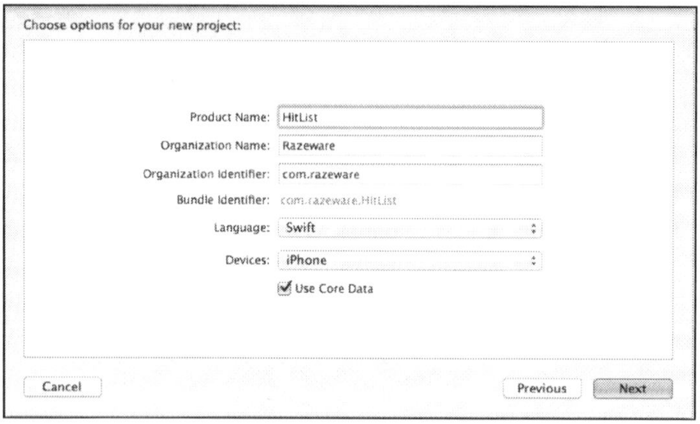

Checking the **Use Core Data** box will cause Xcode to generate boilerplate code for what's known as a **Core Data stack** in **AppDelegate.swift**.

The Core Data stack consists of a set of objects that facilitate saving and retrieving information from Core Data. There's an object to manage the Core Data state as a whole, an object representing the data model, and so on.

You'll learn about each of these pieces in these first few chapters. Later, you'll even have the chance to write your own Core Data stack! The standard stack works just fine for many apps but based on your app and its data, you can customize the stack to be more efficient.

> **Note:** Not all Xcode templates have the option to start with Core Data. In Xcode 6, only the **Master-Detail Application** and the **Single View Application** templates have the **Use Core Data** checkbox.

The idea for this sample app is simple. There will be a table view with a list of names for your very own "hit list". You'll be able to add names to this list and eventually, you'll use Core Data to make sure the data is stored between sessions. We don't condone violence in this book so you can think of this app as a "favorites list" to keep track of your friends too, of course! ;]

Click on **Main.storyboard** to open it in Interface Builder. Select its only view controller and change its size class to Regular Height and Compact Width to match an iPhone in portrait mode:

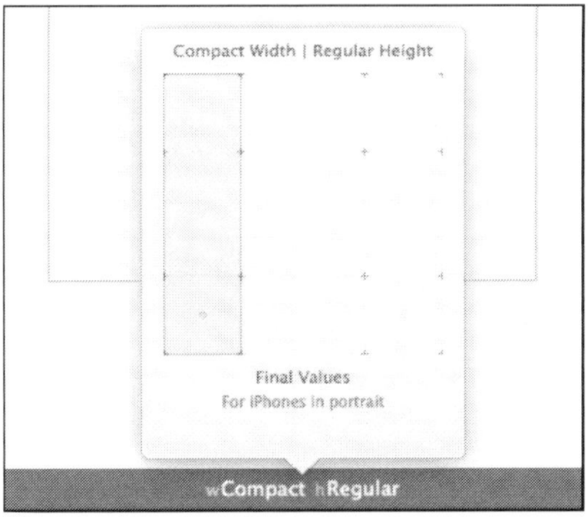

Next, embed the view controller in a navigation controller. From Xcode's **Editor** menu, select **Embed In...\ Navigation Controller**.

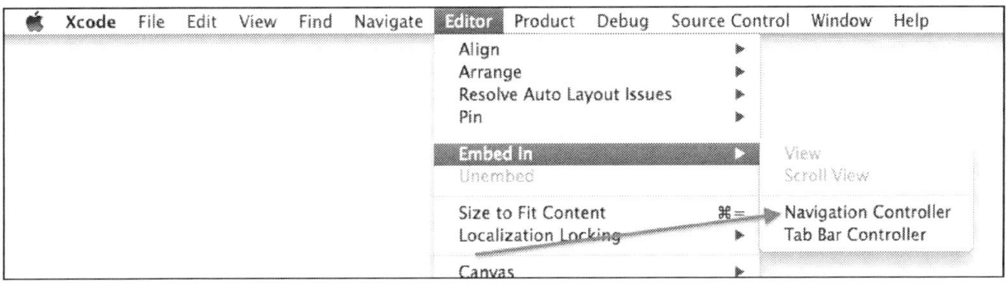

Back in Interface Builder, drag a **Table View** from the object library into the view controller so that it covers the entire view.

Then, drag a **Bar Button Item** and place it on the view controller's newly added navigation bar. Finally, double-click the bar button item to change its text to **Add**.

Your canvas should now look like the following screenshot:

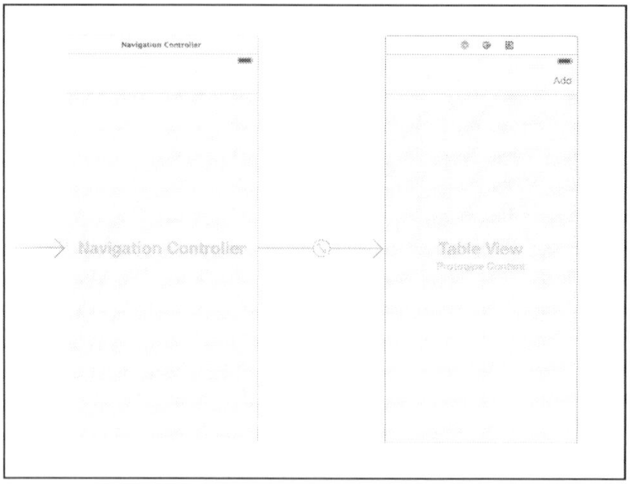

Every time you tap **Add** on the top-right, an alert containing a text field will appear on the screen. From there you'll be able to type someone's name into the text field. Dismissing the alert will save the name and refresh the table view with all the names you've saved up to that point.

Before you can do that, you need to make the view controller the table view's data source. Ctrl-drag from the table view to the yellow view controller icon above the navigation bar, as shown below, and click on **dataSource**:

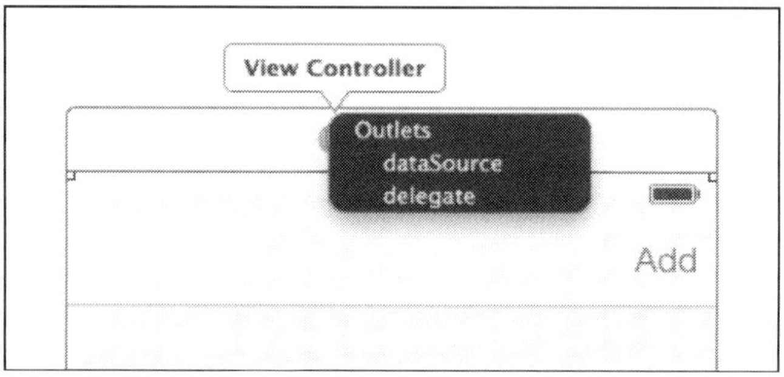

In case you were wondering, you don't need to set up the table view's delegate since tapping on the cells won't trigger any action. It doesn't get simpler than this!

Open the Assistant Editor by hitting Command-Option-Enter or by selecting the middle button on the Editor toolset on the Xcode bar. Ctrl-drag from the table view onto **ViewController.swift**, inside the class definition to insert an outlet:

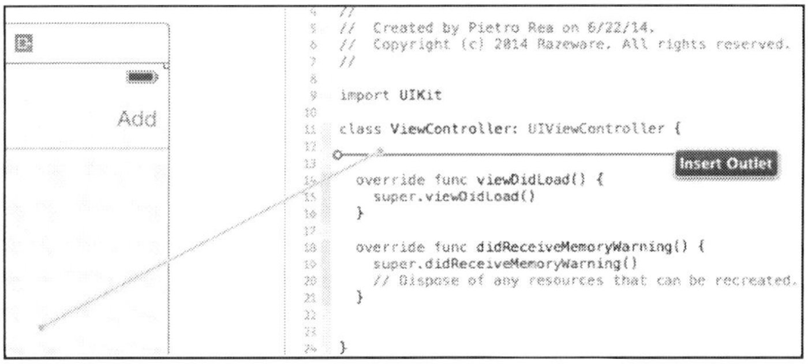

Name the new `IBOutlet` property `tableView`, resulting in the following line:

```
@IBOutlet weak var tableView: UITableView!
```

Ctrl-drag from the **Add** bar button item onto **ViewController.swift**, but this time, create an action instead of an outlet and name the method `addName`:

```
@IBAction func addName(sender: AnyObject) {

}
```

You can now refer to the table view and the bar button item's action in code. Next, set up the model for the table view. Add the following property to **ViewController.swift**:

```
//Insert below the tableView IBOutlet
var names = [String]()
```

`names` is a mutable `Array` to hold the strings for the table view to display.

Replace the implementation of `viewDidLoad` with the following:

```
override func viewDidLoad() {
  super.viewDidLoad()
  title = "\"The List\""
  tableView.registerClass(UITableViewCell.self,
    forCellReuseIdentifier: "Cell")
}
```

This will set a title and register the `UITableViewCell` class with the table view. You do this so that when you dequeue a cell, the table view will return a cell of the correct type.

Still in **ViewController.swift**, declare that `ViewController` will conform to the `UITableViewDataSource` protocol by editing the class declaration:

```
//Add UITableViewDataSource to class declaration
class ViewController: UIViewController, UITableViewDataSource {
```

Immediately, Xcode will complain about `ViewController` not conforming to the protocol. Below `viewDidLoad`, implement the following data source methods to fix the error:

```
// MARK: UITableViewDataSource
func tableView(tableView: UITableView,
    numberOfRowsInSection section: Int) -> Int {
    return names.count
}

func tableView(tableView: UITableView,
  cellForRowAtIndexPath
  indexPath: NSIndexPath) -> UITableViewCell {

    let cell =
        tableView.dequeueReusableCellWithIdentifier("Cell")
        as UITableViewCell

    cell.textLabel.text = names[indexPath.row]

  return cell
}
```

If you've ever worked with `UITableView`, this code should look very familiar. The first method says that the table view will have as many rows as the `names` array has strings.

The second method, `tableView(_:cellForRowAtIndexPath:)`, dequeues table view cells and populates them with the corresponding string in the `names` array.

Don't run the app just yet. First, you need a way to input names so the table view can display them.

Implement the `addName` `IBAction` method you Ctrl-dragged into your code earlier:

```
//Implement the addName IBAction
@IBAction func addName(sender: AnyObject) {

  var alert = UIAlertController(title: "New name",
      message: "Add a new name",
      preferredStyle: .Alert)
```

```
    let saveAction = UIAlertAction(title: "Save",
     style: .Default) { (action: UIAlertAction!) -> Void in

      let textField = alert.textFields![0] as UITextField
      self.names.append(textField.text)
      self.tableView.reloadData()
    }

    let cancelAction = UIAlertAction(title: "Cancel",
      style: .Default) { (action: UIAlertAction!) -> Void in
    }

    alert.addTextFieldWithConfigurationHandler {
      (textField: UITextField!) -> Void in
    }

    alert.addAction(saveAction)
    alert.addAction(cancelAction)

    presentViewController(alert,
        animated: true,
        completion: nil)
  }
```

Every time you tap the **Add** bar button item, this method presents an `UIAlertController` with a text field and two buttons, **Save** and **Cancel**.

Save takes whatever text is currently in the text field, inserts it into the `name` array and reloads the table view. Since the `names` array is the model backing the table view, whatever you typed into the text field will appear in the table view.

Finally it's time to build and run your app for the first time. Tap the **Add** bar button item.

The alert controller will look like this:

Add four or five names to the list. You should wind up with something like this:

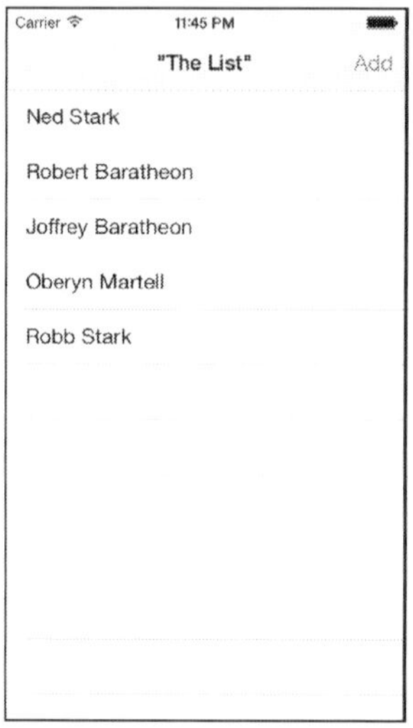

Your table view will display the data and your array will store the names, but the big thing missing here is **persistence**. The array is in memory but if you force quit the app or reboot your device, your hit list will be wiped out.

Core Data provides persistence, meaning it can store data in a more durable state so that it can outlive an app re-launch or a device reboot.

You haven't added any Core Data yet, so nothing should persist after you navigate away from the app. Let's test this out. Press the Home button if you're using a physical device or the equivalent (Shift+⌘+H) if you're on the Simulator. This will take you back to the familiar app grid on the home screen:

From the home screen, tap the **HitList** icon to bring the app back to the foreground. The names are still on the screen. What happened?

When you tap the Home button, the app that's currently in the foreground goes to the background. When this happens, the operating system flash-freezes everything currently in memory, including the strings in the `names` array. Similarly, when it's time to wake up and return to the foreground, the operating system restores what used to be in memory as if you'd never left.

Apple introduced these advances in multitasking back in iOS 4. They create a seamless experience for iOS users but add a wrinkle to the definition of persistence for iOS developers. Are the names really persisted?

No, not really. If you had completely killed the app in the fast app switcher or turned off your phone, those names would be gone. You can verify this, as well.

With the app in the foreground, double tap the Home button to enter the fast app switcher, like so:

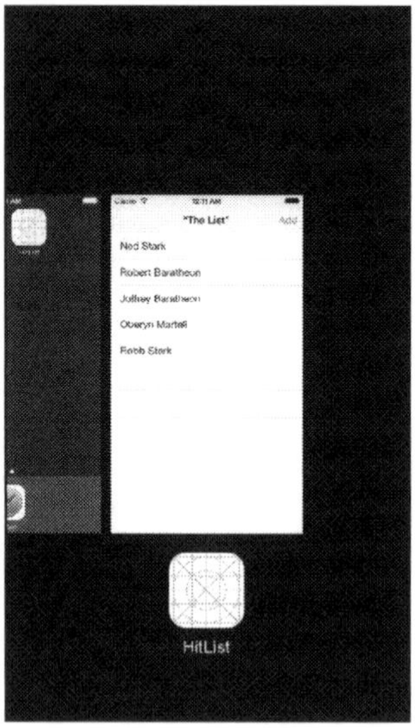

From here, flick the HitList app snapshot upwards to terminate the app. There should be no trace of HitList in living memory (no pun intended). Verify that the names are gone by returning to the home screen and tapping on the HitList icon to trigger a fresh launch.

This difference between flash-freezing and persistence may be obvious if you've been working with iOS for some time and are familiar with the way multitasking works. In a user's mind, however, there is no difference. The user doesn't care if the names are "still there" because the app went into the background and came back, or because the app saved and reloaded them.

All that matters is that the names are still there when she comes back!

So the real test of persistence, the one you will use in this book, is whether your data is still there after a fresh app launch.

Modeling your data

Now that you know how to check for persistence, let's get started with Core Data. Your goal for the HitList app is simple: to persist the names you enter so they're available for viewing after a fresh app launch.

Up to this point, you've been using plain old Swift strings to store the names in memory. In this section, you'll replace these strings with Core Data objects.

The first step is to create a **managed object model**, which spells out the way Core Data represents data on disk. By default, Core Data uses an SQLite database as the persistent store (more on this later), so you can think of the data model as the database schema.

> **Note:** You'll come across the word "managed" quite a bit in this book. If you see "managed" in the name of a class, such as in `NSManagedObjectContext`, chances are you are dealing with a Core Data class. "Managed" refers to Core Data's management of the life cycle of Core Data objects.
>
> However, don't assume that all Core Data classes contain the word "managed"—actually, most don't. For a comprehensive list of Core Data classes, check out the Objective-C umbrella header `<CoreData/CoreData.h>`.

Since you elected to use Core Data when you created the HitList project, Xcode automatically created a data model file for you and named it **HitList.xcdatamodeld**.

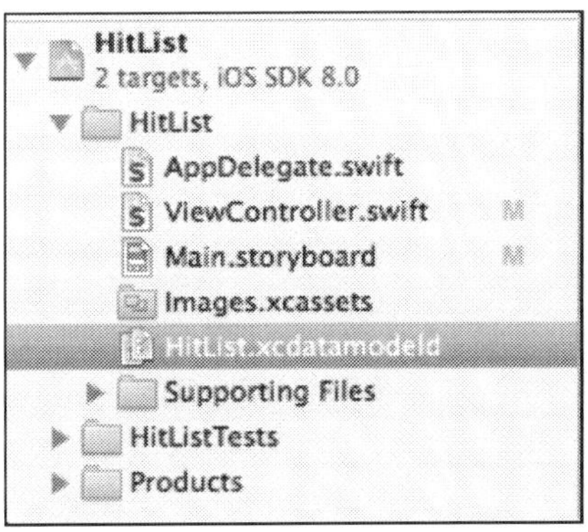

Click on **HitList.xcdatamodeld** to open it. As you can see, Xcode has a powerful data model editor that looks like this:

The data model editor has a lot of features that you'll explore in later chapters. For now, let's focus on creating a single Core Data entity.

Click on **Add Entity** on the lower-left to create a new entity. Double-click on the new entity and change its name to **Person**, like so:

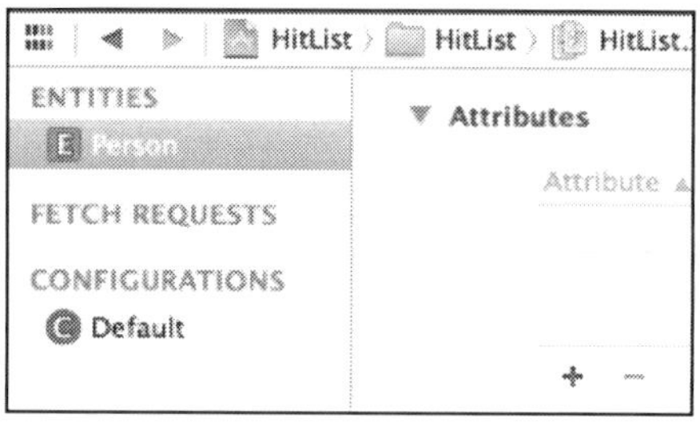

You may be wondering why the model editor uses the term "Entity." Weren't you simply defining a new class? As you'll see shortly, Core Data comes with its own vocabulary. Here's a quick rundown of some of the terms you'll commonly encounter:

- An **entity** is a class definition in Core Data. The classic example is an `Employee` or a `Company`. In a relational database, an entity corresponds to a table.

- An **attribute** is a piece of information attached to a particular entity. For example, an `Employee` entity could have attributes for the employee's name, position and salary. In a database, an attribute corresponds to a particular field in a table.
- A **relationship** is a link between multiple entities. In Core Data, relationships between two entities are called **to-one relationships**, while those between one and many entities are called **to-many relationships**. For example, a `Manager` can have a to-many relationship with a set of employees, whereas an individual `Employee` will have a to-one relationship with his manager.

> **Note:** As you've probably noticed, entities sound a lot like a classes. Likewise, attributes/relationships sound a lot like properties. What's the difference? You can think of a Core Data entity as a class "definition" and the managed object as an instance of that class.

Now that you know what an attribute is, go back to the model editor and add an attribute to `Person`. Select `Person` on the left-hand side and click the plus sign (+) under **Attributes**.

Set the new attribute's name to, well, **name** and change its type to **String**:

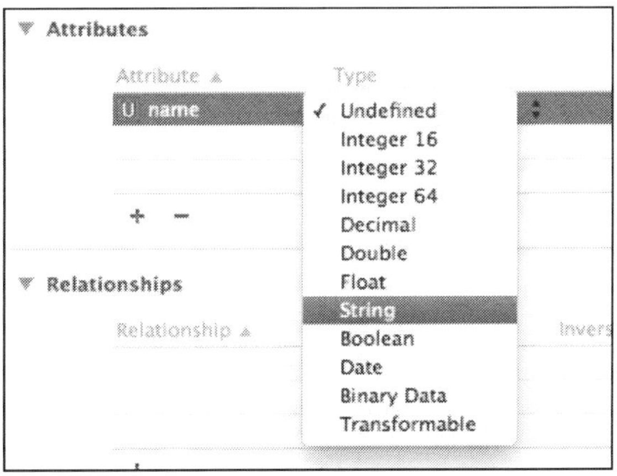

In Core Data, an attribute can be of one of several data types. You will learn about these in the next few chapters.

Saving to Core Data

Import the Core Data module at the top of **ViewController.swift**:

```
//Add below "import UIKit"
import CoreData
```

You may have had to link frameworks manually in your project's Build Phases if you've worked with Objective-C frameworks. In Swift, a simple `import` statement is all you need to start using Core Data APIs in your code.

Next, replace the table view's model with the following:

```
//Change [String] to [NSManagedObject]
var people = [NSManagedObject]()
```

You'll be storing `Person` entities rather than just names, so you rename the `Array` that serves as the table view's data model to `people`. It now holds instances of `NSManagedObject` rather than simple Swift strings.

`NSManagedObject` represents a single object stored in Core Data—you must use it to create, edit, save and delete from your Core Data persistent store. As you'll see shortly, `NSManagedObject` is a shape-shifter. It can take the form of any entity in your data model, appropriating whatever attributes and relationships you defined.

Since you're changing the table view's model, you must also replace both data source methods you implemented earlier with the following to reflect these changes:

```
//Replace both UITableViewDataSource methods
func tableView(tableView: UITableView,
    numberOfRowsInSection section: Int) -> Int {
    return people.count
}

func tableView(tableView: UITableView,
  cellForRowAtIndexPath
  indexPath: NSIndexPath) -> UITableViewCell {

  let cell =
      tableView.dequeueReusableCellWithIdentifier("Cell")
      as UITableViewCell

  let person = people[indexPath.row]
  cell.textLabel.text = person.valueForKey("name") as String?
```

```
    return cell
}
```

The most significant change to these methods occurs in `cellForRowAtIndexPath`. Instead of matching cells with the corresponding string in the model array, you now match cells with the corresponding `NSManagedObject`.

Note how you grab the `name` attribute from the `NSManagedObject`. It happens here:

```
cell.textLabel.text = person.valueForKey("name") as String
```

Why do you have to do this? As it turns out, `NSManagedObject` doesn't know about the `name` attribute you defined in your data model, so there's no way of accessing it directly with a property. The only way Core Data provides to read the value is key-value coding, commonly referred to as KVC.

> **Note:** If you're new to iOS development, you may not be familiar with key-value coding or KVC.
>
> KVC is a mechanism in Cocoa and Cocoa Touch for accessing an object's properties indirectly using strings to identify properties. In this case, KVC makes `NSMangedObject` behave more or less like a dictionary.
>
> Key-value coding is available to all classes that descend from `NSObject`, including `NSManagedObject`. You wouldn't be able to access properties using KVC on a Swift object that doesn't descend from `NSObject`.

Next, replace the save action in the `addName` `@IBAction` method with the following:

```
let saveAction = UIAlertAction(title: "Save",
 style: .Default) { (action: UIAlertAction!) -> Void in

  let textField = alert.textFields![0] as UITextField
  self.saveName(textField.text)
  self.tableView.reloadData()
}
```

This takes the text in the text field and passes it over to a new method called `saveName`. Add `saveName` to **ViewController.swift**, as shown below:

```
func saveName(name: String) {
  //1
  let appDelegate =
  UIApplication.sharedApplication().delegate as AppDelegate

  let managedContext = appDelegate.managedObjectContext!

  //2
  let entity =  NSEntityDescription.entityForName("Person",
    inManagedObjectContext:
    managedContext)

  let person = NSManagedObject(entity: entity!,
    insertIntoManagedObjectContext:managedContext)

  //3
  person.setValue(name, forKey: "name")

  //4
  var error: NSError?
  if !managedContext.save(&error) {
      println("Could not save \(error), \(error?.userInfo)")
  }
  //5
  people.append(person)
}
```

This is where Core Data kicks in! Here's what the code does:

1. Before you can save or retrieve anything from your Core Data store, you first need to get your hands on an `NSManagedObjectContext`. You can think of a managed object context as an in-memory "scratchpad" for working with managed objects.

   Think of saving a new managed object to Core Data as a two-step process: first, you insert a new managed object into a managed object context; then, after you're happy with your shiny new managed object, you "commit" the changes in your managed object context to save it to disk.

   Xcode has already generated a managed object context as part of the new project's template – remember, this only happens if you check the **Use Core Data** checkbox at the beginning. This default managed object context lives as a property of the application delegate. To access it, you first get a reference to the app delegate.

2. You create a new managed object and insert it into the managed object context. You can do this in one step with `NSManagedObject`'s designated initializer: `init(entity:insertIntoManagedObjectContext:)`.

   You may be wondering what an `NSEntityDescription` is all about. Recall that earlier, I called `NSManagedObject` a "shape-shifter" class because it can represent any entity. An entity description is the piece that links the entity definition from your data model with an instance of `NSManagedObject` at runtime.

3. With an `NSManagedObject` in hand, you set the `name` attribute using key-value coding. You have to spell the KVC key ("name" in this case) *exactly* as it appears on your data model, otherwise your app will crash at runtime.

4. You commit your changes to `person` and save to disk by calling `save` on the managed object context. Note that `save` takes one parameter, which is a pointer to an `NSError`; if there is ever an error with the save operation, you can inspect the error and alert the user if necessary.

5. Congratulations! Your new managed object is now safely ensconced in your Core Data persistent store. Insert the new managed object into the `people` array so that it shows up in the table view when it reloads.

That's a little more complicated than an array of strings, but not too bad. Some of the code here—getting the managed object context and entity—could be done just once in your own `init` or `viewDidLoad` and then reused later. For simplicity, you're doing it all at once in one method.

Build and run the app, and add a few names to the table view:

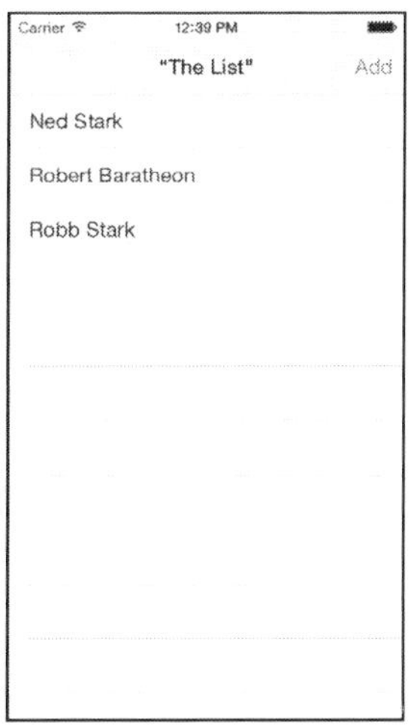

If the names are actually stored in Core Data, the HitList app should pass the persistence test. Double-tap the Home button to bring up the fast app switcher. Terminate the HitList app by flicking it upwards.

From Springboard, tap the HitList app to trigger a fresh launch. Wait, what happened? The table view is empty:

You saved to Core Data, but after a fresh app launch, the `people` array is empty! The data is actually sitting there waiting, but you haven't fetched it yet.

Fetching from Core Data

To get data from your persistent store and into the managed object context, you have to **fetch** it. Add the following method to **ViewController.swift**:

```
override func viewWillAppear(animated: Bool) {
  super.viewWillAppear(animated)

  //1
  let appDelegate =
  UIApplication.sharedApplication().delegate as AppDelegate

  let managedContext = appDelegate.managedObjectContext!

  //2
  let fetchRequest = NSFetchRequest(entityName:"Person")

  //3
  var error: NSError?

  let fetchedResults =
```

```
    managedContext.executeFetchRequest(fetchRequest,
    error: &error) as [NSManagedObject]?

  if let results = fetchedResults {
    people = results
  } else {
    println("Could not fetch \(error), \(error!.userInfo)")
  }
}
```

Step by step, this is what the code does:

1. As mentioned in the previous section, before you can do anything with Core Data, you need a managed object context. Fetching is no different! You pull up the application delegate and grab a reference to its managed object context.

2. As the name suggests, `NSFetchRequest` is the class responsible for fetching from Core Data. Fetch requests are both powerful and flexible. You can use requests to fetch a set of objects that meet particular criteria (e.g., "give me all employees that live in Wisconsin and have been with the company at least three years"), individual values (e.g., "give me the longest name in the database") and more.

   Fetch requests have several qualifiers that refine the set of results they return. You'll learn more about these qualifiers in Chapter 4, "Intermediate Fetching"; for now, you should know that `NSEntityDescription` is one of these qualifiers (one that is required!).

   Setting a fetch request's `entity` property, or alternatively initializing it with `init(entityName:)`, fetches *all* objects of a particular entity. This is what you do here to fetch all `Person` entities.

3. You hand the fetch request over to the managed object context to do the heavy lifting. `executeFetchRequest(_:error:)` returns an optional array of managed objects that meets the criteria specified by the fetch request.

> **Note:** If there are no objects that match the fetch request's criteria, the method returns an optional value containing an empty array.
>
> If an error occurred during the fetch, the method returns an optional value that contains nil. If this happens, you can inspect the `NSError` and respond appropriately.

Build and run the application once again. Immediately, you should see the list of names you added earlier:

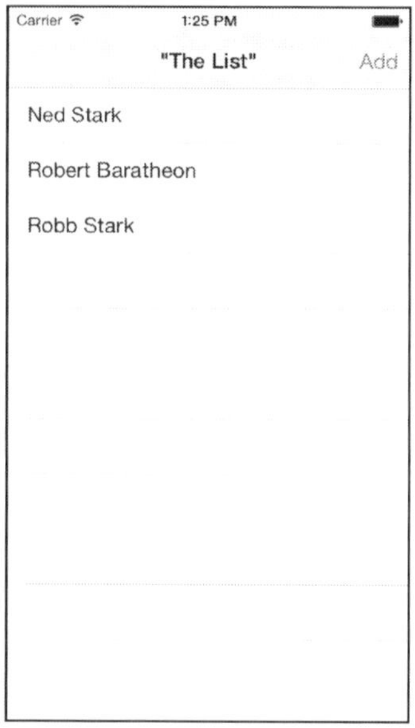

Great! They're back from the dead. Add a few more names to the list and restart the app to verify that saving and fetching are working properly. Short of deleting the app, resetting the Simulator or throwing your phone off a tall building, the names will appear in the table view no matter what.

Where to go from here?

In just a few pages, you've already experienced several fundamental Core Data concepts: data models, entities, attributes, managed objects, managed object contexts and fetch requests.

There were a few rough edges in HitList: you had to get the managed object context from the app delegate each time, and you used KVC to access the attributes rather than a more natural object-style `person.name`.

The best way to get familiar with Core Data is to play with it, so that's exactly what you'll do in the next chapter! You'll file away some of those rough edges and also work with a more complex data model as you learn more about Core Data.

Chapter 2: NSManagedObject Subclasses

By Pietro Rea

You got your feet wet with a simple Core Data app in chapter 1; now it's time to explore more of what Core Data has to offer!

At the core of this chapter is subclassing `NSManagedObject` to make your own classes for each entity. This creates a direct one-to-one mapping between entities in the data model editor and classes in your code. It means in some parts of your code, you can work with objects and properties without worrying too much about the Core Data side of things.

Along the way, you'll learn about all the data types available in Core Data entities, including a couple that are outside the usual string and number types. And with all the data type options available, you'll also learn about validating data to automatically check values before saving.

Getting started

Head over to the files that accompany this book and open the sample project named **Bow Ties**. Like HitList, this project uses Xcode's Core Data-enabled **Single View Application** template. And like before, this means Xcode generated its own ready-to-use Core Data stack located in **AppDelegate.swift**.

Go to **Main.storyboard**. Here you'll find the sample project's single-page UI:

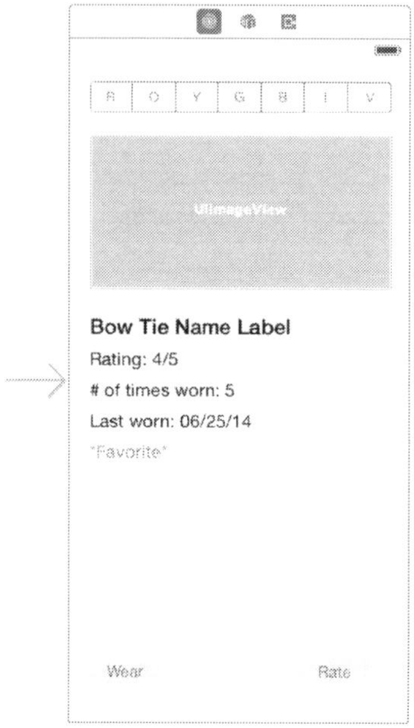

As you can probably guess, Bow Ties is a lightweight bow tie management application. You can switch between the different colors of bow tie you own—the app assumes one of each—using the topmost segmented control—tap "R" for red, "O" for orange and so on.

Tapping on a particular color pulls up an image of the tie and populates several labels on the screen with specific information about the tie. This includes:

- The name of the bow tie (so you can tell similarly-colored ones apart);
- The number of times you've worn the tie;
- The date you last wore the tie;
- Whether the tie is a favorite of yours.

The **Wear** button on the bottom-left increments the number of times you've worn that particular tie and sets the "last worn" date to today.

Orange is not your color? Not to worry. The **Rate** button on the bottom-right changes a bow tie's rating. This particular rating system uses a scale from 0 to 5, allowing for decimal values.

That's what the application is *supposed* to do in its final state. Open **ViewController.swift** to see what it currently does:

```
import UIKit

class ViewController: UIViewController {

  @IBOutlet weak var segmentedControl: UISegmentedControl!
  @IBOutlet weak var imageView: UIImageView!
  @IBOutlet weak var nameLabel: UILabel!
  @IBOutlet weak var ratingLabel: UILabel!
  @IBOutlet weak var timesWornLabel: UILabel!
  @IBOutlet weak var lastWornLabel: UILabel!
  @IBOutlet weak var favoriteLabel: UILabel!

  override func viewDidLoad() {
    super.viewDidLoad()

  }

  @IBAction func segmentedControl(control: UISegmentedControl) {

  }

  @IBAction func wear(sender: AnyObject) {

  }

  @IBAction func rate(sender: AnyObject) {

  }
}
```

The bad news is that in its current state, Bow Ties doesn't do anything. The good news is that you don't need to do any Ctrl-dragging!

The segmented control and all the labels on the user interface are already connected to `@IBOutlets` in code. In addition, the segmented control, the Wear button and the Rate button all have corresponding `@IBActions`.

It looks like you have everything you need to get started adding some Core Data… but wait, what are you going to display onscreen? There's no input method to speak of, so the app must ship with sample data.

That's exactly right. Bow Ties includes a property list called **SampleData.plist** that contains the information for seven sample ties, one for each color of the rainbow:

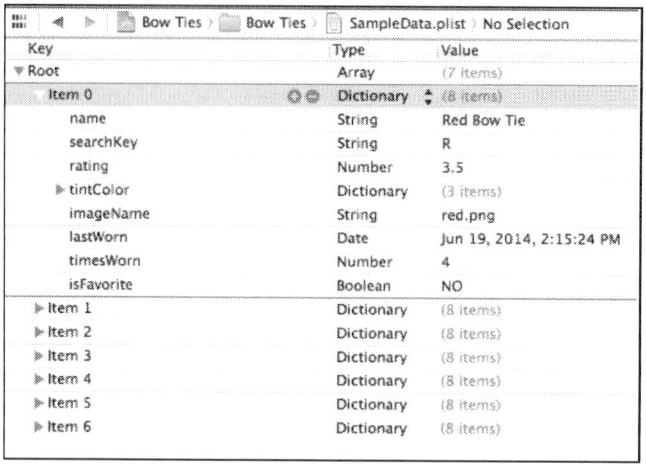

Furthermore, the application's asset catalog—**Images.xcassets**—contains seven images corresponding to the seven bow ties in **SampleData.plist**.

What you have to do now is take this sample data, store it in Core Data and use it to implement the bow tie management functionality.

Modeling your data

In the previous chapter, you learned that one of the first things you have to do when starting a new Core Data project is create your data model.

Open **Bow_Ties.xcdatamodeld** and click **Add Entity** on the lower-left to create a new entity. Double-click on the new entity and change its name to **Bowtie**, like so:

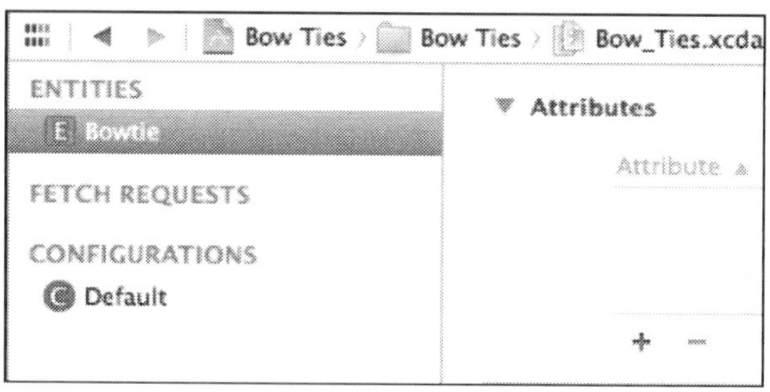

In the previous chapter, you created a simple `Person` entity with a single string attribute to hold the person's name. Core Data supports several other primitive data types, and you'll use most of them for the new `Bowtie` entity.

An attribute's data type determines what kind of data you can store in it and how much space it will occupy on disk. In Core Data, an attribute's data type begins as `Undefined` so you'll have to change it to something else.

If you remember from **SampleData.plist**, each bow tie has eight associated pieces of information. This means the `Bowtie` entity will end up with at least eight attributes in the model editor.

Select `Bowtie` on the left-hand side and click the plus sign (+) under **Attributes**. Change the new attribute's name to **name** and set its type to **String**:

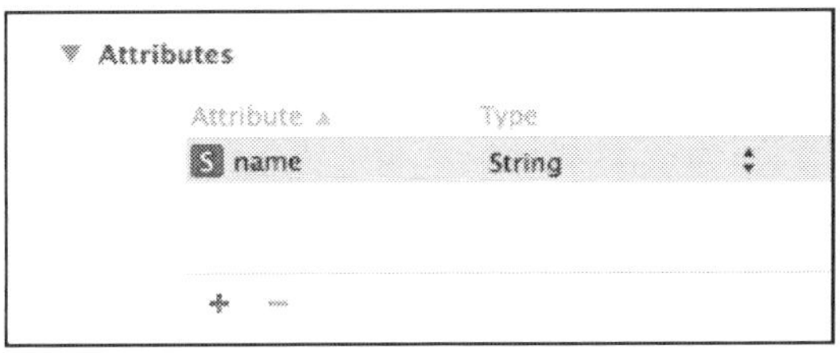

Repeat this process five more times to add the following attributes:

- A **Boolean** named **isFavorite**;
- A **Date** named **lastWorn**;
- A **Double** named **rating**;
- A **String** named **searchKey**;
- An **Integer 32** named **timesWorn**.

When you're finished, your Attributes section should look like this:

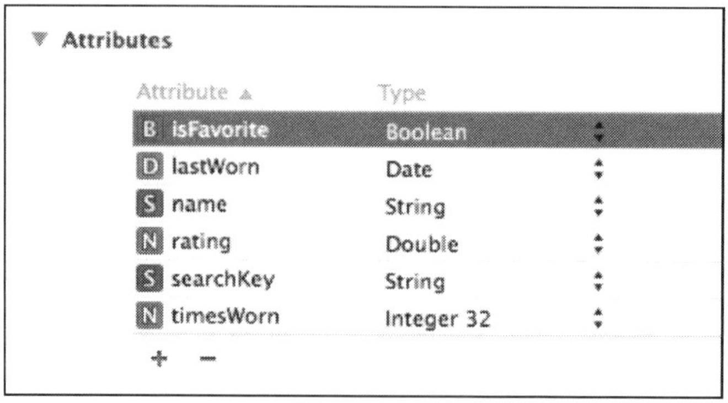

Don't worry if the order of the attributes is different – all that matters is that the attribute names and types are correct.

> **Note:** You may have noticed you have three options for the `timesWorn` integer attribute: **Integer 16**, **Integer 32** or **Integer 64**.
>
> 16, 32 and 64 refer to the number of bits that represent the integer. This is important for two reasons: the number of bits reflects how much space an integer takes up on disk as well as how many values it can represent, or its "range." Here are the ranges for the three types of integers:
>
> Range for 16-bit integer: -32768 to 32767
> Range for 32-bit integer: –2147483648 to 2147483647
> Range for 64-bit integer: –9223372036854775808 to 9223372036854775807
>
> How do you choose? The source of your data will dictate the best type of integer. You are assuming your users *really* like bow ties, so a 32-bit integer should offer enough storage for a lifetime of bow tie wear. :]

Each bow tie has an associated image. How will you store it in Core Data? Add one more attribute to the `Bowtie` entity, naming it **photoData** and changing its data type to **Binary Data**:

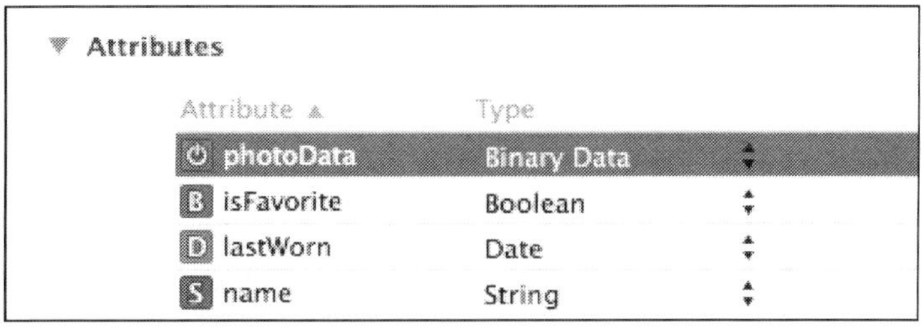

Core Data also provides the option of storing arbitrary blobs of binary data directly in your data model. These could be anything from images to PDF files, or anything else that can be serialized into zeroes and ones.

As you can imagine, this convenience can come at a steep cost. Storing a large amount of binary data in the same SQLite database as your other attributes will likely impact your app's performance. That means a giant binary blob would be loaded into memory each time you access an entity, even if you only need to access its name!

Luckily, Core Data anticipates this problem. With the `photoData` attribute selected, open the **Attributes** inspector and check the **Allows External Storage** option:

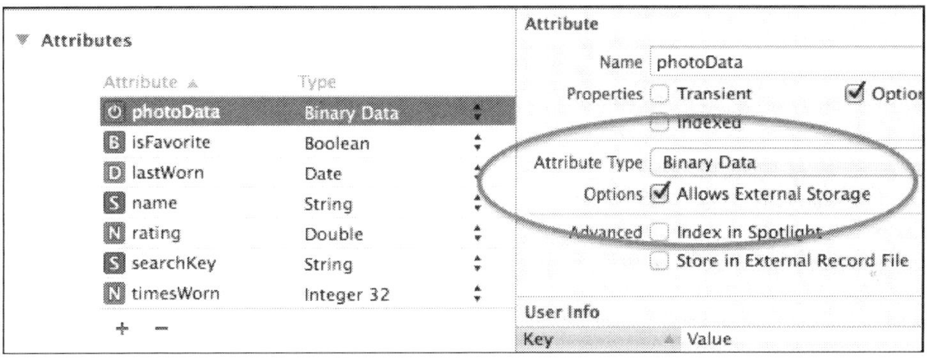

When you enable **Allows External Storage**, Core Data heuristically decides on a per-value basis if it should save the data directly in the database or store a URI that points to a separate file.

> **Note:** The **Allows External Storage** option is only available for the binary data attribute type. In addition, if you turn it on, you won't be able to query Core Data using this attribute.

In sum, besides strings, integers, doubles, Booleans and dates, Core Data can also save binary data, and it can do so efficiently and intelligently.

Storing non-standard data types in Core Data

Still, there are many other types of data you may want to save. For example, what would you do if you had to store an instance of `UIColor`?

With the options presented so far, you would have to deconstruct the color into its individual components and save them as integers (e.g., red: 255, green: 101, blue: 155). Then, after fetching these components, you'd have to reconstitute your color at runtime.

Alternatively, you could serialize the `UIColor` instance to `NSData` and save it as binary data. Then again, you'd also have to "add water" afterward to convert the binary data back to the `UIColor` object you wanted in the first place.

Once again, Core Data has your back. If you took a close look at **SampleData.plist**, you probably noticed that each bow tie has an associated color.

Select the `Bowtie` entity in the model editor and add a new attribute named **tintColor** of data type **Transformable**:

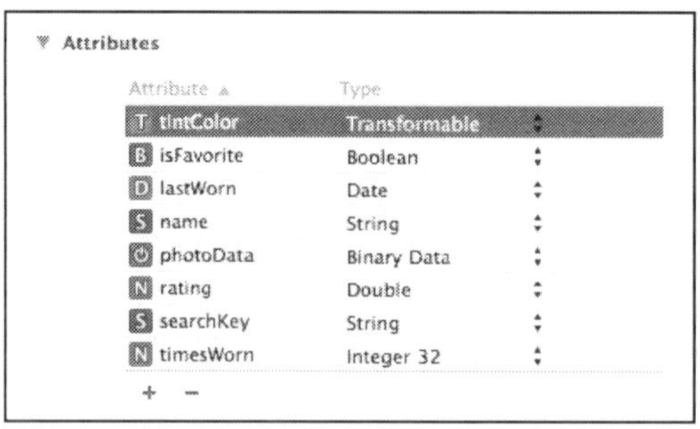

You can save any data type to Core Data (even ones you define) using the transformable type as long as your type conforms to the `NSCoding` protocol.

`UIColor` conforms to `NSSecureCoding`, which inherits from `NSCoding`, so it can use the transformable type out of the box. If you wanted to save your own custom object, you would first have to implement the `NSCoding` protocol.

> **Note:** The `NSCoding` protocol is a simple way to archive and unarchive objects into data buffers so they can be saved to disk.
>
> If you want to familiarize yourself with `NSCoding`, check out Ray's `NSCoding` tutorial for a quick introduction:
>
> http://www.raywenderlich.com/1914/nscoding-tutorial-for-ios-how-to-save-your-app-data

Your data model is now complete. The `Bowtie` entity has the eight attributes it needs to store all the information in **SampleData.plist**.

Managed object subclasses

In the sample project from the last chapter, you used key-value coding to access the attributes on the `Person` entity. It looked something like this:

```
//Set the name
person.setValue(name1, forKey: "name")

//Get the name
let name = person.valueForKey("name")
```

Even though you can do everything directly on `NSManagedObject` using key-value coding, that doesn't mean you should!

The biggest problem with key-value coding is the fact that you're accessing of data using strings instead of strongly-typed classes. This is often jokingly referred to as writing *stringly typed* code. :]

As you probably know from experience, "stringly typed" code is vulnerable to silly human errors such as mistyping and misspelling. Key-value coding also doesn't take full advantage of Swift's type-checking and Xcode's auto-completion.

The best alternative to key-value coding is to create `NSManagedObject` subclasses for each entity in your data model. That means there will be a `Bowtie` class with correct types for each property!

Xcode can automatically generate the subclass for you. Make sure you still have **Bow_Ties.xcdatamodeld** open, and go to **Editor\Create NSManagedObject Subclass...**. Select the data model and then the `Bowtie` entity in the next two dialog boxes, then select **Swift** as the language option in the final box. If you're asked, say **No** to creating an Objective-C bridging header. Click **Create** to save the file.

Go to **Bowtie.swift**. It should look like this:

```
import Foundation
import CoreData

class Bowtie: NSManagedObject {

  @NSManaged var name: String
  @NSManaged var isFavorite: NSNumber
  @NSManaged var lastWorn: NSDate
  @NSManaged var rating: NSNumber
  @NSManaged var searchKey: String
  @NSManaged var timesWorn: NSNumber
  @NSManaged var photoData: NSData
  @NSManaged var tintColor: AnyObject

}
```

The editor has created a class with a property for each attribute in your data model.

Note that there is a corresponding Foundation class or Swift class for every attribute type. Here's the full mapping of attribute types to runtime classes:

- **String** maps to `String`
- **Integer 16/32/64, Float, Double** and **Boolean** map to `NSNumber`
- **Decimal** maps to `NSDecimalNumber`
- **Date** maps to `NSDate`
- **Binary data** maps to `NSData`
- **Transformable** maps to `AnyObject`

Core Data persists an **object graph** to disk, so by default it works with objects. This is why you see primitive types like integers, doubles and Booleans boxed inside `NSNumber`. You can retrieve the actual attribute value with one of `NSNumber`'s convenience methods such as `boolValue`, `doubleValue`, and `integerValue`.

If you want to work directly with primitive data types such as `Double` and `Int32`, you could have checked the box next to **Use scalar properties for primitive data types** in the last dialog when you were generating the managed object subclass:

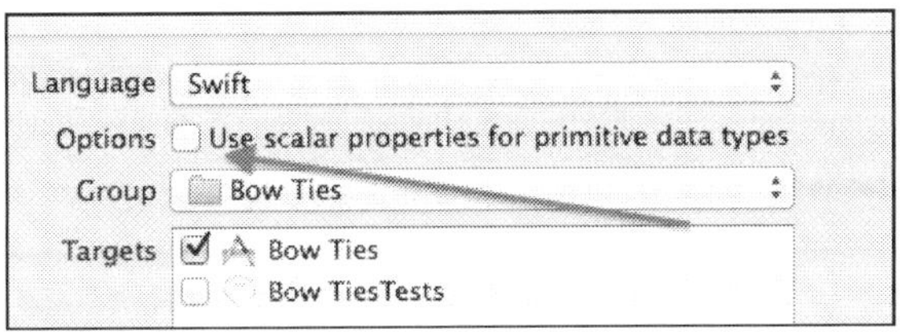

You'll focus on the object-oriented approach in this chapter, which is why you left that box unchecked. Just be aware that there's an option out there if you don't want to deal with `NSNumber` anymore!

> **Note:** Similar to `@dynamic` in Objective-C, the `@NSManaged` attribute informs the Swift compiler that the backing store and implementation of a property will be provided at runtime instead of at compile time.
>
> The normal pattern is for a property to be backed by an instance variable in memory. A property on a managed object is different: It's backed by the managed object context, so the source of the data is not known at compile time.

There's one more thing you need to do to before you can start using your new managed object subclass. Open the model editor and with the `Bowtie` entity selected, open the **Attributes** inspector. Make the following change:

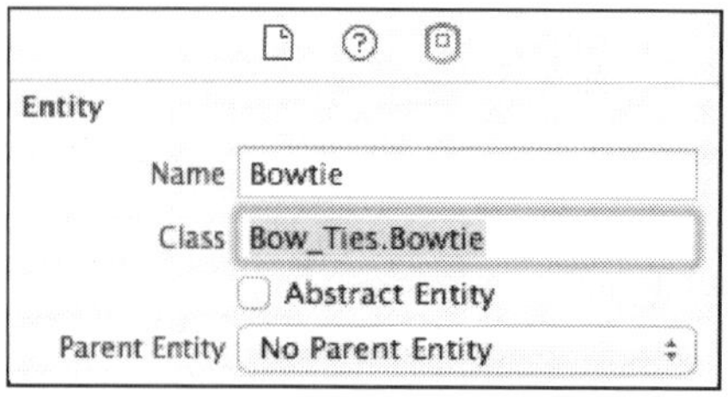

Next to **Class**, replace **Bowtie** with **Bow_Ties.Bowtie**. This is the fully specified class name for **Bowtie.swift**. This last step links the runtime `Bowtie` class to the `Bowtie` entity in the data model editor.

Congratulations, you've just made your first managed object subclass in Swift! Compared with key-value coding, this is a much better way of working with Core Data entities. There are two main benefits:

1. Managed object subclasses unleash the syntactic power of Swift properties. By accessing attributes using properties instead of key-value coding, you again befriend Xcode and the compiler.
2. You gain the ability to override existing methods or to add your own convenience methods. Note that there are some `NSManagedObject` methods you must never override. Check Apple's documentation of `NSManagedObject` for a complete list.

To make sure everything is hooked up correctly between the data model and your new managed object subclass, let's perform a small test.

Open **AppDelegate.swift** and replace `didFinishLaunchingWithOptions` with the following implementation:

```
func application(application: UIApplication,
  didFinishLaunchingWithOptions
  launchOptions: [NSObject: AnyObject]?) -> Bool {

    /* Save test bow tie */

    let entity =  NSEntityDescription.entityForName("Bowtie",
      inManagedObjectContext: managedObjectContext!)

    let bowtie = Bowtie(entity: entity!,
      insertIntoManagedObjectContext: managedObjectContext)
```

```
    bowtie.name = "My bow tie"
    bowtie.lastWorn = NSDate()

    managedObjectContext!.save(nil)

    /* Retrieve test bow tie */

    let request = NSFetchRequest(entityName: "Bowtie")

    let ties =
    managedObjectContext!.executeFetchRequest(request,
      error: nil) as [Bowtie]

    let sample = ties[0]

    println("Name: \(sample.name),  Worn: \(sample.lastWorn)")

    return true
}
```

On app launch, this test creates a bow tie and sets its `name` and `lastWorn` properties before saving the managed object context.

Immediately after that, it fetches all `Bowtie` entities and prints the name and the last worn date of the first one to the console (there should only be one).

> **Note:** This code doesn't do any error checking because it's meant to be a quick and easy test. When you're writing a real application, always check for errors. It makes the difference between a good app and a great app!

Build and run the application and pay close attention to the console:

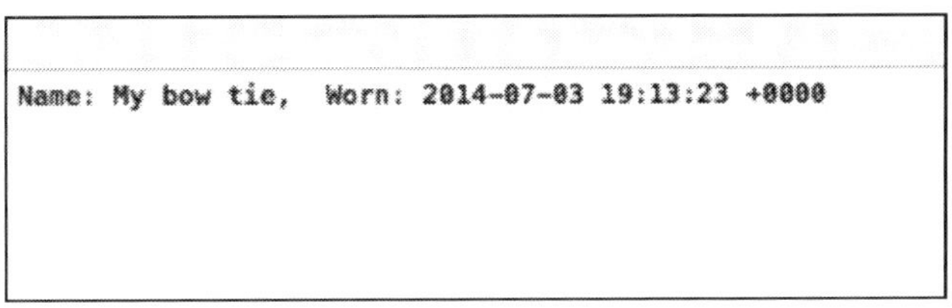

If you've been following along carefully, the name and last worn date print to the console as expected. This means you were able to save and fetch a `Bowtie` managed object subclass successfully. With this new knowledge under your belt, it's time to implement the entire sample app.

Propagating a managed context

Go to **ViewController.swift** and import Core Data below where you import UIKit:

```
import CoreData
```

Now add the following below the last `@IBOutlet` property:

```
var managedContext: NSManagedObjectContext!
```

To reiterate, before you can do anything in Core Data, you first have to get a managed context to work on. Knowing how to **propagate** a managed context to different parts of your app is an important aspect of Core Data programming.

Switch to **AppDelegate.swift** and replace `didFinishLaunchingWithOptions` (which currently contains the test code) with the following implementation:

```
func application(application: UIApplication,
  didFinishLaunchingWithOptions
  launchOptions: [NSObject: AnyObject]?) -> Bool {

    let viewController =
    self.window!.rootViewController as ViewController

    viewController.managedContext = self.managedObjectContext

    return true
}
```

In the previous chapter, you gained access to the app delegate's managed context using the delegate more or less as a global variable. In this sample project, you'll use another approach: pass the managed context from class to class via a property.

Since the caller is responsible for setting the managed context, `ViewController` can use it without needing to know where it came from. The benefit here is cleaner code since the context moves "down" the chain rather than each object accessing some global state.

You've got seven bowties that are dying to enter your Core Data store. Satisfy them by switching to **ViewController.swift** once again and adding the following two methods:

```
//Insert sample data
func insertSampleData() {
  let fetchRequest = NSFetchRequest(entityName:"Bowtie")
  fetchRequest.predicate = NSPredicate(
    format: "searchKey != nil")
  let count = managedContext.countForFetchRequest(fetchRequest,
   error: nil);

  if count > 0 { return }

  let path = NSBundle.mainBundle().pathForResource("SampleData",
    ofType: "plist")

  let dataArray = NSArray(contentsOfFile: path!)!

  for dict : AnyObject in dataArray {

    let entity =  NSEntityDescription.entityForName("Bowtie",
    inManagedObjectContext: managedContext)

    let bowtie = Bowtie(entity: entity!,
    insertIntoManagedObjectContext: managedContext)

    let btDict = dict as NSDictionary

    bowtie.name = btDict["name"] as NSString
    bowtie.searchKey = btDict["searchKey"] as NSString
    bowtie.rating = btDict["rating"] as NSNumber
    let tintColorDict = btDict["tintColor"] as NSDictionary
    bowtie.tintColor = colorFromDict(tintColorDict)

    let imageName = btDict["imageName"] as NSString
    let image = UIImage(named:imageName)
    let photoData = UIImagePNGRepresentation(image)
    bowtie.photoData = photoData

    bowtie.lastWorn = btDict["lastWorn"] as NSDate
    bowtie.timesWorn = btDict["timesWorn"] as NSNumber
    bowtie.isFavorite = btDict["isFavorite"] as NSNumber
  }

  var error: NSError?
  if !managedContext.save(&error) {
    println("Could not save \(error), \(error!.userInfo)")
  }
}

func colorFromDict(dict: NSDictionary) -> UIColor {
```

```
    let red = dict["red"] as NSNumber
    let green = dict["green"] as NSNumber
    let blue = dict["blue"] as NSNumber

    let color = UIColor(red: CGFloat(red)/255.0,
    green: CGFloat(green)/255.0,
    blue: CGFloat(blue)/255.0,
    alpha: 1)

    return color;
}
```

That's quite a bit of code, but it's all fairly simple. The first method, `insertSampleData`, checks for any bow ties (you'll learn how this works later) and if none are present, it grabs the bow tie information in **SampleData.plist**, iterates through each bow tie dictionary and inserts a new `Bowtie` entity into your Core Data store. At the end of this iteration, it saves the managed context property to commit these changes to disk.

The second method, `colorFromDict`, is also simple. **SampleData.plist** stores colors in a dictionary that contains three keys: red, green and blue. This method takes in this dictionary and returns a bona fide `UIColor`.

Notice two things:

1. **The way you store images in Core Data.** The property list contains a file name for each bow tie, not the file image—the actual images are in the project's asset catalog. With this file name, you instantiate the `UIImage` and immediately convert it into `NSData` by means of `UIImagePNGRepresentation()` before storing it in the `imageData` property.
2. **The way you store the color.** Even though the color is stored in a transformable attribute, it doesn't require any special treatment before you store it in `tintColor`. You simply set the property and you're good to go.

The previous methods insert all the bow tie data you had in **SampleData.plist** into Core Data. Now you need to access the data from somewhere!

Replace `viewDidLoad` with the following implementation:

```
override func viewDidLoad() {
  super.viewDidLoad()

  //1
  insertSampleData()
```

```
  //2
  let request = NSFetchRequest(entityName:"Bowtie")
  let firstTitle = segmentedControl.titleForSegmentAtIndex(0)

  request.predicate =
    NSPredicate(format:"searchKey == %@", firstTitle!)

  //3
  var error: NSError? = nil

  var results =
    managedContext.executeFetchRequest(request,
    error: &error) as [Bowtie]?

  //4
  if let bowties = results {
    populate(bowties[0])
  } else {
    println("Could not fetch \(error), \(error!.userInfo)")
  }
}
```

This is where you fetch the `Bowties` from Core Data and populate the UI. Step by step, here's what you're doing with this code:

1. You call the `insertSampleData` method you implemented earlier. Since `viewDidLoad` can be called every time the app is launched, `insertSampleData` itself performs a fetch to make sure it isn't inserting the sample data into Core Data multiple times.

2. You create a fetch request for the purpose of fetching the newly inserted `Bowtie` entities. The segmented control has tabs to filter by color, so the predicate adds the condition to find the bow ties that match the selected color. Predicates are both very flexible and very powerful—you'll read more about them in chapter 4.

   For now, you should know that this particular predicate is looking for bow ties that have their `searchKey` property set to the segmented control's first button title, "R" in this case.

3. As always, the managed context does the heavy lifting for you. It executes the fetch request you crafted moments earlier and returns an array of `Bowtie` objects.

4. You populate the user interface with the first bow tie in the results array. If there was an error, print the error to the console.

You haven't defined the populate method yet, so Xcode throws a warning. Implement it as follows:

```
func populate(bowtie: Bowtie) {
  imageView.image = UIImage(data:bowtie.photoData)
  nameLabel.text = bowtie.name
  ratingLabel.text = "Rating: \(bowtie.rating.doubleValue)/5"

  timesWornLabel.text =
  "# times worn: \(bowtie.timesWorn.integerValue)"

  let dateFormatter = NSDateFormatter()
  dateFormatter.dateStyle = .ShortStyle
  dateFormatter.timeStyle = .NoStyle

  lastWornLabel.text = "Last worn: " +
    dateFormatter.stringFromDate(bowtie.lastWorn)

  favoriteLabel.hidden = !bowtie.isFavorite.boolValue

  view.tintColor = bowtie.tintColor as UIColor
}
```

There's a UI element for every one of the attributes defined in a bow tie. Since Core Data only stores the image as a blob of binary data, it's your job to reconstitute it back into an image so the view controller's image view can use it.

Similarly, you can't use the lastWorn date attribute directly. You first need to create a date formatter to be able to turn the date into a string that humans can understand.

Finally, the tintColor transformable attribute that stores your bow tie's color changes the color of not one, but *all* the elements on the screen. Simply set the tint color on the view controller's view and voila! Everything is now tinted the same color.

Build and run the app. The red bow tie appears on the screen, like so:

The Wear and Rate buttons do nothing. Tapping on the different parts of the segmented controls also does nothing. You've still got work to do!

First, you need to keep track of the currently selected bow tie so you can reference it from anywhere in your class. Add a new property to do this below `var managedContext: NSManagedObjectContext!`:

```
var currentBowtie: Bowtie!
```

Next, replace the last `if-let` statement in `viewDidLoad` to use your new property:

```
//4
if let bowties = results {
  currentBowtie = bowties[0]
  populate(currentBowtie)
} else {
  println("Could not fetch \(error), \(error!.userInfo)")
}
```

Keeping track of the currently selected bow tie is necessary to implement the Wear and Rate buttons since these actions only affect the current bow tie.

Every time the user taps on Wear, the button executes the `wear` action method. But `wear` is empty at the moment. Implement it as shown below:

```
@IBAction func wear(sender: AnyObject) {
  let times = currentBowtie.timesWorn.integerValue
  currentBowtie.timesWorn = NSNumber(integer: (times + 1))

  currentBowtie.lastWorn = NSDate()

  var error: NSError?
  if !managedContext.save(&error) {
  println("Could not save \(error), \(error!.userInfo)")
  }

  populate(currentBowtie)
}
```

This method takes the currently selected bow tie and increments its `timesWorn` attribute by one. Since the `timesWorn` property is an `NSNumber`, you have to first unbox the integer, increment it and wrap it up nicely into another `NSNumber`.

Then, you change the `lastWorn` date to today and save the managed context to commit these changes to disk. Finally, you populate the user interface to visualize these changes.

Run the application and tap **Wear** as many times as you'd like. It looks like you thoroughly enjoy the timeless elegance of a red bow tie!

Similarly, every time the user taps on Rate, it executes the `rate` action in your code. This action is currently empty. Implement it as shown below:

```
@IBAction func rate(sender: AnyObject) {
  let alert = UIAlertController(title: "New Rating",
    message: "Rate this bow tie",
    preferredStyle: UIAlertControllerStyle.Alert)

  let cancelAction = UIAlertAction(title: "Cancel",
    style: .Default,
    handler: { (action: UIAlertAction!) in

  })

  let saveAction = UIAlertAction(title: "Save",
    style: .Default,
    handler: { (action: UIAlertAction!) in

      let textField = alert.textFields![0] as UITextField
      self.updateRating(textField.text)

  })

  alert.addTextFieldWithConfigurationHandler {
    (textField: UITextField!) in

  }

  alert.addAction(cancelAction)
  alert.addAction(saveAction)

  self.presentViewController(alert,
    animated: true,
    completion: nil)
}
```

Tapping on Rate now brings up an alert view with a single text field, a cancel button and a save button. Tapping the save button calls the method `updateRating`, which…

Whoops, you haven't defined it yet. Appease Xcode by implementing it below:

```
func updateRating(numericString: String) {
  currentBowtie.rating = (numericString as NSString).doubleValue

  var error: NSError?
  if !managedContext.save(&error) {
    println("Could not save \(error), \(error!.userInfo)")
```

```
    }

    populate(currentBowtie)
  }
```

You convert the text from the alert view's text field into a double and use it to update the current bow ties rating property.

Finally, you commit your changes as usual by saving the managed context and refresh the UI to see your changes in real time.

Try it out. Build and run the app and tap **Rate**:

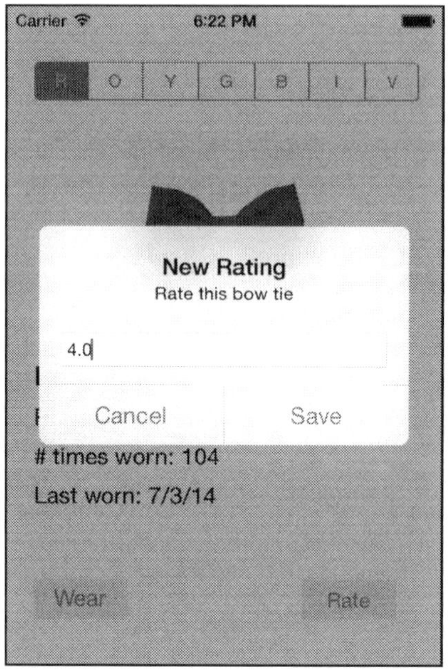

Enter any decimal number from 0 to 5 and tap **Save**. As you would expect, the rating label updates to the new value you entered.

Now tap **Rate** one more time. Remember the timeless elegance of a red bow tie? Let's say you like it so much that you decide to rate it a 6 out of 5. Tap **Save** to refresh the user interface:

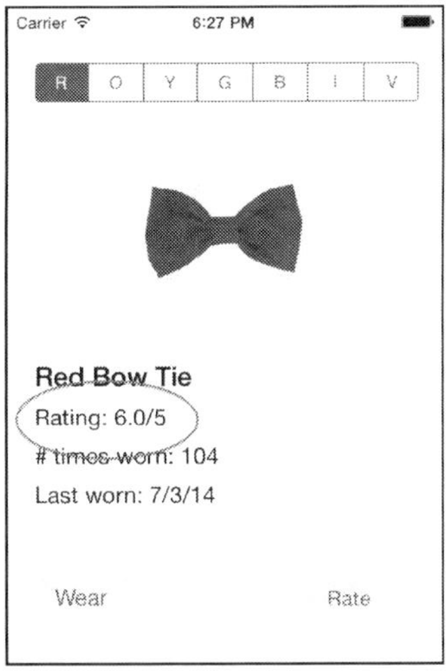

While you may absolutely *love* the color red, this is neither the time nor the place for hyperbole. Your app let you save a 6 for a value that's only supposed to go up to 5. You've got invalid data on your hands.

Data validation in Core Data

Your first instinct may be to write client-side validation—something like, "Only save the new rating if the value is greater than 0 and less than 5." Fortunately, you don't have to write this code yourself. Core Data supports validation for most attribute types out of the box.

Open your data model, select the **rating** attribute and open the data model inspector:

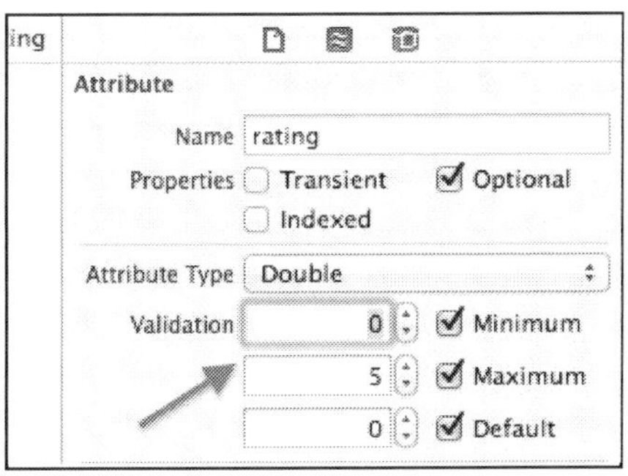

Next to **Validation**, type **0** for minimum and **5** for maximum. That's it! No need to write any Swift to reject invalid data.

> **Note:** Normally, you have to **version** your data model if you want to change it after you've shipped your app. You'll learn more about this in Chapter 6, "Versioning and Migration."
>
> Attribute validation is one of the few exceptions. If you add it to your app after shipping, you don't have to version your data model. Lucky you!

But what does this do, exactly?

Validation kicks in immediately after you call `save` on your managed object context. The managed object context checks with the model to see if any of the new values conflict with the validation rules you've put in place.

If there's a validation error, the save fails. Remember that `NSError` pointer you pass into the save method? Up until now, you've had no reason to do anything special if there's an error. Validation changes that.

If the save fails, Core Data populates the `NSError` you pass in by reference and lets you decide what to do. It's time to see this in action.

Build and run the app once more. Give the red bowtie a rating of 6 out of 5 and save. A rather cryptic error message will spill out onto your console:

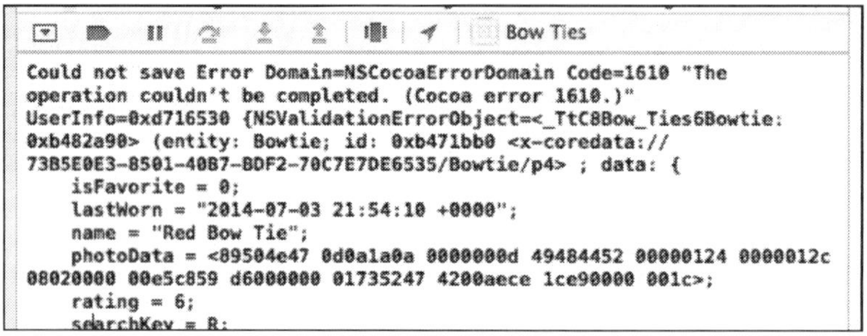

The `userInfo` dictionary that comes with the error contains all kinds of useful information about why Core Data aborted your save operation. It even has a localized error message that you can show your users, under the key `NSLocalizedDescription`: "The operation couldn't be completed."

What you do with this error, however, is entirely up to you. Re-implement `updateRating` to handle the error appropriately:

```
func updateRating(numString: String) {

  currentBowtie!.rating = (numString as NSString).doubleValue

  var error: NSError?
  if !self.managedContext.save(&error) {

    if error!.code == NSValidationNumberTooLargeError ||
       error!.code == NSValidationNumberTooSmallError {

        rate(currentBowtie)
    }
  } else {
    populate(currentBowtie)
  }
}
```

If there's an error and it happened because the new rating was either too large or too small, then you present the alert view again. Otherwise, you populate the user interface with the new rating.

But wait... Where did `NSValidationNumberTooLargeError` and `NSValidationNumberTooSmallError` come from? Go back to the previous console reading and look closely at the first line:

```
Could not save Error Domain=NSCocoaErrorDomain Code=1610
"The operation couldn't be completed.
```

`NSValidationNumberTooLargeError` is an enumeration value that maps to the integer 1610. For a full list of Core Data errors and code definitions, you can consult **CoreDataErrors.h** in Xcode by Cmd-clicking on `NSValidationNumberTooLargeError`.

> **Note:** When an `NSError` is involved, it's standard practice to check the domain and code for the error to determine what went wrong. You can read more about this in Apple's *Error Handling Programming Guide*:
>
> https://developer.apple.com/library/mac/documentation/Cocoa/Conceptual/ErrorHandlingCocoa/CreateCustomizeNSError/CreateCustomizeNSError.html

Build and run the app. Verify that the new validation rules work properly by once again showing the red tie some love:

If you enter any value above 5 and try to save, the app rejects your rating and asks you to try again with a new alert view. Voila!

Tying everything up

The Wear and Rate buttons are working properly but the app can only display one tie. Tapping the different values on the segmented control is supposed to switch ties. You will finish up this sample project by implementing that feature.

Every time the user taps the segmented control, it executes the `segmentedControl` action method in your code. This method is currently blank; implement it as shown below:

```
@IBAction func segmentedControl(control: UISegmentedControl) {

    let selectedValue =
    control.titleForSegmentAtIndex(control.selectedSegmentIndex)

    let fetchRequest = NSFetchRequest(entityName:"Bowtie")

    fetchRequest.predicate =
    NSPredicate(format:"searchKey == %@", selectedValue!)
```

```
    var error: NSError?

    let results =
      managedContext.executeFetchRequest(fetchRequest,
      error: &error) as [Bowtie]?

    if let bowties = results {
      currentBowtie = bowties.last!
      populate(currentBowtie)
    } else {
      println("Could not fetch \(error), \(error!.userInfo)")
    }
  }
```

The title of each segment in the segmented control conveniently corresponds to a particular tie's `searchKey` attribute. Grab the title of the currently selected segment and fetch the appropriate bow tie using a well-crafted `NSPredicate`.

Then, use the last bow tie in the array of results (there should only be one per `searchKey`) to populate the user interface.

Once again, build and run the app. Tap different letters on the segmented control for a psychedelic treat:

You did it! With this bow tie app under your belt, you're well on your way to becoming a Core Data master.

Where to go from here?

In this chapter, on top of practicing what you already knew about fetching and saving, you learned how to create your own managed object subclasses in Swift, explored different types of Core Data attributes and learned about validation.

Even though this is just the second chapter, you've probably already started to appreciate the flexibility and power of Core Data as a framework. But you've only scratched the surface. There's a lot more to learn!

Chapter 3: The Core Data Stack

By Pietro Rea

Until now, you've been relying on Xcode's Core Data template. There's nothing wrong with getting help from Xcode (that's what it's there for!), but if you really want to know how Core Data works, building your own stack is a must.

The stack is made up of four Core Data classes:

- `NSManagedObjectModel`
- `NSPersistentStore`
- `NSPersistentStoreCoordinator`
- `NSManagedObjectContext`

Of these four classes, you've only encountered `NSManagedObjectContext` so far in this book. But the other three were there behind the scenes the whole time, supporting your managed context!

In this chapter, you'll learn the details of what these four classes do. Rather than rely on the default starter template, you'll build your own Core Data stack: a customizable "wrapper" around these classes that works as a unit.

Getting started

The sample project for this chapter is a simple dog-walking app. This application lets you save the date and time of your dog walks in a simple table view. Use this app regularly and your pooch (and his bladder) will love you.

You'll find the sample project Dog Walk in the resources that accompany this book. Open **Dog Walk.xcodeproj** to open the project in Xcode, and build and run the starter project:

As you can see, the sample app is already a fully-working (albeit simple) prototype. Tapping on the plus (+) button on the top-right adds a new entry to the list of walks. The image represents the dog you're currently walking, but otherwise does nothing.

The app has all the functionality it needs, except for one important feature: The list of walks doesn't persist. If you terminate **Dog Walk** and re-launch, your entire history is gone. How will you remember if you walked your pooch this morning?

Your task in this chapter is to save the list of walks in Core Data. If that sounds like something you've already done in chapters 1 and 2, here's the twist: you'll be writing your own Core Data stack to really understand what's really going on under the hood!

Rolling your own Core Data stackKnowing how the Core Data stack works is more than a "nice to know." If you're working with a more advanced setup, such as syncing with iCloud or migrating data from an old persistent store, digging into the stack is essential.

Before you jump into the code, let's consider what each of the four classes in the Core Data stack—`NSManagedObjectModel`, `NSPersistentStore`, `NSPersistentStoreCoordinator` and `NSManagedObjectContext`—does in detail.

> **Note:** This is one of the few parts of the book where you'll read about the theory before using the concepts in practice. It's almost impossible to separate one component from the rest of the stack and use it in isolation.

The managed object model

The `NSManagedObjectModel` represents each object type in your app's data model, the properties they can have, and the relationship between them. Other parts of the Core Data stack use the model to create objects, store properties and save data.

As mentioned earlier in the book, it can be helpful to think about `NSManagedObjectModel` as a database schema. If your Core Data stack uses SQLite under the hood, that is absolutely what `NSManagedObjectModel` represents.

However, SQLite is only one of many persistent store types you can use in Core Data (more on this later), so it's better to think of the managed object model in more general terms.

> **Note:** You may be wondering how `NSManagedObjectModel` relates to the data model editor you've been using all along. Good question!
>
> The visual editor creates and edits an **xcdatamodel** file. There's a special compiler, `momc`, that compiles the model file into a set of files in a `momd` folder.
>
> Just as your Swift code is compiled and optimized so it can run on a device, the compiled model can be accessed efficiently at runtime. Core Data uses the compiled contents of the `momd` folder to initialize an `NSManagedObjectModel` at runtime.

The persistent store

`NSPersistentStore` reads and writes data to whichever storage method you've decided to use. Core Data provides four types of `NSPersistentStore` out of the box: three atomic and one non-atomic.

An **atomic** persistent store needs to be completely deserialized and loaded into memory before you can make any read or write operations. In contrast, a **non-atomic** persistent store can load chunks of itself onto memory as needed.

Here's a brief overview of the four built-in Core Data store types:

1. **NSQLiteStoreType** is backed by an SQLite database. It is the only non-atomic store type that Core Data supports out of the box, giving it a lightweight and efficient memory footprint. This makes it the best choice for most iOS projects. Xcode's Core Data template uses this store type by default.
2. **NSXMLStoreType** is backed by an XML file, making it the most human-readable of all the store types. This store type is atomic, so it can have a large memory footprint. `NSXMLStoreType` is only available on OS X.
3. **NSBinaryStoreType** is backed by a binary data file. Like `NSXMLStoreType`, it is also an atomic store, so the entire binary file must be loaded onto memory before you can do anything with it. You'll rarely find this type of persistent store in real world applications.
4. **NSInMemoryStoreType** is the in-memory persistent store type. In a way, this store type is not really "persistent." Terminate the app or turn off your phone, and the data stored in an in-memory store type disappears into thin air. Although this may seem to defeat the purpose of Core Data, in-memory persistent stores can be helpful for unit testing and some types of caching.

> **Note:** Were you holding your breath for a persistent store type backed by a JSON file or a CSV file? Bummer. The good news is that you can create your own type of persistent store by subclassing `NSIncrementalStore`.
>
> Refer to Apple's Incremental Store Programming Guide if you're curious about this option:
>
> https://developer.apple.com/library/ios/documentation/DataManagement/Conceptual/IncrementalStorePG/Introduction/Introduction.html

The persistent store coordinator

`NSPersistentStoreCoordinator` is the bridge between the managed object model and the persistent store. It is responsible for using the model and the persistent stores to do most of the hard work in Core Data. It understands the `NSManagedObjectModel` and knows how to send information to, and fetch information from, the `NSPersistentStore`.

`NSPersistentStoreCoordinator` also hides the implementation details of how your persistent store or stores are configured. This is useful for two reasons:

1. `NSManagedObjectContext` (coming next!) doesn't have to know if it's saving to an SQLite database, XML file or even iCloud.
2. If you have multiple persistent stores, the persistent store coordinator presents a unified interface to the managed context. As far as the managed context is concerned, it always interacts with a single, aggregate persistent store.

The managed object context

On a day-to-day basis, you'll work with `NSManagedObjectContext` the most out of the four stack components. You'll probably only see the other three components when you set up your stack or do a migration.

Therefore, understanding how contexts work is very important! Here are some things you may have already picked up from the book so far:

- A context is an in-memory scratchpad for working with your managed objects.
- You do all of the work with your Core Data objects within a managed object context.
- Any changes you make won't affect the underlying data on disk until you call `save()` on the context.

Now here are five things about contexts that weren't mentioned before. A few of them are very important for later chapters, so pay close attention:

1. The context *manages* the lifecycle of the objects that it creates or fetches. This lifecycle management includes powerful features such as faulting, inverse relationship handling and validation.

2. A managed object cannot exist without an associated context. In fact, a managed object and its context are so tightly coupled that every managed object keeps a reference to its context, which can be accessed like so:

```
let employeeContext = employee.managedObjectContext
```

3. Contexts are very territorial; once a managed object has associated with a particular context, it will remain associated with the same context for the duration of its lifecycle.

4. An application can use more than one context—most non-trivial Core Data applications fall into this category. Since a context is an in-memory scratch pad for what's on disk, you can actually load the same Core Data object onto two different contexts simultaneously.

5. A context is not thread safe. The same goes for a managed object—you can only interact with contexts and managed objects on the same thread in which they were created. Apple has provided many ways to work with contexts in multithreaded applications. You'll read all about different concurrency models in Chapter 10, "Multiple Managed Object Contexts."

Creating your stack object

Now that you know what each component does, it's time to return to Dog Walk and implement your own Core Data stack.

As you know from previous chapters, Xcode creates its Core Data stack in the app delegate. You're going to do it differently. Instead of mixing app delegate code with Core Data code, you'll create a separate class to encapsulate the stack.

Go to **File\New\File...**, select the **iOS\Source\Swift File** template and click **Next**. Name the file **CoreDataStack** and click **Create** to save the file.

Go to the newly created **CoreDataStack.swift** and replace the contents of the file with the following:

```
import CoreData

class CoreDataStack {
  let context:NSManagedObjectContext
  let psc:NSPersistentStoreCoordinator
  let model:NSManagedObjectModel
```

```
  let store:NSPersistentStore?
}
```

These properties correspond to the stack components you read about in the previous section. You aren't setting them to anything at the moment, so you should be seeing warnings telling you that the Swift class is missing an initializer. Ignore this warning for now—it will disappear in a few minutes.

Below the properties you just added, add the following method:

```
func applicationDocumentsDirectory() -> NSURL {
  let fileManager = NSFileManager.defaultManager()

  let urls = fileManager.URLsForDirectory(.DocumentDirectory,
    inDomains: .UserDomainMask) as [NSURL]

  return urls[0]
}
```

This is a simple helper method that returns a URL to your application's documents directory. Why do you need this? You're going to store the SQLite database (which is simply a file) in the documents directory. This is the recommended place to store the user's data, whether or not you're using Core Data.

Now add the initializer method below the properties you declared earlier:

```
init() {
  //1
  let bundle = NSBundle.mainBundle()
  let modelURL =
  bundle.URLForResource("Dog Walk", withExtension:"momd")
  model = NSManagedObjectModel(contentsOfURL: modelURL!)!

  //2
  psc = NSPersistentStoreCoordinator(managedObjectModel:model)

  //3
  context = NSManagedObjectContext()
  context.persistentStoreCoordinator = psc

  //4
  let documentsURL = applicationDocumentsDirectory()
  let storeURL =
  documentsURL.URLByAppendingPathComponent("Dog Walk")
```

```
    let options =
    [NSMigratePersistentStoresAutomaticallyOption: true]

    var error: NSError? = nil
    store = psc.addPersistentStoreWithType(NSSQLiteStoreType,
      configuration: nil,
      URL: storeURL,
      options: options,
      error:&error)

    if store == nil {
      println("Error adding persistent store: \(error)")
      abort()
    }

  }
```

The initializer is responsible for configuring each individual component in your Core Data stack. It's a large chunk of code that probably looks very cryptic at the moment, so let's go over each section in turn:

1. The first step is to load the managed object model from disk into a `NSManagedObjectModel` object. You do this by getting a URL to the `momd` directory that contains the compiled version of the `.xcdatamodeld` file.
2. Once you've initialized `NSManagedObjectModel`, the next step is to create `NSPersistentStoreCoordinator`. Remember that the persistent store coordinator mediates between the persistent store and `NSManagedObjectModel`. Initialize one using the `NSManagedObjectModel` you just created.
3. The `NSManagedObjectContext` takes no arguments to initialize. However, it won't be very useful until you connect it to an `NSPersistentStoreCoordinator`. You can do this easily by setting the context's `persistentStoreCoordinator` property to the persistent store coordinator you just created in the previous step.
4. The way you create a persistent store is a bit unintuitive—you don't initialize it directly. Instead, the persistent store coordinator hands you an `NSPersistentStore` object as a side effect of attaching a persistent store type. You simply have to specify the store type (`NSSQLiteStoreType` in this case), the URL location of the store file and some configuration options.

> **Note:** Chapter 6, "Versioning and Migration," covers `NSMigratePersistentStoresAutomaticallyOption`. For now, you just need to know that setting this options tells Core Data to do its best to automatically merge different versions of a managed object model when the model's entities or attributes change.

Finally, under the initializer method, add the following method:

```
func saveContext() {
  var error: NSError? = nil
  if context.hasChanges && !context.save(&error) {
    println("Could not save: \(error), \(error?.userInfo)")
  }
}
```

This is a convenience method to save the stack's managed object context and handle any errors that might result.

Switch to **ViewController.swift** and make the following changes. First, import the Core Data framework below `import UIKit`:

```
import CoreData
```

Then, add a property inside the class definition to hold the managed object context:

```
var managedContext: NSManagedObjectContext!
```

As in the previous chapter, you'll follow the pattern of each view controller having a reference to the managed object context.

Now open **AppDelegate.swift** and make the following changes. Again, you need to import the Core Data framework below `import UIKit`:

```
import CoreData
```

Then, below `var window: UIWindow?`, add a variable to hold the Core Data stack:

```
lazy var coreDataStack = CoreDataStack()
```

You initialize the Core Data stack object as a lazy variable on the application delegate. This means the stack won't be set up until the first time you access the property.

Still in **AppDelegate.swift**, implement `application(_:didFinishLaunchingWithOptions:)` as shown below:

```
func application(application: UIApplication,
  didFinishLaunchingWithOptions
  launchOptions: [NSObject: AnyObject]?) -> Bool {

  let navigationController =
  self.window!.rootViewController as UINavigationController

  let viewController =
  navigationController.topViewController as ViewController

  viewController.managedContext = coreDataStack.context

  return true
}
```

This code propagates the managed context from your `CoreDataStack` object (initializing the whole stack in the process) to `ViewController`.

Finally, add the following two `UIApplicationDelegate` methods to the `AppDelegate` class:

```
func applicationDidEnterBackground(application: UIApplication) {
  coreDataStack.saveContext()
}

func applicationWillTerminate(application: UIApplication) {
  coreDataStack.saveContext()
}
```

These methods ensure that Core Data saves any pending changes before the app is either sent to the background or terminated for whatever reason.

Modeling your data

Now that your shiny new Core Data stack is securely fastened to your application delegate, it's time to create your data model.

Head over to your Project Navigator and… Wait a second. There's no data model file! That's right. Since I generated this sample application without enabling the option to use Core Data, there's no **.xcdatamodel** file.

No worries. Go to **File\New\File...**, select the **iOS\Core Data\Data Model** template and click **Next**. Name the file **Dog Walk.xcdatamodeld** and click **Create** to save the file:

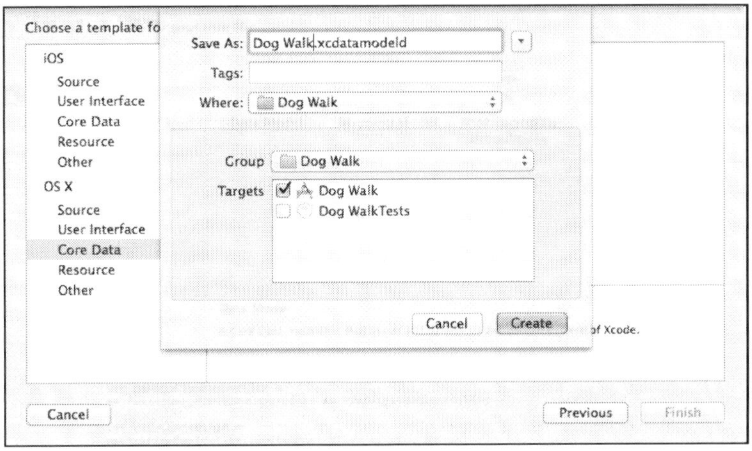

> **Note:** You'll have problems at runtime if you don't name your data model file precisely **Dog Walk.xcdatamodel**. This is because **CoreDataStack.swift** expects to find the compiled version at **Dog Walk.momd**.

Open the data model file and create a new entity named **Dog**. You should be able to do this on your own by now, but in case you forgot how, click the **Add Entity** button on the bottom left.

Add an attribute named **name** of type **String**. Your data model should look like this:

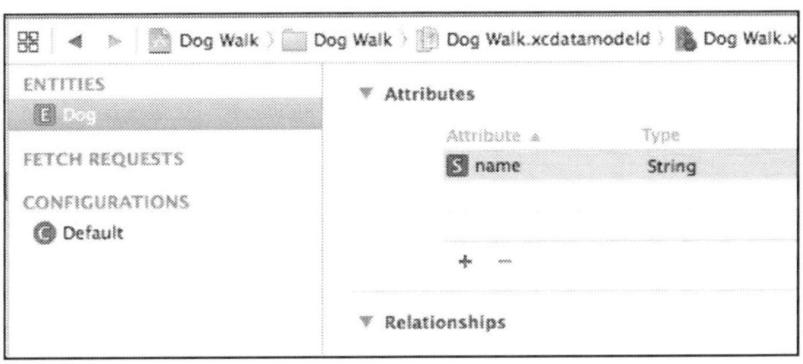

You also want to keep track of the walks for a particular dog. After all, that's the whole point of the app!

Define another entity and name it **Walk**. Then add an attribute named **date** and set its type to **Date**.

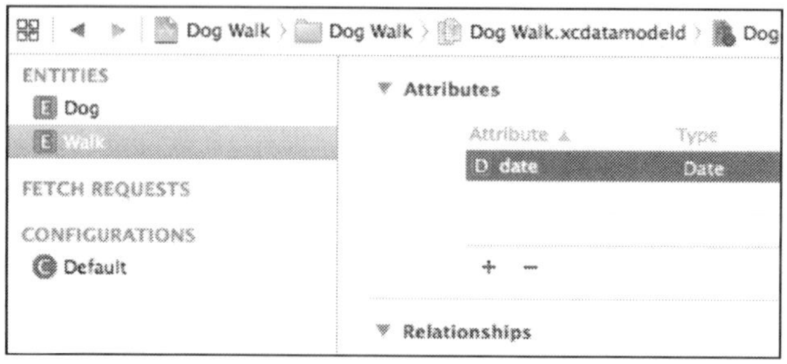

Go back to the `Dog` entity. You might think you need to add a new attribute of type **Array** to hold the walks, but there is no Array type in Core Data. Instead, the way to do this is to model it as a relationship. Add a new relationship and name it **walks**:

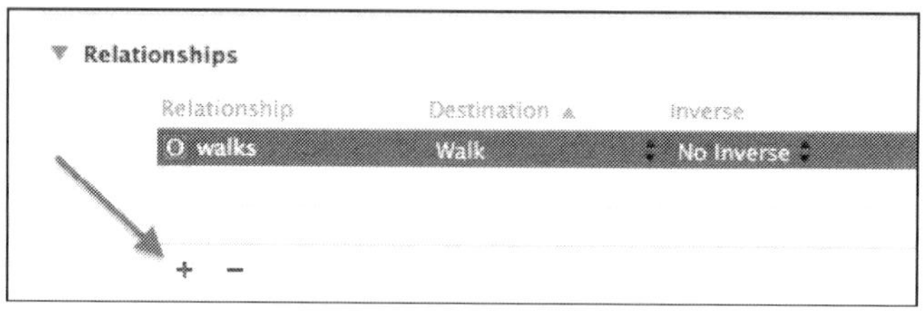

Set the destination to **Walk**. You can think of the destination as the receiving end of a relationship.

Every relationship begins as a to-one relationship by default, which means you can only track one walk per dog at the moment. Unless you don't plan on keeping your dog for very long, you probably want to track more than one walk.

To fix this, with the **walks** relationship selected, open the **Data Model** inspector:

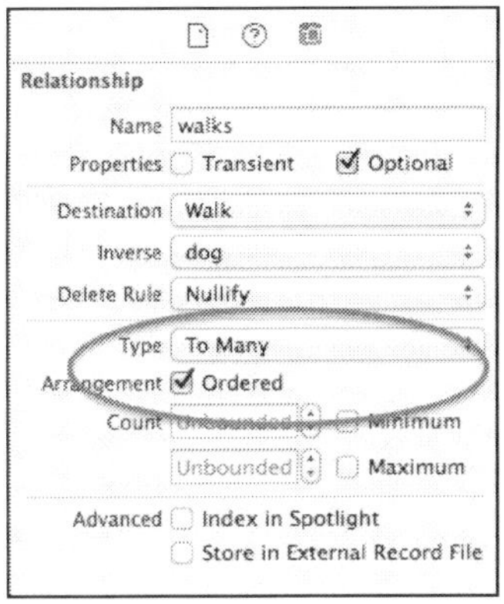

Click on the **Type** dropdown, select **To Many** and check **Ordered**. This means one dog can have many walks and the order of the walks matters, since you'll be displaying the walks sorted by date.

Select the **Walk** entity and create an inverse relationship back to **Dog**. Set the destination as **dog** and the inverse as **walks**.

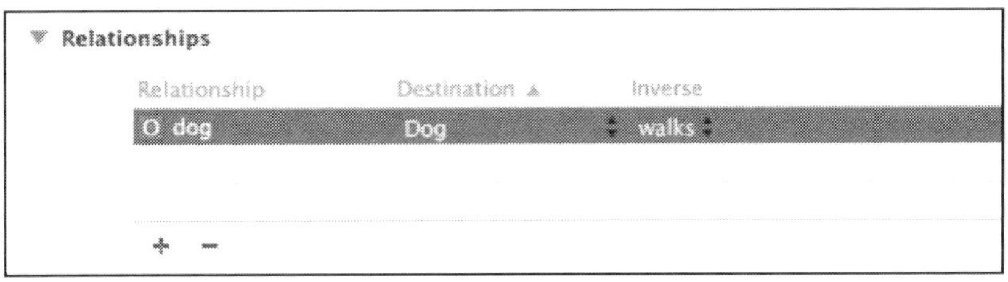

It's OK to leave this relationship as a to-one relationship. A dog can have many walks, but a walk can only belong to one dog—for the purposes of this app, at least. :]

The inverse lets the model know how to find its way back, so to speak. Given a walk record, you can follow the relationship to the dog. Thanks to the inverse, the model knows to follow the **walks** relationship to get back to the walk record.

This is a good time to let you know that the data model editor has another view style. This entire time you've been looking at the table editor style. Toggle the segmented control on the bottom-right to switch to the graph editor style:

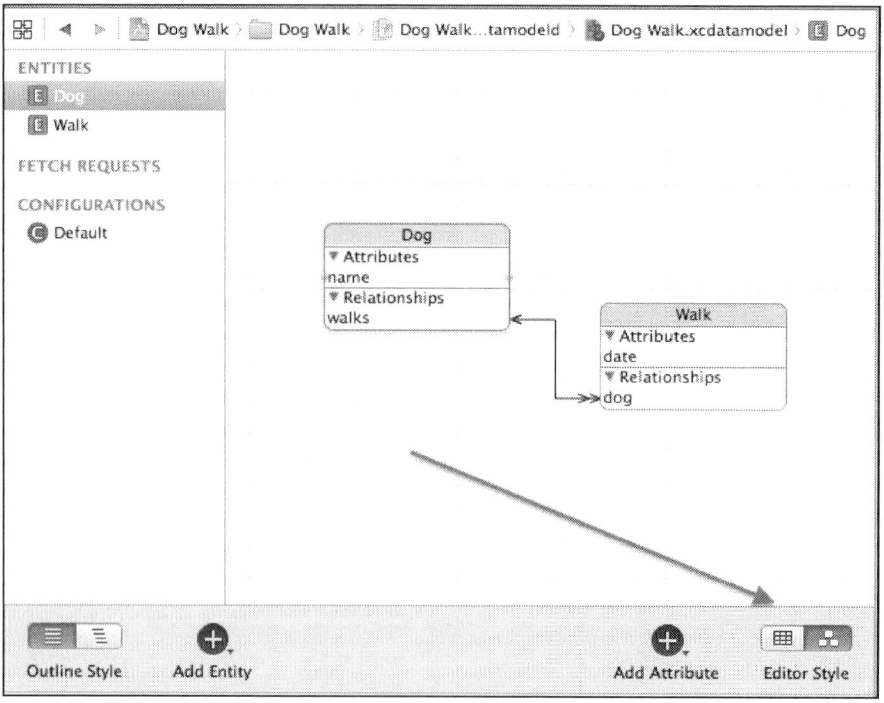

The graph editor style is a great tool to visualize the relationships between your Core Data entities. Here the to-many relationship from `Dog` to `Walk` is represented with a double arrow. `Walk` points back to `Dog` with a single arrow (to-one relationship).

Feel free to switch back and forth between the two editor styles. You might find it easier to use the table style to add and remove entities and attributes, and the graph style to see the big picture of your data model.

Adding managed object subclasses

In the previous chapter you learned how to create custom managed object subclasses for your Core Data entities. It's more convenient to work this way, so this is what you'll do for `Dog` and `Walk` as well.

Go to **Editor\Create NSManagedObject Subclass...** and choose the **Dog Walk** model and then both the **Dog** and **Walk** entities. Make sure you choose **Swift** as the language and click **Create**.

Dog.swift should look like this:

```
import Foundation
import CoreData

class Dog: NSManagedObject {
  @NSManaged var name: String
  @NSManaged var walks: NSOrderedSet
}
```

Like before, the `name` attribute is a `String`. But what about the `walks` relationship? Core Data represents to-many relationships using sets, not arrays. Because you made the `walks` relationship ordered, you've got an ordered set.

> **Note:** `NSSet` seems like an odd choice, doesn't it? Unlike arrays, sets don't allow accessing their members by index. In fact, there's no ordering at all! Core Data uses `NSSet` because a set forces uniqueness in its members. The same object can't feature more than once in a to-many relationship.
>
> If you need to access individual objects by index, you can check the **Ordered** checkbox in the visual editor, as you've done here. Core Data will then represent the relationship as an `NSOrderedSet`.

Walk.swift should look like this:

```
import Foundation
import CoreData

class Walk: NSManagedObject {

  @NSManaged var date: NSDate
  @NSManaged var dog: Dog

}
```

The inverse relationship back to `Dog` is simply a variable of type `Dog`. Easy as pie.

> **Note:** Sometimes Xcode will create relationship properties with the generic `NSManagedObject` type instead of the specific class, especially if you're making lots of subclasses at the same time. If this happens, just correct the type yourself or generate the specific file again.

There is one more step before you can use your managed object subclasses. Click into the data model, select the `Dog` entity and open the **Data Model** inspector:

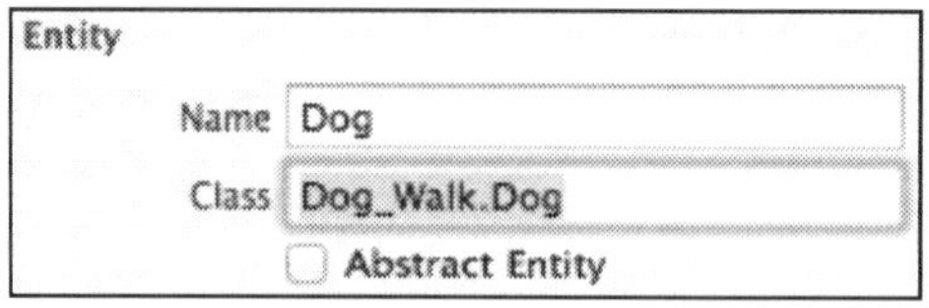

Next to **Class**, replace **Dog** with **Dog_Walk.Dog**. Do the same for the `Walk` entity, swapping **Walk** with **Dog_Walk.Walk**. You did this in the last chapter, but in case you forgot why it's necessary, this step connects the fully specified class name for your managed object subclasses with the entities in your data model.

A walk down persistence lane

All your setup is complete: your Core Data stack, your data model and your managed object subclasses. It's time to convert Dog Walk to use Core Data. You've done this several times before, so this should be an easy section for you.

Pretend for a moment that this application will at some point support tracking multiple dogs. The first step is to track the currently selected dog. Switch to **ViewController.swift** and replace the `walks` array with the following property:

```
var currentDog: Dog!
```

Then, add the following code to the end of `viewDidLoad`:

```
//Insert Dog entity

let dogEntity = NSEntityDescription.entityForName("Dog",
  inManagedObjectContext: managedContext)

let dog = Dog(entity: dogEntity!,
  insertIntoManagedObjectContext: managedContext)
```

```
let dogName = "Fido"
let dogFetch = NSFetchRequest(entityName: "Dog")
dogFetch.predicate = NSPredicate(format: "name == %@", dogName)

var error: NSError?

let result =
  managedContext.executeFetchRequest(dogFetch,
  error: &error) as [Dog]?

if let dogs = result {

  if dogs.count == 0 {

    currentDog = Dog(entity: dogEntity!,
    insertIntoManagedObjectContext: managedContext)
    currentDog.name = dogName

    if !managedContext.save(&error) {
      println("Could not save: \(error)")
    }
  } else {
    currentDog = dogs[0]
  }

} else {
  println("Could not fetch: \(error)")
}
```

First, you fetch all `Dog` entities with names of "Fido" from Core Data. If the fetch request comes back with zero results, this probably means it's the user's first time opening the app. If this is the case, you insert a new dog, name it "Fido", and set it as the currently selected dog.

If the fetch request came back with results, you set the first entity (there should only be one) as the currently selected dog.

Next, replace the implementation of `tableView(_:numberOfRowsInSection:)` with the following:

```
func tableView(tableView: UITableView,
  numberOfRowsInSection section: Int) -> Int {

    var numRows = 0
```

```
    if let dog = currentDog? {
      numRows =  dog.walks.count
    }

    return numRows;
}
```

As you can probably guess, this ties the number of rows in the table view to the number of walks set in the currently selected dog.

Next, replace `tableView(_:cellForRowAtIndexPath:)` as follows:

```
func tableView(tableView: UITableView,
  cellForRowAtIndexPath
  indexPath: NSIndexPath) -> UITableViewCell {

  let cell =
  tableView.dequeueReusableCellWithIdentifier("Cell",
      forIndexPath: indexPath) as UITableViewCell

  let dateFormatter = NSDateFormatter()
  dateFormatter.dateStyle = .ShortStyle
  dateFormatter.timeStyle = .MediumStyle

  //the next two statements have changed
  let walk = currentDog.walks[indexPath.row] as Walk

  cell.textLabel.text =
    dateFormatter.stringFromDate(walk.date)

  return cell
}
```

Only two lines of code have changed. Now, you take the date of each walk and display it in the corresponding table view cell.

The `add` method still has a reference to the old `walks` array. Remove it for now—you'll re-implement this method in the next step:

```
@IBAction func add(sender: AnyObject) {
  //remove walks.append(NSDate())
  tableView.reloadData()
}
```

Build and run to make sure you've hooked up everything correctly:

Hooray! You've inserted a dog into Core Data and are currently populating the table view with his list of walks. This list doesn't have any walks at the moment, so the table doesn't look very exciting.

Tap the plus (+) button and it understandably does nothing. You haven't implemented it yet! Before the transition to Core Data, this method simply added an `NSDate` object to an array and reloaded the table view. Re-implement it as shown below:

```
@IBAction func add(sender: AnyObject) {

  //Insert new Walk entity into Core Data
  let walkEntity = NSEntityDescription.entityForName("Walk",
    inManagedObjectContext: managedContext)

  let walk = Walk(entity: walkEntity!,
    insertIntoManagedObjectContext: managedContext)

  walk.date = NSDate()

  //Insert the new Walk into the Dog's walks set
  var walks =
    currentDog.walks.mutableCopy() as NSMutableOrderedSet

  walks.addObject(walk)

  currentDog.walks = walks.copy() as NSOrderedSet
```

```
    //Save the managed object context
    var error: NSError?
    if !managedContext!.save(&error) {
      println("Could not save: \(error)")
    }

    //Reload table view
    tableView.reloadData()
}
```

As you can see, the Core Data version of this method is much more complicated. First, you have to create a new `Walk` entity and set its date attribute to now. Then, you have to insert this walk into the currently selected dog's list of walks.

However, the `walks` attribute is of type `NSOrderedSet`. `NSOrderedSet` is immutable, so you first have to create a mutable copy (`NSMutableOrderedSet`), insert the new walk and *then* reset an immutable copy of this mutable ordered set back on the dog.

> **Note:** Is adding a new object into a to-many relationship making your head spin? Many people can sympathize, which is why many of the Core Data open source projects have convenience methods to do this.
>
> Core Data can make things easier for you, though. If the relationship weren't ordered, you'd just be able to set the "one" side of the relationship (e.g., `walk.dog = currentDog`) rather than the "many" side and Core Data would use the inverse relationship defined in the model editor to add the walk to the dog's set of walks.

Finally, you commit your changes to the persistent store by calling `save` on the managed object context, and you reload the table view.

Build and run the app, and tap the plus (+) button a few times:

Great! The list of walks should now be saved in Core Data. Verify this by terminating the app in the fast app switcher and re-launching from scratch.

Deleting objects from Core Data

Let's say you were too trigger-friendly and tapped the plus (+) button when you didn't mean to. You didn't actually walk your dog, so you want to delete the walk you just added.

You've added objects to Core Data, you've fetched them, modified them and saved them again. What you haven't yet done is delete them—but you're about to do that next.

First, add the following method to **ViewController.swift**:

```
func tableView(tableView: UITableView,
    canEditRowAtIndexPath indexPath: NSIndexPath) -> Bool {
    return true
}
```

You're going to use `UITableView`'s default behavior for deleting items: swipe left to reveal the red **Delete** button, then tap on it to delete. The table view calls this

UITableViewDataSource method to ask if a particular cell is editable, and returning true means all the cells should be editable.

Next, add the following method:

```
func tableView(tableView: UITableView,
  commitEditingStyle
  editingStyle: UITableViewCellEditingStyle,
  forRowAtIndexPath indexPath: NSIndexPath) {

    if editingStyle == UITableViewCellEditingStyle.Delete {

      //1
      let walkToRemove =
      currentDog.walks[indexPath.row] as Walk

      //2
      managedContext.deleteObject(walkToRemove)

      //3
      var error: NSError?
      if !managedContext.save(&error) {
        println("Could not save: \(error)")
      }

      //4
      tableView.deleteRowsAtIndexPaths([indexPath],
        withRowAnimation: UITableViewRowAnimation.Automatic)
    }
}
```

This table view data source method is called when you tap the red Delete button. Let's go step by step through the code:

1. First, you get a reference to the walk you want to delete.
2. Remove the walk from Core Data by calling NSManagedObjectContext's deleteObject method. Core Data also takes care of removing the deleted walk from the current dog's walks relationship.
3. No changes are final until you save your managed object context, not even deletions!
4. Finally, you animate the table view to tell the user about the deletion.

Build and run the app one more time. You should have several walks from previous runs. Pick any and swipe to the left:

Tap on the Delete button to remove the walk. Verify that the walk is actually gone by terminating the app and re-launching from scratch.

The walk you just removed is gone for good. Core Data giveth and Core Data taketh away.

Where to go from here?

If you followed this chapter all the way through, then you've spent a lot of time on setup and the underlying pieces that make up Core Data. This was intentional! Core Data has a reputation for its steep learning curve. This is partly because of all the setup it requires just to get started: the stack, the data model, the managed object subclasses, et cetera. In addition, you got some firsthand experience with relationships and deletion.

These last three chapters were not only a tour of Core Data but also a thorough introduction to the entire framework. Even though you didn't spend long on any one particular topic, you're now familiar with the basics of fetching, saving, editing and deleting objects from a Core Data store backed by an SQLite database.

In the next chapter, you'll spend less time on setup and dig much deeper into fetching and other advanced topics in iOS 8. You got a small taste of the basic operations in this chapter, but there's a lot more to learn. Are you ready to continue your journey?

Chapter 4: Intermediate Fetching

By Pietro Rea

In the first three chapters of this book, you began exploring the foundations of Core Data, including very basic ways of saving and fetching data to and from your Core Data persistent store.

For example, you performed simple, unrefined fetches such as "fetch *all* Bowtie entities." Sometimes this is all you need to do, but often you'll want to exert more control over how you retrieve information from Core Data.

Building on what you've learned so far, this chapter dives deep into the topic of **fetching**. Fetching is a large topic in Core Data, and you have many tools at your disposal. By the end of this chapter, you'll know how to:

- fetch only what you need to;
- refine your fetched results using predicates;
- fetch in the background to avoid blocking the UI; and
- avoid unnecessary fetching by updating objects directly in the persistent store.

This chapter is a toolbox sampler: Its aim is to expose you to many of the things you can do with fetching so that when the time comes, you can use the right tool.

NSFetchRequest: the star of the show

As you've learned in previous chapters, the way to fetch records from Core Data is to create an instance of `NSFetchRequest`, configure it as you like it and hand it over to `NSManagedObjectContext` to do the heavy lifting for you.

Simple enough, right? There are actually *four* different ways to get ahold of a fetch request. Some are more popular than others, but you'll likely encounter all of them at some point as a Core Data developer.

Before jumping to the starter project for this chapter, let's quickly go over the different ways to set up a fetch request so you're not caught by surprise. They are demonstrated below:

```
//1
let fetchRequest1 = NSFetchRequest()

let entity = NSEntityDescription.entityForName("Person",
  inManagedObjectContext: managedObjectContext!)

fetchRequest1.entity = entity!

//2
let fetchRequest2 = NSFetchRequest(entityName: "Person")

//3
let fetchRequest3 =
 managedObjectModel.fetchRequestTemplateForName("peopleFR")

//4
let fetchRequest4 =
 managedObjectModel.fetchRequestFromTemplateWithName("peopleFR",
  substitutionVariables: ["NAME" : "Ray"])
```

Let's go through them in turn:

1. In the first example, you initialize an instance of `NSFetchRequest` as if it were any other object. At a minimum, you must specify an `NSEntityDescription` for the fetch request. In this case, the entity is `Person`. You initialize an instance of `NSEntityDescription` and use it to set the fetch request's `entity` property.
2. Here, you use `NSFetchRequest`'s convenience initializer. It initializes a new fetch request and sets its entity property in one step. You simply need to provide a string for the entity name rather than a full-fledged `NSEntityDescription`.

3. In the third example, you retrieve your fetch request from your `NSManagedObjectModel`. You can configure and store commonly used fetch requests in Xcode's data model editor. You'll learn how to do this later in the chapter.

4. The last case is similar to the third. You get a fetch request from your managed object model, but this time, you pass in some extra variables. These "substitution" variables are used in a predicate to refine your fetched results.

The first two examples are the simple cases you've already seen. You'll see even more of these simple cases in the rest of this chapter, in addition to stored fetch requests and other tricks of `NSFetchRequest`!

Introducing the Bubble Tea app

This chapter's sample project is a bubble tea app. For those of you who don't know about bubble tea (also known as "boba tea"), it is a Taiwanese tea-based drink that contains large tapioca pearls. It's very yummy!

You can think of this bubble tea app as an ultra-niche Yelp. Using this app, you can find the locations near you that sell your favorite Taiwanese drink. For this chapter, you'll only be working with static venue data from Foursquare—around 30 locations in New York City that sell bubble tea. You'll use this data to build the filter/sort screen to arrange the list of static venues as you see fit.

Go to this chapter's files and open **Bubble Tea Finder.xcodeproj**. Build and run the starter project, and you'll see the following:

The sample app consists of a number of table view cells with static information. Although the sample project isn't very exciting at the moment, there's a lot of setup that's already been done for you.

Open the project navigator and take a look at the full list of files in the starter project:

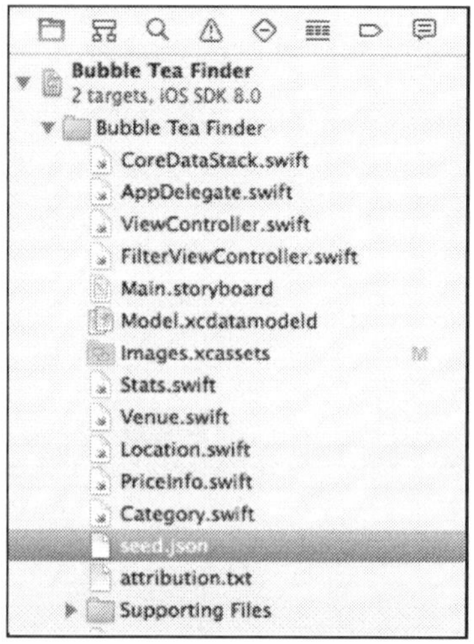

It turns out that most of the Core Data setup you had to do in the first section of the book comes ready for you to use. Here's a quick overview of the components that you get in the starter project. It's quite a lot, so I've grouped the files into categories below:

- **Seed data:** **seed.json** is a JSON file that contains real-world venue data for venues in New York City that serve bubble tea. Since this is real data coming from Foursquare, the structure is more complex than previous seed data used in this book.
- **Data model:** Click on **Model.xcdatamodeld** to open Xcode's model editor. The top-level entity is `Venue`. It contains attributes for a venue's name, phone number and the number of specials it's offering at the moment.

  Since the JSON data is rather complex, the data model breaks down a venue's information into other entities. These are `Category`, `Location`, `PriceInfo` and `Stats`. For example, `Location` has attributes for city, state, country, et cetera.
- **Managed object subclasses:** All the entities in your data model also have corresponding `NSManagedObject` subclasses. These are **Venue.swift**, **Location.swift**, **PriceInfo.swift**, **Category.swift** and **Stats.swift**.
- **App Delegate:** On first launch, the app delegate reads from **seed.json**, creates corresponding Core Data objects and saves them to the persistent store.

- **CoreDataStack**: As in previous chapters, this object contains the cadre of Core Data objects known as the "stack": the context, the model, the persistent store and the persistent store coordinator. No need to set this up—it comes ready for you to use it.
- **View Controllers:** The initial view controller that shows you the list of venues is **ViewController.swift**. Tapping the Filter button on the top-right brings up **FilterViewController.swift**. There's not much going on here at the moment. You'll be adding code to these two files throughout the chapter.

When you first launched the sample app, you saw only static information. However, your app delegate had already read the seed data from **seed.json**, parsed it into Core Data objects and saved them into the persistent store.

Your first task will be to fetch this data and display it on a table view. However, this time you'll do it with a twist.

Stored fetch requests

As previously mentioned, you can store frequently used fetch requests right in the data model. Not only does this make them easier to access, but you also get the benefit of using a GUI tool to set up the fetch request parameters.

Let's give it a try. Open **Model.xcdatamodeld** and long-click the **Add Entity** button:

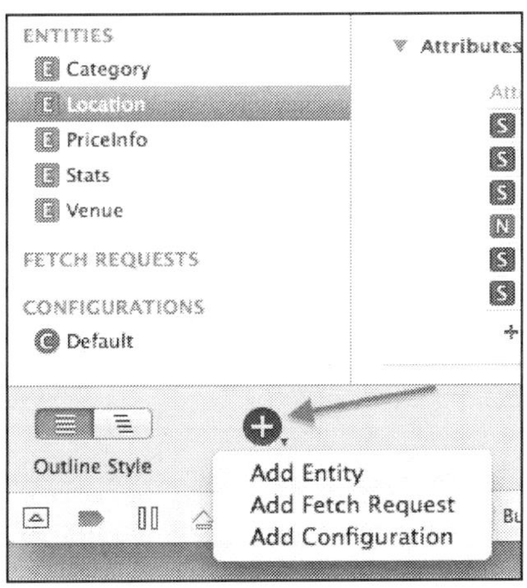

Select **Add Fetch Request** from the menu. This will create a new fetch request on the left-side bar and take you to a special fetch request editor:

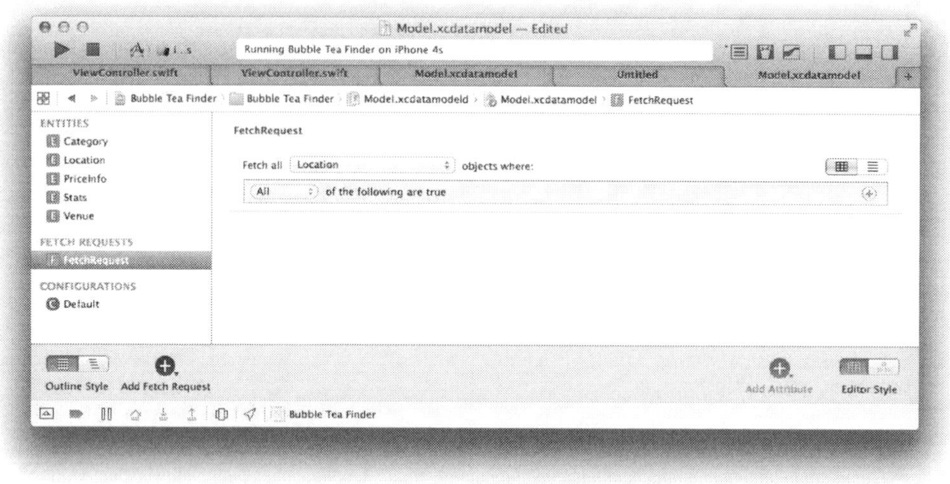

You can click on the newly created fetch request on the left-hand sidebar to change its name. Leave it with the default "FetchRequest" for now.

You can make your fetch request as general or as specific as you want using this visual tool in Xcode's data model editor. To start, create a fetch request that retrieves all `Venue` objects from the persistent store.

You only need to make one change here: click the dropdown menu next to **Fetch all** and select **Venue**.

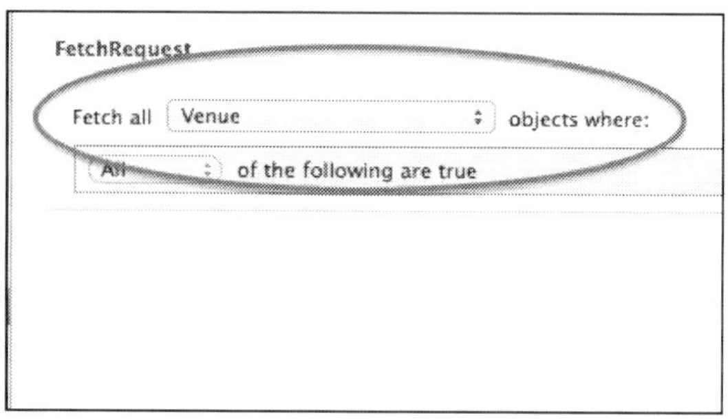

That's all you need to do. If you wanted to refine your fetch request with an additional predicate, you could also add conditions from the fetch request editor.

Let's take your newly created fetch request out for a spin. Switch to **ViewController.swift** and import the Core Data framework:

```
import CoreData
```

Then, add the following two properties to the top of the file:

```
//Add below var coreDataStack: CoreDataStack!
var fetchRequest: NSFetchRequest!
var venues: [Venue]!
```

The first property will hold your fetch request. The second property is the array of `Venue` objects that you'll use to populate the table view.

Next, make the following additions to the currently empty `viewDidLoad`:

```
fetchRequest =
coreDataStack.model.fetchRequestTemplateForName("FetchRequest")

fetchAndReload()
```

The first line connects the `fetchRequest` property you set up moments ago to the one you created using Xcode's data model editor. There are two things to remember here:

1. Unlike other ways of getting a fetch request, this one involves the managed object model. This is why you must go through `CoreDataStack`'s `model` property to retrieve your fetch request.
2. `NSManagedObjectModel`'s `fetchRequestTemplateForName()` takes a string identifier. This identifier must exactly match whatever name you chose for your fetch request in the model editor. Otherwise, your app will throw an exception and crash. Whoops!

The second line calls a method you haven't defined yet, so Xcode will complain about it. Declare this method at the bottom of the file to appease Xcode:

```
//MARK - Helper methods

func fetchAndReload(){

  var error: NSError?
  let results =
coreDataStack.context.executeFetchRequest(fetchRequest,
    error: &error) as [Venue]?

  if let fetchedResults = results {
```

```
    venues = fetchedResults
  } else {
    println("Could not fetch \(error), \(error!.userInfo)")
  }

  tableView.reloadData()
}
```

As its name suggests, `fetchAndReload()` executes the fetch request and reloads the table view. Other methods in this class will need to see the fetched objects, so you store the fetched results in the `venues` property you defined earlier.

There's one more thing you have to do before you can run the sample project for the first time: You have to hook up the table view's data source with the fetched `Venue` objects.

Replace the placeholder implementations of `numberOfRowsInSection` and `cellForRowAtIndexPath` with the following:

```
func tableView(tableView: UITableView?,
  numberOfRowsInSection section: Int) -> Int {
    return venues.count
}

func tableView(tableView: UITableView!,
  cellForRowAtIndexPath
  indexPath: NSIndexPath!) -> UITableViewCell! {

    var cell =
      tableView.dequeueReusableCellWithIdentifier("VenueCell")
      as UITableViewCell

    let venue = venues[indexPath.row]
    cell.textLabel.text = venue.name
    cell.detailTextLabel!.text = venue.priceInfo.priceCategory

    return cell
}
```

You've implemented these methods many times in this book, so you're probably familiar with what they do. The first method, `numberOfRowsInSection`, matches the number of cells in the table view with the number of fetched objects in the `venues` array.

The second method, `cellForRowAtIndexPath`, dequeues a cell for a given index path and populates it with the information of the corresponding `Venue` in the `venues` array.

In this case, the main label gets the venue's name and the detail label, in turn, gets a price category that is one of three possible values: $, $$ or $$$.

Build and run the project, and you'll see the following:

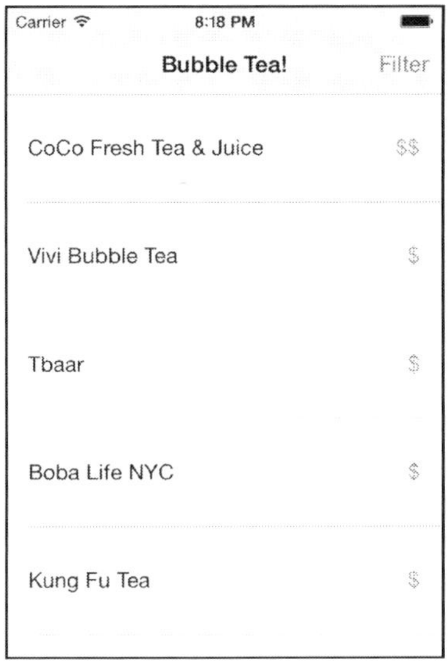

You can scroll down the list of bubble tea venues. These are all real places in New York City that sell the delicious drink.

> **Note:** When should you store fetch requests in your data model?
>
> If you know you'll be making the same fetch over and over in different parts of your app, you can use this feature to save you from writing the same code multiple times. A drawback of stored fetch requests is that there is no way to specify a sort order for the results.

Fetching different result types

All this time, you've probably been thinking of `NSFetchRequest` as a fairly simple tool. You give it some instructions and you get some objects in return. What else is there to it?

If this is the case, you've been underestimating this class. `NSFetchRequest` is the multi-function Swiss army knife of the Core Data framework! You can use it to fetch individual values, compute statistics on your data such as the average, minimum and maximum, and more.

How is this possible, you ask? `NSFetchRequest` has a property named `resultType`. So far, you've only used the default value, `NSManagedObjectResultType`. Here are all the possible values for a fetch request's result type:

- **NSManagedObjectResultType:** Returns managed objects (default value).
- **NSCountResultType**: Returns the count of the objects that match the fetch request.
- **NSDictionaryResultType**: This is a catch-all return type for returning the results of different calculations.
- **NSManagedObjectIDResultType**: Returns unique identifiers instead of full-fledged managed objects.

Let's go back to the sample project and apply these concepts in practice.

With the sample project running, tap **Filter** in the top-right corner to bring up the UI for the filter screen. You won't implement the actual filters/sorts right now. Instead, you'll focus on the following four labels:

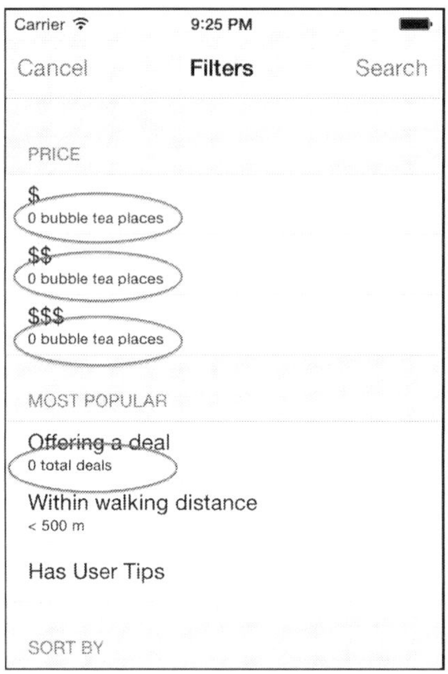

The filter screen is divided into three sections: Price, Most Popular and Sort By. That last section is not technically made up of "filters," but sorting usually goes hand in hand with filters, so we'll leave it like that. :]

Below each price filter is space for the total number of venues that fall into that price category. Similarly, there's a spot for the total number of deals across all venues. You'll implement these next.

Returning a count

Open **FilterViewController.swift** and, as always, import the Core Data framework at the top of the file:

```
import CoreData
```

Then add the following property below the last `@IBOutlet` property:

```
var coreDataStack: CoreDataStack!
```

This will hold the `CoreDataStack` object you've been using in the app delegate and in **ViewController.swift**.

Switch to **ViewController.swift** and make the following modification to the already implemented `prepareForSegue`:

```
override func prepareForSegue(segue: UIStoryboardSegue,
  sender: AnyObject?) {
  if segue.identifier == "toFilterViewController" {
    let navController = segue.destinationViewController
      as UINavigationController

    let filterVC = navController.topViewController
      as FilterViewController

    //add the line below
    filterVC.coreDataStack = coreDataStack
  }
}
```

The new line of code propagates the `CoreDataStack` object from `ViewController` to `FilterViewController`. The filter screen is now ready to use Core Data.

Go back to **FilterViewController.swift** and add the following lazy property:

```
lazy var cheapVenuePredicate: NSPredicate = {
  var predicate =
```

```
  NSPredicate(format: "priceInfo.priceCategory == %@", "$")
  return predicate!
  }()
```

You'll use this lazily instantiated `NSPredicate` to calculate the number of venues that fall into the lowest price category.

> **Note:** `NSPredicate` supports key paths. This is why you can drill down from the `Venue` entity into the `PriceInfo` entity using `priceInfo.priceCategory`.

Next, implement the following method in `FilterViewController`:

```
func populateCheapVenueCountLabel()
{
  // $ fetch request

  let fetchRequest = NSFetchRequest(entityName: "Venue")
  fetchRequest.resultType = .CountResultType
  fetchRequest.predicate = cheapVenuePredicate

  var error: NSError?

  let result =
  coreDataStack.context.executeFetchRequest(fetchRequest,
    error: &error) as [NSNumber]?

  if let countArray = result {

    let count = countArray[0].integerValue

    firstPriceCategoryLabel.text =
    "\(count) bubble tea places"

  } else {
    println("Could not fetch \(error), \(error!.userInfo)")
  }
}
```

This method creates a fetch request to fetch `Venue` entities. You then set the result type to `.CountResultType` and set the fetch request's predicate to the lazy variable you defined moments ago.

When you set a fetch result's result type to NSCountResultType, the return value becomes an optional Swift array containing a single NSNumber. The integer inside the NSNumber is the total count you're looking for.

Once again, you execute the fetch request against CoreDataStack's NSManagedObjectContext property. Then you extract the integer from the resulting NSNumber and use it to populate firstPriceCategoryLabel.

Before you run the sample app, implement viewDidLoad to invoke the method you just implemented:

```
override func viewDidLoad() {
  super.viewDidLoad()
  populateCheapVenueCountLabel()
}
```

Now build and run to test if these changes took effect. Tap **Filter** to bring up the filter/sort menu:

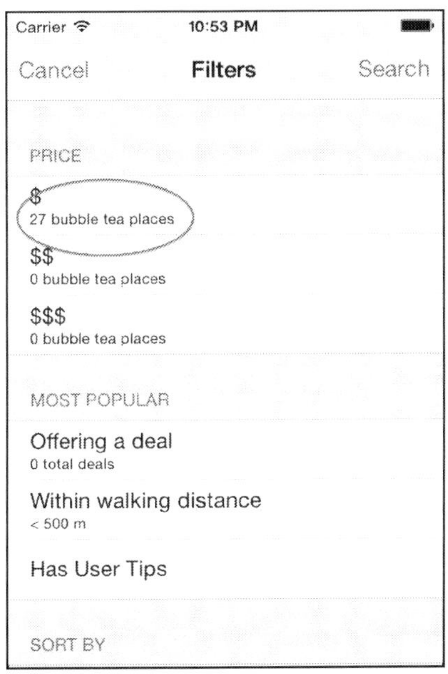

The label under the first price filter now says "27 bubble tea places." Hooray! You've successfully used NSFetchRequest to calculate a count.

> **Note:** You may be thinking that you could have just as easily fetched the actual `Venue` objects and gotten the count from the array's `count` property.
>
> That's true. Fetching counts instead of objects is mainly a performance optimization. For example, if you had census data for New York City and wanted to know how many people lived in its metropolitan area, would you prefer Core Data gave you the number 8,300,000 (an integer) or an array of 8,300,000 records? Obviously, getting the count directly is more memory-efficient.
>
> There's a whole chapter devoted to Core Data performance. If you want to learn more about performance optimization in Core Data, check out Chapter 9, "Measuring and Boosting Performance."

Now that you're acquainted with the count result type, let's quickly implement the count for the second price category filter.

Add the following lazy property below the first one you added earlier:

```
lazy var moderateVenuePredicate: NSPredicate = {
  var predicate =
    NSPredicate(format: "priceInfo.priceCategory == %@", "$$")
  return predicate!
  }()
```

This `NSPredicate` is almost identical to the cheap venue predicate, except that this one matches against $$ instead of $.

Similarly, add the following method below `populateCheapVenueCountLabel`:

```
func populateModerateVenueCountLabel() {
  // $$ fetch request

  let fetchRequest = NSFetchRequest(entityName: "Venue")
  fetchRequest.resultType = .CountResultType
  fetchRequest.predicate = moderateVenuePredicate

  var error: NSError?
  let result =
  coreDataStack.context.executeFetchRequest(fetchRequest,
    error: &error) as [NSNumber]?

  if let countArray = result {
```

```
    let count = countArray[0].integerValue

    secondPriceCategoryLabel.text =
    "\(count) bubble tea places"

  } else {
    println("Could not fetch \(error), \(error!.userInfo)")
  }
}
```

Finally, modify `viewDidLoad` to invoke your newly defined method:

```
override func viewDidLoad() {
  super.viewDidLoad()

  populateCheapVenueCountLabel()

  //add the line below
  populateModerateVenueCountLabel()
}
```

Build and run the sample project. As before, tap **Filter** on the top right to reach the filter/sort screen:

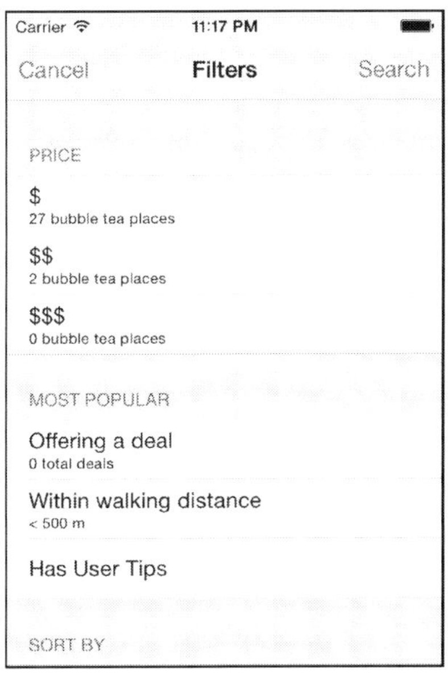

Great news for bubble tea lovers! Only two places are moderately expensive. Bubble tea as a whole seems to be quite accessible. :]

An alternate way to fetch a count

Now that you're familiar with NSCountResultType, it's a good time to mention that there's an alternate API for fetching a count directly from Core Data.

Since there's one more price category count to implement, let's use this alternate API now. Add the follow lazy property below the one you added previously:

```
lazy var expensiveVenuePredicate: NSPredicate = {
  var predicate =
    NSPredicate(format: "priceInfo.priceCategory == %@", "$$$")
  return predicate!
  }()
```

Now implement the following method below populateModerateVenueCountLabel:

```
func populateExpensiveVenueCountLabel()
{
  // $$$ fetch request

  let fetchRequest = NSFetchRequest(entityName: "Venue")
  fetchRequest.predicate = expensiveVenuePredicate

  var error: NSError?
  let count =
  coreDataStack.context.countForFetchRequest(fetchRequest,
    error: &error)

  if count == NSNotFound {
    println("Could not fetch \(error), \(error!.userInfo)")
  }

  thirdPriceCategoryLabel.text =
  "\(count) bubble tea places"
}
```

Like in the previous two scenarios, here you create a fetch request for retrieving Venue objects. Then you set the predicate that you defined as a lazy property moments earlier, expensiveVenuePredicate.

The difference between this scenario and the last two is that here, you don't set the result type to NSCountResultType. Rather than the usual executeFetchRequest(), you use NSManagedObjectContext's method countForFetchRequest() instead.

The return value for countForFetchRequest() is an integer that you can use directly to populate the third price category label.

Finally, modify `viewDidLoad` to invoke the method you just defined:

```
override func viewDidLoad() {
  super.viewDidLoad()

  populateCheapVenueCountLabel()
  populateModerateVenueCountLabel()

  //add the line below
  populateExpensiveVenueCountLabel()
}
```

Build and run to see if your latest changes took effect. The filter/sort screen should look like this:

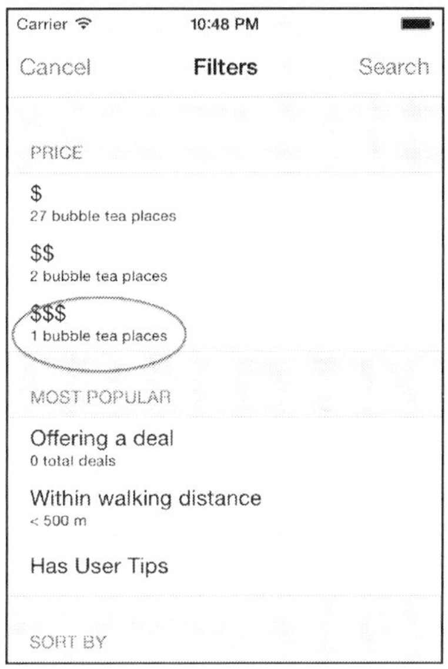

There's only one bubble tea venue that falls into the $$$ category. Maybe they use real pearls instead of tapioca?

Performing calculations with fetch requests

All three price category labels are populated with the number of venues that fall into each category. The next step is to populate the label under "Offering a deal." It currently says "0 total deals." That can't be right!

Where exactly does this information come from? `Venue` has a `specialCount` attribute that captures the number of deals the venue is currently offering. Unlike the labels under the price category, you now need to know the total sum of deals across *all* venues since a particularly savvy venue could have many deals at once.

The naïve approach would be to load all venues into memory and sum their deals using a `for`-loop. If you're hoping for a better way, you're in luck: Core Data has built-in support for a number of different functions such as average, sum, min and max.

Still in **FilterViewController.swift**, implement the following method:

```
func populateDealsCountLabel() {
  //1
  let fetchRequest = NSFetchRequest(entityName: "Venue")
  fetchRequest.resultType = .DictionaryResultType

  //2
  let sumExpressionDesc = NSExpressionDescription()
  sumExpressionDesc.name = "sumDeals"

  //3
  sumExpressionDesc.expression =
    NSExpression(forFunction: "sum:",
      arguments:[NSExpression(forKeyPath: "specialCount")])

  sumExpressionDesc.expressionResultType =
    .Integer32AttributeType

  //4
  fetchRequest.propertiesToFetch = [sumExpressionDesc]

  //5
  var error: NSError?
  let result =
  coreDataStack.context.executeFetchRequest(fetchRequest,
    error: &error) as [NSDictionary]?

  if let resultArray = result {

    let resultDict = resultArray[0]
    let numDeals: AnyObject? = resultDict["sumDeals"]
    numDealsLabel.text = "\(numDeals!) total deals"

  } else {
    println("Could not fetch \(error), \(error!.userInfo)")
  }
}
```

This method contains a few classes you've not encountered in the book before, so let's explain each step in turn:

1. You begin by creating your typical fetch request for retrieving `Venue` objects. Next, you specify the result type to be `DictionaryResultType`.
2. You create an `NSExpressionDescription` to request the sum, and give it the name `"sumDeals"` so you can read its result out of the result dictionary that you'll get back from the fetch request.
3. You give the expression description an `NSExpression` to specify that you want the sum function. Then you give *that* expression another `NSExpression` to specify what property you want to sum over—in this case, `specialCount`. Lastly, you have to set the return data type of your expression description, so you set it to `Integer32AttributeType`.
4. You tell your original fetch request that you want to fetch the sum by setting its `propertiesToFetch` property to the expression description you just created.
5. Finally, you can execute the fetch request. You cast the return value of this fetch request to an optional dictionary, fish out the result of your expression using your expression description's name (`sumDeals`) and you're done!

> **Note:** What other functions does Core Data support? To name a few: count, min, max, average, median, mode, absolute value and many more. For a comprehensive list, check out Apple's documentation for `NSExpression`.

Fetching a calculated value from Core Data requires you to follow many, often unintuitive steps, so make sure you have a good reason for using this technique—like performance considerations.

Next, add the following line to the bottom of `viewDidLoad`:

```
populateDealsCountLabel()
```

Build the sample project and head to the filter/sort screen to verify your changes:

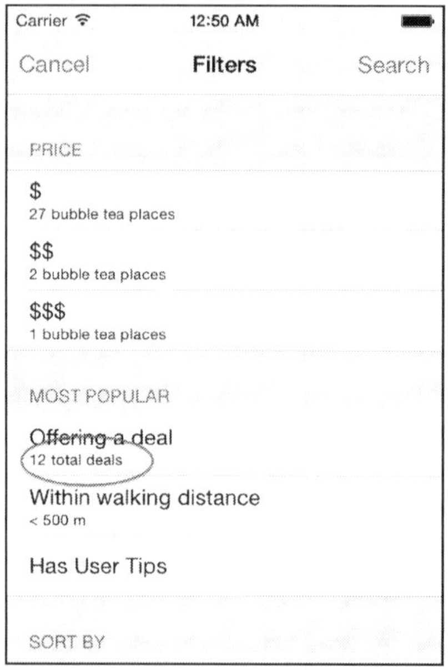

Great! There are 12 total deals across all the venues that you have stored in Core Data.

You've now used three of the four supported `NSFetchRequest` result types: `.ManagedObjectResultType`, `.CountResultType` and `.DictionaryResultType`.

The remaining result type is `.ManagedObjectIDResultType`. When you fetch with this type, the result is an array of `NSManagedObjectID` objects rather the actual managed objects they represent. An `NSManagedObjectID` is a compact, universal identifier for a managed object. It works like the primary key in the database!

Prior to iOS 5, fetching by IDs was popular because it conformed to the thread confinement concurrency model. Now that thread confinement has been deprecated in favor of more modern concurrency models, there's little reason to fetch by object ID anymore.

> **Note:** You can set up multiple managed object contexts to run concurrent operations and keep long-running operations off the main thread. For more information, check out Chapter 10, "Multiple Managed Object Contexts."Predicates in fetch requests

You've gotten a taste of all the things a fetch request can do for you. But just as important as the information a fetch request returns is the information it *doesn't* return. For practical reasons, you have cap the incoming data at some point.

Why? Imagine a perfectly connected object graph, one where each Core Data object is connected to every other object through a series of relationships. If Core Data didn't put limits on the information a fetch request returned, you'd be fetching the entire object graph every single time! That's not memory efficient.

There are ways you can manually limit the information you get back from a fetch request. For example, `NSFetchRequest` supports fetching batches. You can use the properties `fetchBatchSize`, `fetchLimit` and `fetchOffset` to control the batching behavior.

Core Data also tries to minimize its memory consumption for you by using a technique called **faulting**. A fault is a placeholder object representing a managed object that hasn't yet been fully brought into memory.

Yet another way to limit your object graph is to use predicates, as you've done to populate the venue count labels above. Let's add the filters to the sample app using predicates.

Still in **FilterViewController.swift**, add the following protocol declaration outside of the main class definition:

```
protocol FilterViewControllerDelegate: class {
  func filterViewController(filter: FilterViewController,
    didSelectPredicate predicate:NSPredicate?,
    sortDescriptor:NSSortDescriptor?)
}
```

This protocol defines a delegate method that will notify the delegate that the user selected a new sort/filter combination.

Next, define the following delegate property in `FilterViewController`:

```
weak var delegate: FilterViewControllerDelegate?
var selectedSortDescriptor: NSSortDescriptor?
var selectedPredicate: NSPredicate?
```

This first property will hold a reference to `FilterViewController`'s delegate. The second and third properties will hold references to the currently selected `NSSortDescriptor` and `NSPredicate`, respectively.

Next, re-implement the `saveButtonTapped` as shown below:

```
@IBAction func saveButtonTapped(sender: UIBarButtonItem) {

  delegate!.filterViewController(self,
    didSelectPredicate: selectedPredicate,
    sortDescriptor: selectedSortDescriptor)

  dismissViewControllerAnimated(true, completion:nil)
}
```

This means every time you tap Search in the top-right corner of the filter/sort screen, you'll notify the delegate of your selection and dismiss the filter/sort screen to reveal the list of venues behind it.

You need to make one more change in this file. Scroll down to `didSelectRowAtIndexPath` and implement it as shown below:

```
override func tableView(tableView: UITableView,
  didSelectRowAtIndexPath indexPath: NSIndexPath) {

    let cell = tableView.cellForRowAtIndexPath(indexPath)!

    switch cell {
      // Price section
    case cheapVenueCell:
      selectedPredicate = cheapVenuePredicate
    case moderateVenueCell:
      selectedPredicate = moderateVenuePredicate
    case expensiveVenueCell:
      selectedPredicate = expensiveVenuePredicate
    default:
      println("default case")
    }

    cell.accessoryType = .Checkmark
}
```

When the user taps on any of the first three price category cells, this method will map the selected cell to the appropriate predicate. You store a reference to this predicate in `selectedPredicate` to have ready when you notify the delegate of the user's selection.

Now, switch to **ViewController.swift** and make the following change to the class declaration:

```
class ViewController: UIViewController,
FilterViewControllerDelegate {
```

Adding `FilterViewControllerDelegate` to the class declaration tells the compiler that this class will conform to this protocol. You haven't implemented the delegate method yet, so Xcode will complain until you do. You'll fix this in a second.

Next, add the following delegate method at the bottom of the class:

```
//MARK - FilterViewControllerDelegate methods

func filterViewController(filter: FilterViewController,
  didSelectPredicate predicate:NSPredicate?,
  sortDescriptor:NSSortDescriptor?) {

    fetchRequest.predicate = nil
    fetchRequest.sortDescriptors = nil

    if let fetchPredicate = predicate {
      fetchRequest.predicate = fetchPredicate
    }

    if let sr = sortDescriptor {
      fetchRequest.sortDescriptors = [sr]
    }

    fetchAndReload()
}
```

This delegate method fires every time the user selects a new filter/sort combination. Here, you reset your fetch request's `predicate` and `sortDescriptors`, then unwrap the predicate and sort descriptor passed into the method and reload.

There's one more thing you need to do before you can test your price category filters. Head over to `prepareForSegue` and add the following line inside the `if` statement:

```
//add line below filterVC.coreDataStack = coreDataStack
filterVC.delegate = self
```

This formally declares `ViewController` as `FilterViewController`'s delegate.

Now build and run the sample project. Go to the Filter screen, tap the first price category cell (**$**) and then tap **Search** in the top-right corner.

What happened? Your app crashes with the following error message in the console:

```
2014-09-27 00:51:29.501 Bubble Tea Finder[23672:1975276] *** Terminating
app due to uncaught exception 'NSInternalInconsistencyException', reason:
'Can't modify a named fetch request in an immutable model.'
*** First throw call stack:
(
    0   CoreFoundation                        0x005cfdf6
```

Remember how earlier in the chapter, you defined your fetch request in the data model? It turns out that if you use that technique, the fetch request becomes immutable. You can't change its predicate at runtime, or else this will happen. If you want to set a fetch request in advance, you have to do it in the data model editor.

Still in **ViewController.swift**, go back to `viewDidLoad` and make the following change:

```
override func viewDidLoad() {
  super.viewDidLoad()

//  fetchRequest =
//
coreDataStack.model.fetchRequestTemplateForName("FetchRequest")

  fetchRequest = NSFetchRequest(entityName: "Venue")

  fetchAndReload()
}
```

Comment out the line that retrieves the fetch request from the template in the managed object model. Instead, create an instance of `NSFetchRequest` directly.

Build and run the sample app one more time. Go to the Filter screen, tap the second price category cell (**$$**) and then tap **Search** in the top-right corner. This is the result:

As expected, there are only two venues in this category. Test the first ($) and third ($$$) price category filters as well and make sure the filtered list contains the correct number of venues for each.

Let's practice writing a few more predicates for the remaining filters. The process is similar to what you've done already, so this time you'll do it with less explanation.

Switch to **FilterViewController.swift** once more and add these three lazy properties to the top of the class:

```
lazy var offeringDealPredicate: NSPredicate = {
  var pr = NSPredicate(format: "specialCount > 0")
  return pr!
  }()

lazy var walkingDistancePredicate: NSPredicate = {
  var pr = NSPredicate(format: "location.distance < 500")
  return pr!
  }()

lazy var hasUserTipsPredicate: NSPredicate = {
  var pr = NSPredicate(format: "stats.tipCount > 0")
  return pr!
  }()
```

The first predicate specifies venues that are currently offering one or more deals, the second predicate specifies venues that are less than 500 meters away from your current location and the third predicate specifies venues that have at least one user tip.

> **Note:** So far in the book, you've written predicates with a single condition. You can write predicates that check two conditions instead of one by using compound predicate operators such as `AND`, `OR` and `NOT`.
>
> Alternatively, you can string two simple predicates into one compound predicate by using the class `NSCompoundPredicate`.
>
> `NSPredicate` isn't technically part of Core Data (it's part of Foundation) so this book won't cover it in depth, but you can seriously improve your Core Data chops by learning the ins and outs of this nifty class. For more information, make sure to check out Apple's Predicate Programming Guide:
>
> https://developer.apple.com/library/mac/documentation/Cocoa/Conceptual/Predicates/predicates.html

Next, scroll down to `didSelectRowAtIndexPath`. You're going to add three more cases to the `switch` statement you added earlier:

```
override func tableView(tableView: UITableView,
  didSelectRowAtIndexPath indexPath: NSIndexPath) {

    let cell = tableView.cellForRowAtIndexPath(indexPath)!

    switch cell {
      // Price section
    case cheapVenueCell:
      selectedPredicate = cheapVenuePredicate
    case moderateVenueCell:
      selectedPredicate = moderateVenuePredicate
    case expensiveVenueCell:
      selectedPredicate = expensiveVenuePredicate
      //Most Popular section
    case offeringDealCell:
      selectedPredicate = offeringDealPredicate
    case walkingDistanceCell:
      selectedPredicate = walkingDistancePredicate
    case userTipsCell:
      selectedPredicate = hasUserTipsPredicate
    default:
      println("default case")
    }

    cell.accessoryType = .Checkmark
}
```

Above, you added cases for `offeringDealCell`, `walkingDistanceCell` and `userTipsCell`. These are the three new filters for which you're now adding support.

That's all you need to do. Build and run the sample app. Go to the filters page, select the **Offering Deals** filter and tap **Search**:

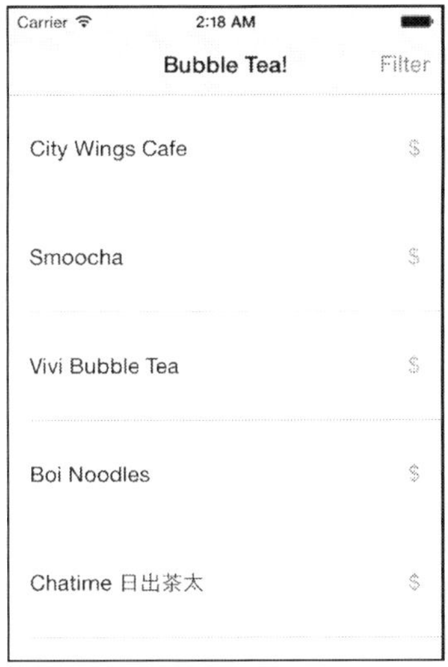

You'll see a total of six venues, starting with City Wings Cafe. You can verify that these venues have specials by looking them up in **seed.json**. For example, City Wing Cafe is currently offering four specials. Woo-hoo!

Sorting fetched results

Another powerful feature of `NSFetchRequest` is its ability to sort fetched results for you. It does this by using yet another handy Foundation class, `NSSortDescriptor`. These sorts happen at the SQLite level, not on memory. This makes sorting in Core Data fast and efficient.

In this section, you'll implement four different sorts to complete the filter/sort screen.

Begin by adding the following three lazy properties to the top of **FilterViewController.swift**:

```
lazy var nameSortDescriptor: NSSortDescriptor = {
  var sd = NSSortDescriptor(key: "name",
    ascending: true,
    selector: "localizedStandardCompare:")
  return sd
  }()

lazy var distanceSortDescriptor: NSSortDescriptor = {
  var sd = NSSortDescriptor(key: "location.distance",
```

```
      ascending: true)
    return sd
    }()

  lazy var priceSortDescriptor: NSSortDescriptor = {
    var sd = NSSortDescriptor(key: "priceInfo.priceCategory",
      ascending: true)
    return sd
    }()
```

The way to add sorts is very similar to the way you added filters. Each sort maps to one of these three lazy `NSSortDescriptor` properties.

To initialize an instance of `NSSortDescriptor` you need three things: a key path to specify the attribute by which you want to sort, a specification of whether the sort is ascending or descending and an optional selector.

> **Note:** If you've worked with `NSSortDescriptor` before, then you probably know there's a block-based API that takes a comparator instead of a selector. Unfortunately, Core Data doesn't support this way of defining a sort descriptor.
>
> The same thing goes for the block-based way of defining an `NSPredicate`. Core Data doesn't support this either. The reason is related to the fact that filtering/sorting happens in the SQLite database, so the predicate/sort descriptor has to match nicely to something that can be written as an SQLite statement.

The three sort descriptors are going to sort by name, distance and price category, respectively, and they are all ascending. Before moving on, take a closer look at the first sort descriptor, `nameSortDescriptor`. The initializer takes in an optional selector called `localizedStandardCompare`. What is that?

Any time you're sorting user-facing strings, Apple recommends that you pass in `localizedStandardCompare` to sort according to the language rules of the current locale. That means the sort will "just work" and do the right thing for languages with accented characters, for example. It's the little things that matter. :]

Next, go down to `didSelectRowAtIndexPath` and add the following cases to the end of the `switch` statement:

```
//Sort By section
case nameAZSortCell:
```

```
    selectedSortDescriptor = nameSortDescriptor
  case nameZASortCell:
    selectedSortDescriptor =
      nameSortDescriptor.reversedSortDescriptor
      as? NSSortDescriptor
  case distanceSortCell:
    selectedSortDescriptor = distanceSortDescriptor
  case priceSortCell:
    selectedSortDescriptor = priceSortDescriptor
```

Like before, this `switch` statement matches the cell the user tapped with the appropriate sort descriptor, so that it's ready to pass to the delegate when the user taps Search.

The only wrinkle is the `nameZA` sort descriptor. Rather than creating a separate sort descriptor, you can reuse the one for A-Z and simply call the method `reversedSortDescriptor`. How handy!

Everything else is hooked up for you to test the sorts you just implemented. Build and run the sample app and go to the Filter screen. Tap the **Z-A name filter** and then tap **Search**. You'll see search results ordered like so:

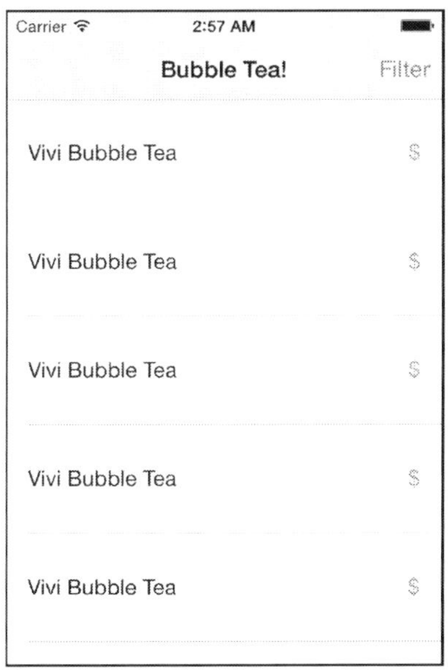

No, you're not seeing double. There really are six Vivi Bubble Tea venues in the data set—it's a popular bubble tea chain in NYC. As you scroll down the table view, you'll see that the app has indeed sorted the venues alphabetically from Z to A. Woo-hoo!

You've now completed your Filter screen, setting it up such that the user can combine any one filter with any one sort. Try different combinations to see what you get. The venue cell doesn't show much information, so if you need to verify a sort, you can go straight to the source and consult **seed.json**.

Asynchronous fetching

If you've gotten this far, there's both good news and bad news (and then more good news). The good news it that you've learned a lot about what you can do with a plain, old `NSFetchRequest`. The bad news is that every fetch request you've executed so far has blocked the main thread while you waited for your results to come back.

When you block the main thread, it makes the screen unresponsive to incoming touches and creates a slew of other problems. You haven't felt this blocking of the main thread because you've made simple fetch requests that only fetch a few objects at a time.

Since the beginning of Core Data, the framework has given developers several techniques to perform fetches in the background. New in iOS 8, Core Data now has an API for performing long-running fetch requests in the background and getting a completion callback when the fetch is completed.

Let's see this new API in action. Go back to **ViewController.swift** and add the following property:

```
var asyncFetchRequest: NSAsynchronousFetchRequest!
```

There you have it. The new class responsible for this asynchronous magic is aptly called `NSAsynchronousFetchRequest`. Don't be fooled by its name, though. It isn't directly related to `NSFetchRequest`; it's actually a subclass of `NSPersistentStoreRequest`.

Go to `viewDidLoad()` and re-implement it as shown below:

```
override func viewDidLoad() {
  super.viewDidLoad()

  //1
  fetchRequest = NSFetchRequest(entityName: "Venue")

  //2
  asyncFetchRequest =
  NSAsynchronousFetchRequest(fetchRequest: fetchRequest)
    { [unowned self] (result: NSAsynchronousFetchResult! )
```

```
      -> Void in

      self.venues = result.finalResult as [Venue]
      self.tableView.reloadData()
  }

  //3
  var error: NSError?
  let results =
  coreDataStack.context.executeRequest(asyncFetchRequest,
    error: &error)

  if let persistentStoreResults = results {
    //Returns immediately, cancel here if you want
  } else {
    println("Could not fetch \(error), \(error!.userInfo)")
  }
}
```

There's a lot that you haven't seen before, so let's cover it step by step:

1. Notice here than an asynchronous fetch request doesn't replace the regular fetch request. Rather, you can think of an asynchronous fetch request as a *wrapper* around the fetch request you already had.

2. To create an `NSAsynchronousFetchRequest` you need two things: a regular `NSFetchRequest` and a completion handler. Your fetched venues are contained in `NSAsynchronousFetchResult`'s `finalResult` property. Within the completion handler, you update the `venues` property and reload the table view.

3. Specifying the completion handler is not enough! You still have to execute the asynchronous fetch request. Once again, `CoreDataStack`'s `context` property handles the heavy lifting for you. However, notice that the method you use is different—this time, it's `executeRequest()` instead of the usual `executeFetchRequest()`.

4. `executeRequest()` returns immediately. You don't need to do anything with the return value since you're going to update the table view from within the completion block. The return type is `NSAsynchronousFetchResult`.

> **Note:** As an added bonus to this API, you can cancel the fetch request with `NSAsynchronousFetchResult`'s `cancel()` method.

If you were to build and run the sample app at this point, it would crash on launch. There are two more changes you need to make.

First, go to **CoreDataStack.swift** and replace `context = NSManagedObjectContext()` with the following code:

```
context = NSManagedObjectContext(concurrencyType:
 .MainQueueConcurrencyType)
```

A managed object context can have one of three concurrency types. If you don't specify a concurrency type, it defaults to `.ConfinementConcurrencyType`. The problem is that this concurrency type is an old pattern that is all but deprecated.

As such, asynchronous fetching doesn't work with the confinement concurrency type, so you have to be explicit and set your concurrency type to `.MainQueueConcurrencyType`.

> **Note**: The third concurrency type is `.PrivateQueueConcurrencyType`. You'll learn about this type in Chapter 10, "Multiple Managed Object Contexts."

Second, go to the `venues` property in **ViewController.swift** and change it to the following:

```
var venues: [Venue]! = []
```

Since the original fetch request is asynchronous, it will finish after the table view does its initial load. The table view will try to unwrap the `venues` property but since there are no results yet, your app will crash.

You fix this issue by initializing `venues` to an empty array. This way, on first load, if there are no results yet, your table view will simply be empty.

Let's see if your asynchronous fetch delivers as promised. If everything goes well, you shouldn't notice any difference in the user interface. Build and run the sample app. You'll see the usual list of venues as before:

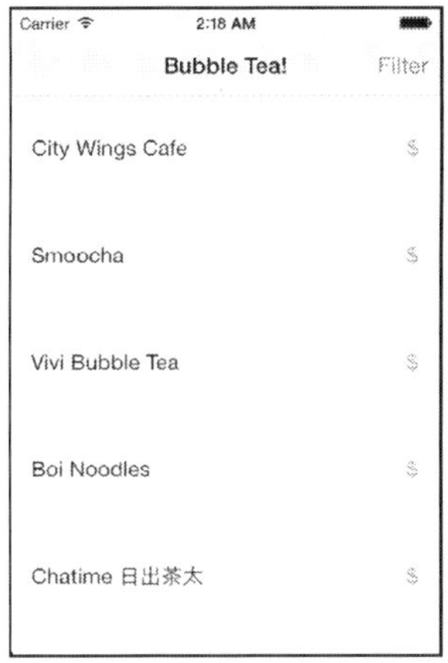

Hooray! You've mastered asynchronous fetching. The filters and sorts will also work as usual, except they still use a plain `NSFetchRequest` to reload the table view.

Batch updates: no fetching required

Sometimes, the only reason you fetch objects from Core Data is to mutate an attribute. Then, after you make your changes, you have to commit the Core Data objects back to the persistent store and call it a day. This is the normal process you've been following all along.

But what if you want to update a hundred thousand records all at once? It would take a lot of time and a lot of memory to fetch all of those objects just to update one attribute. No amount of tweaking your fetch request would save your user from having to stare at a spinner for a long, long time.

Luckily, in iOS 8 Apple introduced batch updates, a new way to update Core Data objects without having to fetch anything into memory. This new technique greatly reduces the amount of time and memory that you need to make those huge kinds of updates.

The new technique bypasses the `NSManagedObjectContext` and goes straight to the persistent store. Let's see this in practice.

Go to `viewDidLoad()` and add the following lines of code after `super.viewDidLoad()`:

```
let batchUpdate = NSBatchUpdateRequest(entityName: "Venue")
batchUpdate.propertiesToUpdate
  = ["favorite" : NSNumber(bool: true)]
batchUpdate.affectedStores = coreDataStack.psc.persistentStores
batchUpdate.resultType = .UpdatedObjectsCountResultType

var batchError: NSError?
let batchResult =
coreDataStack.context.executeRequest(batchUpdate,
  error: &batchError) as NSBatchUpdateResult?

if let result = batchResult {
  println("Records updated \(result.result!)")
} else {
  println("Could not update \(batchError),
\(batchError!.userInfo)")
}
```

The classic use case for batch updates is the "Mark all as read" feature in a messaging application or an e-mail client. For this sample app, you're going to do something more fun. Since you love bubble tea so much, you're going to mark every `Venue` in Core Data as your favorite. :]

You create an instance of `NSBatchUpdateRequest` with the entity that you want to update—`Venue` in this case. You set up your batch update request by setting `propertiesToUpdate` to a dictionary that contains the key path of the attribute you want to update, `favorite`, and its new value.

You also have to set `affectedStores` to your persistent store coordinator's `persistentStores` array. Finally, you set the result type to return a count and execute your batch update request.

Build and run your sample app. If everything works properly, you'll see the following printed to your console log:

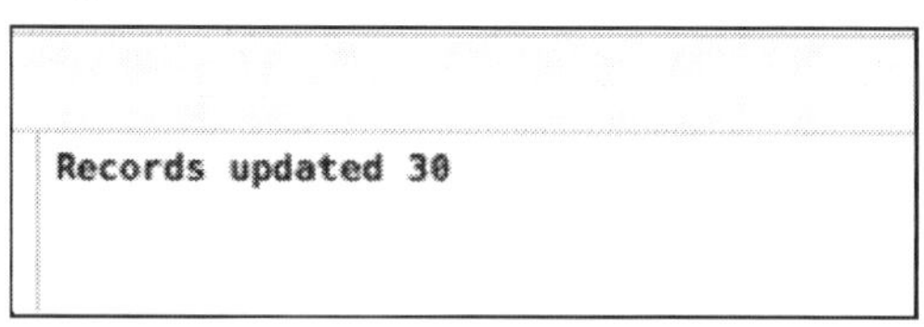

Great! You've surreptitiously marked every bubble tea venue in New York City as your favorite. :]

Note: Since you're sidestepping your `NSManagedObjectContext`, you won't get any validation if you use a batch update request. Make sure you're sanitizing and validating your data properly before using this new feature!

Where to go from here?

Whew! If you followed the chapter all the way through, then you've spent a lot of time fetching from your Core Data persistent store. I hope these examples gave you insight into how powerful and flexible fetching is in Core Data.

Among other things, you learned how to store fetch requests in your data model and how to refine your fetched results using predicates and sort descriptors. In addition, you got to experience firsthand Apple's exciting new developments in Core Data in iOS 8: asynchronous fetching and batch updates.

There is much more to learn about fetching! In the next chapter, you'll work with `NSFetchedResultsController`, a helpful class that makes using table views a breeze.

If you're thirsty and need a break before continuing – perhaps you now feel like a nice refreshing bubble tea?

Chapter 5: NSFetchedResultsController

By Pietro Rea

If you followed the previous chapters closely, you probably noticed that most of the sample projects use table views. That's because Core Data fits nicely with table views.

Set up your fetch request, fetch an array of managed objects and plug the result into the table view's data source. This is a common, everyday scenario.

If you see a tight relationship between Core Data and `UITableView`, you're in good company. The authors of the Core Data framework at Apple thought the same way! In fact, they saw *so* much potential for a close connection between `UITableView` and Core Data that they penned a class to formalize this bond: `NSFetchedResultsController`.

As the name suggests, `NSFetchedResultsController` is a controller, but it is not a *view* controller. It has no user interface. Its purpose is to make developers' lives easier by abstracting away much of the code needed to synchronize a table view with a data source backed by Core Data.

Set up an `NSFetchedResultsController` correctly, and your table will "magically" mimic its data source without you have to write more than a few lines of code. In this chapter, you'll learn the ins and outs of this class. You'll also learn when to use it and when not to use it. Are you ready?

Introducing the World Cup app

This chapter's sample project is a World Cup scoreboard app for iOS. A very simple one! On startup, the one-page application will list all the teams contesting for the World Cup. Tapping on a country's cell will increase the country's wins by one. In this simplified version of the World Cup, the country with the most taps wins the tournament. This ranking simplifies the real elimination rules quite a bit, but it's good enough for demonstration purposes.

Go to this chapter's files and find the **WorldCup-Starter** folder. Open **WorldCup.xcodeproj**. Build and run the starter project:

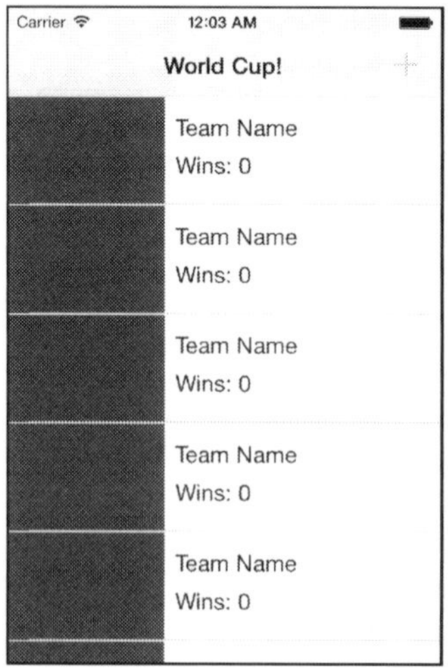

The sample application consists of 20 static cells in a table view. Those bright blue boxes are where the teams' flags should be. Instead of real names, you see "Team Name." Although the sample project isn't too exciting, it actually does a lot of the setup for you.

Open the project navigator and take a look at the full list of files in the starter project:

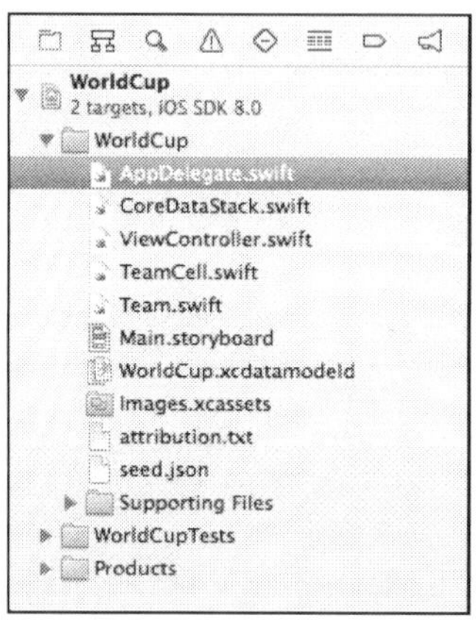

Before jumping into the code, let's briefly go over what each class does for you out of the box. You'll find that a lot of the setup that you did manually in previous chapters comes already implemented for you. Hooray!

- **AppDelegate**: On first launch, the app delegate reads from **seed.json**, creates corresponding Core Data objects and saves them to the persistent store.
- **CoreDataStack**: As in previous chapters, this object contains the cadre of Core Data objects known as the "stack": the context, the model, the persistent store and the persistent store coordinator. No need to set this up. It comes ready to be used.
- **ViewController**: The sample project is a one-page application, and this file represents that one page. If you're curious about its UI elements, head over to **Main.storyboard**. There's a table, a navigation bar and a single prototype cell.
- **Team**: This class represents a country's team. It is an `NSManagedObject` subclass with properties for each of its four attributes: `teamName`, `qualifyingZone`, `imageName` and `wins`. If you're curious about its entity definition, head over to **WorldCup.xcdatamodel**.
- **Images.xcassets**: The sample project's asset catalog contains a flag image for every country in **seed.json**.

The first three chapters of this book covered the Core Data concepts mentioned above. If "managed object subclass" doesn't ring a bell or if you're unsure what a Core Data stack is supposed to do, you may want to go back and reread the relevant chapters. `NSFetchedResultsController` will be here when you return. :]

Otherwise, if you're ready to proceed, let's begin implementing the World Cup application. You probably already know who won the World Cup last time, but this is your chance to rewrite history for the country of your choice, with just a few taps!

It all begins with a fetch request...

At its core, `NSFetchedResultsController` is a wrapper around the results of an `NSFetchRequest`. Right now, the sample project contains static information. You're going to create a fetched results controller to display the list of teams from Core Data in the table view.

Go to **ViewController.swift** and import the Core Data framework:

```
import CoreData
```

Then, add a property to hold your fetched results controller:

```
var fetchedResultsController : NSFetchedResultsController!
```

Add the following code to the end of `viewDidLoad` to set up your fetched results controller property:

```
//1
let fetchRequest = NSFetchRequest(entityName: "Team")

//2
fetchedResultsController =
  NSFetchedResultsController(fetchRequest: fetchRequest,
    managedObjectContext: coreDataStack.context,
    sectionNameKeyPath: nil,
    cacheName: nil)

//3
var error: NSError? =  nil
if (!fetchedResultsController.performFetch(&error)) {
  println("Error: \(error?.localizedDescription)")
}
```

Setting up a fetched results controller is a little more complicated than setting up a simple fetch request. Let's go step by step through the process:

1. The fetched results controller handles the coordination between Core Data and your table view, but it still needs you to provide an `NSFetchRequest`. Remember that the `NSFetchRequest` class is highly customizable. It can take sort descriptors, predicates, etc.

   In this example, you simply initialize a fetch request with an entity description, because you want to fetch all `Team` objects.

2. The initializer method for a fetched results controller takes four parameters: first is the fetch request you just created.

   The second parameter is an instance of `NSManagedObjectContext`. Like `NSFetchRequest`, the fetched results controller class needs a managed object context to execute the fetch. It can't actually fetch anything by itself.

   The other two parameters are optional: `sectionNameKeyPath` and `cacheName`. Leave them blank for now; you'll read more about them later in the chapter.

3. You execute the fetch request. If there's an error, you log the error to the console.

Note that fetching with `NSFetchRequest` returns an array of results. Fetching with `NSFetchedResultsController` returns a Boolean to denote success or failure. Wait a minute... where are your fetched results?

`NSFetchedResultsController` is both a wrapper around a fetch request *and* a container for its fetched results. You can get at them either with the `fetchedObjects` property or the `objectAtIndexPath` method.

Next, you'll connect the fetched results controller to the usual table view data source methods. The fetched results determine both the number of sections and the number of rows per section.

With this in mind, re-implement `numberOfSectionsInTableView` and `numberOfRowsInSection`, as shown below:

```
func numberOfSectionsInTableView
  (tableView: UITableView) -> Int {
  return fetchedResultsController.sections!.count
}

func tableView(tableView: UITableView,
  numberOfRowsInSection section: Int) -> Int {
  let sectionInfo = fetchedResultsController.sections![section]
    as NSFetchedResultsSectionInfo

  return sectionInfo.numberOfObjects
}
```

The number of sections in the table view corresponds to the number of sections in the fetched results controller. You may be wondering how this table view can have more than one section. Aren't you simply fetching and displaying all `Teams`?

That's correct. You will only have one section this time around, but keep it in the back of your mind that `NSFetchedResultsController` can split up your data into sections. You'll see an example of this later in the chapter.

Furthermore, the number of rows in each table view section corresponds to the number of objects in each fetched results controller section. You can query information about a fetched results controller section through its `sections` property.

> **Note:** The `sections` array contains opaque objects that implement the `NSFetchedResultsSectionInfo` protocol. This lightweight protocol provides information about a section, such as its title and number of objects.

Implementing `tableView(_:cellForRowAtIndexPath:)` would typically be the next step. A quick look at the method, however, reveals that it is already vending `TeamCell` cells as needed. What you need to change is the helper method that populates the cell.

Below `cellForRowAtIndexPath`, re-implement `configureCell`:

```
func configureCell(cell: TeamCell, indexPath: NSIndexPath) {
  let team =
   fetchedResultsController.objectAtIndexPath(indexPath) as Team

  cell.flagImageView.image = UIImage(named: team.imageName)
  cell.teamLabel.text = team.teamName
  cell.scoreLabel.text = "Wins: \(team.wins)"
}
```

This method takes in a `TeamCell` object and an index path. You use this index path to grab the corresponding `Team` object from the fetched results controller. Then you use this Core Data object to populate the cell's flag image, team name and score label.

Notice again that there's no array variable holding your teams. They're all stored inside the fetched results controller and you access them via `objectAtIndexPath`.

It's time to test your creation. Build and run the app. Ready, set and... crash?

```
2014-08-08 00:04:42.307 WorldCup[6883:332389] *** Terminating app due to uncaught exception
'NSInvalidArgumentException', reason: 'An instance of NSFetchedResultsController requires a fetch
request with sort descriptors'
*** First throw call stack:
(
    0   CoreFoundation                      0x008c6df6 __exceptionPreprocess + 182
    1   libobjc.A.dylib                     0x02274837 objc_exception_throw + 44
    2   CoreData                            0x0052941d -[NSFetchedResultsController
initWithFetchRequest:managedObjectContext:sectionNameKeyPath:cacheName:] + 2285
    3   WorldCup                            0x0006cb36
_TTOFCSo26NSFetchedResultsControllercfMS_FT12fetchRequestGSQCSo14NSFetchRequest_20managedObjectCont
extGSQCSo22NSManagedObjectContext_18sectionNameKeyPathGSQSS_9cacheNameGSQSS__S_ + 1350
    4   WorldCup                            0x0006bcce
_TFCSo26NSFetchedResultsControllerCfMS_FT12fetchRequestGSQCSo14NSFetchRequest_20managedObjectContex
tGSQCSo22NSManagedObjectContext_18sectionNameKeyPathGSQSS_9cacheNameGSQSS__S_ + 222
    5   WorldCup                            0x0006855c
_TFC8WorldCup14ViewController11viewDidLoadfS0_FT_T_ + 908
    6   WorldCup                            0x00069102
All Output
```

What happened? `NSFetchedResultsController` is helping you out here, though it may not feel like it! If you want to use it to populate a table view and have it know which managed object should appear at which index path, you can't just throw it a basic fetch request. The key part of the crash log is this:

```
'An instance of NSFetchedResultsController requires a fetch
request with sort descriptors'
```

A regular fetch request doesn't *require* a sort descriptor. Its minimum requirement is that you set an entity description, and it will fetch all objects of that type of entity. `NSFetchedResultsController`, however, requires at least one sort descriptor. Otherwise, how would it know the right order for your table view?

Go back to `viewDidLoad` and add the following lines after you initialize the fetch request:

```
let sortDescriptor =
  NSSortDescriptor(key: "teamName", ascending: true)

fetchRequest.sortDescriptors = [sortDescriptor]
```

Adding this sort descriptor will show the teams in alphabetical order from A to Z and fix the earlier crash.

Build and run the application. Your screen will look like this:

Success! The full list of World Cup participants is on your device or iOS Simulator. Notice, however, that every country has zero wins and there's no way to increment the score. Some people say that soccer is a low-scoring sport, but this is absurd!

Modifying data

Let's fix everyone's zero score and add some code to increment the number of wins. Replace the currently empty implementation of the table view delegate method `tableView(_:didSelectRowAtIndexPath:)` as shown below:

```
func tableView(tableView: UITableView,
 didSelectRowAtIndexPath indexPath: NSIndexPath) {
  tableView.deselectRowAtIndexPath(indexPath, animated: true)

  let team =
  fetchedResultsController.objectAtIndexPath(indexPath) as Team

  let wins = team.wins.integerValue
  team.wins = NSNumber(integer: wins + 1)
  coreDataStack.saveContext()
}
```

When the user taps on a row, you grab the `Team` that corresponds to the selected index path, increment its number of wins and commit the change to Core Data's persistent store.

Remember from earlier chapters that Core Data stores integers as `NSNumber`s, so you have to unwrap the number of wins before you can modify it, and you have to rewrap it before you can save it.

You might think a fetched *results* controller is only good for getting results, but the `Team` objects you get back are the same old managed object subclasses. You can update their values and save just as you've always done.

Build and run once again, and tap on the first country on the list (Algeria) five times:

What's going on here? You're tapping away but the number of cells is not going up. You're updating Algeria's number of wins in Core Data's underlying persistent store, but you aren't triggering a UI refresh.

Go back to Xcode, stop the app, and build and run again:

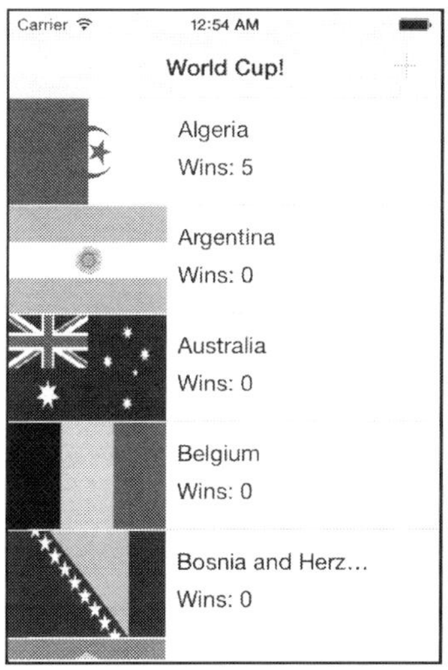

Just as you suspected, re-launching the app from scratch forced a UI refresh, showing Algeria's real score of 5. `NSFetchedResultsController` has a nice solution to this problem, but for now, let's use the brute force solution.

Add the follow line at the end of your current implementation of `didSelectRowAtIndexPath`:

```
tableView.reloadData()
```

In addition to incrementing a team's number of wins, tapping a cell now reloads the entire table view. This approach is heavy-handed but it does the job for now.

Build and run the app one more time. Tap as many countries as you want as many times as you want. Verify that the UI is always up to date.

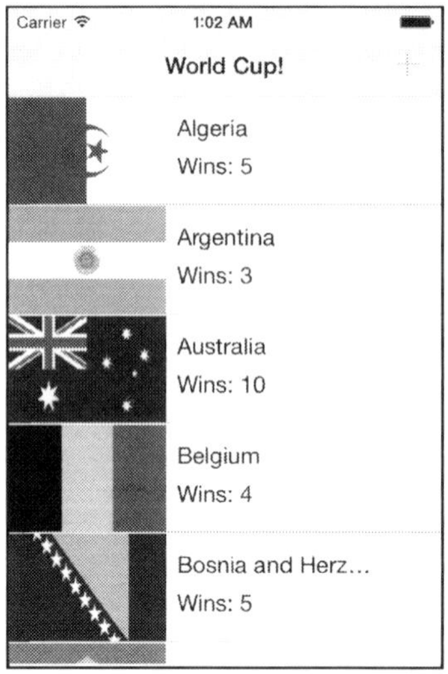

There you go. You've got a fetched results controller up and running. Excited?

If this were all `NSFetchedResultsController` could do, you would probably feel a little disappointed. After all, you can accomplish the same thing using an `NSFetchRequest` and a simple array.

The real magic comes in the remaining sections of this chapter. `NSFetchedResultsController` earned its keep in the Cocoa Touch frameworks with features such as section handling and change monitoring, covered next.

Grouping results into sections

There are six qualifying zones in the World Cup: Africa, Asia, Oceania, Europe, South America and North/Central America. The `Team` entity has a string attribute named `qualifyingZone` that stores this information.

In this section, you'll split up the list of countries into their respective qualifying zones. `NSFetchedResultsController` makes this very simple.

Let's see it in action. Go back to `viewDidLoad` and make the following change to the fetched results controller's initializer:

```
fetchedResultsController =
  NSFetchedResultsController(fetchRequest: fetchRequest,
    managedObjectContext: coreDataStack.context,
    sectionNameKeyPath: "qualifyingZone",
    cacheName: nil)
```

The difference here is you're passing in a value for the optional `sectionNameKeyPath` parameter. You can use this parameter to specify an attribute that the fetched results controller should use to group the results and generate sections.

How exactly are these sections generated? Each unique attribute value becomes a section. `NSFetchedResultsController` then groups its fetched results into these sections. In this case, it will generate sections for each unique value of `qualifyingZone` such as "Africa", "Asia", "Oceania" and so on. This is exactly what you want!

> **Note:** `sectionNameKeyPath` takes a `keyPath` string. It can take the form of an attribute name such as "`qualifyingZone`" or "`teamName`", or it can drill deep into a Core Data relationship, such as "`employee.address.street`".

The fetched results controller will now report the sections and rows to the table view, but the current UI won't look any different. To fix this problem, add the following method to the class:

```
func tableView(tableView: UITableView,
 titleForHeaderInSection section: Int) -> String? {
  let sectionInfo = fetchedResultsController.sections![section]
    as NSFetchedResultsSectionInfo
  return sectionInfo.name
}
```

Implementing this data source method adds section headers to the table view, making it easy to see where one section ends and another one begins. In this case, the section gets its title from the qualifying zone. Like before, this information comes directly from the `NSFetchedResultsSectionInfo` protocol.

Build and run the application. Your app will look something like the following:

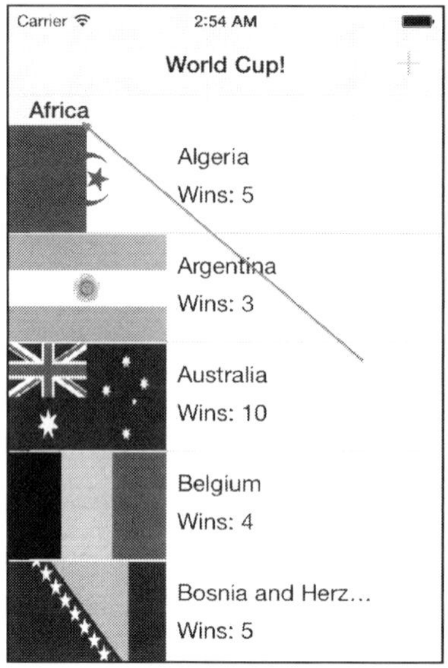

Scroll down the page. There's good news and bad news. The good news is that the app accounts for all six sections. Hooray! The bad news is that the world is upside down.

Take a closer look at the sections. You'll see Argentina in Africa, Cameroon in Asia and Russia in South America. How did this happen? It's not a problem with the data; you can open **seed.json** and verify that each team lists the correct qualifying zone.

Have you figured it out? The list of countries is still shown alphabetically and the fetched results controller is simply splitting up the table into sections as if all teams of the same qualifying zone were grouped together.

Go back to `viewDidLoad` and make the following change to fix the problem. Replace the existing code that creates and sets the sort descriptor on the fetch request with the following:

```
let zoneSort =
    NSSortDescriptor(key: "qualifyingZone", ascending: true)
let scoreSort =
```

```
    NSSortDescriptor(key: "wins", ascending: false)
let nameSort =
    NSSortDescriptor(key: "teamName", ascending: true)

fetchRequest.sortDescriptors = [zoneSort, scoreSort, nameSort]
```

The problem was the sort descriptor. This is another `NSFetchedResultsController` "gotcha" to keep in mind. If you want to separate fetched results using a section `keyPath`, *the first sort descriptor's attribute must match the key path's attribute.*

The documentation for `NSFetchedResultsController` makes this point emphatically, and with good reason! You saw what happened when the sort descriptor doesn't match the key path—your data ends up making no sense.

Build and run one more time to verify that this change fixed the problem:

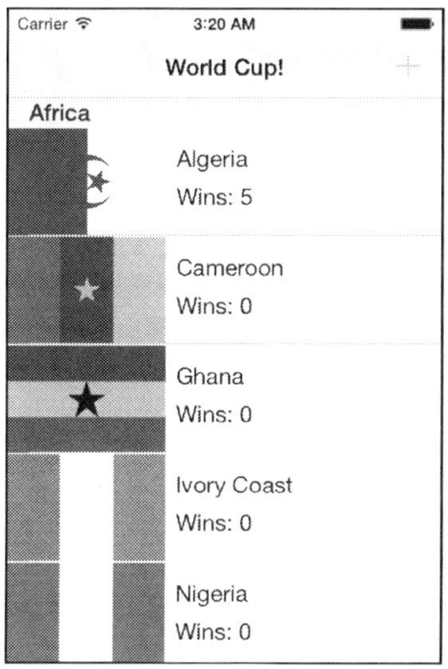

Indeed it did. Changing the sort descriptor restored the geopolitical balance in your sample application. African teams are in Africa, European teams are in Europe and so on.

> **Notes:** The only team that may still raise eyebrows is Australia, which appears under Asia's qualifying zone. This is how FIFA categorizes Australia. If you don't like it, you can file a bug report with them! ;]

Notice that within each qualifying zone, teams are sorted by number of wins from highest to lowest, then by name. This is because in the previous code snippet, you added three sort descriptors: first sort by qualifying zone, then by number of wins, then finally by name.

Before moving on, take a moment to think of what you'd have needed to do to separate the teams by qualifying zone without the fetched results controller. First, you would've had to create a dictionary and iterated over the teams to find unique qualifying zones. As you traversed the array of teams, you would have had to associate each team with the correct qualifying zone. Once you have the list of teams by zone, you'd then need to sort the data.

Of course it's not impossible to do this yourself, but it is tedious. This is what `NSFetchedResultsController` saved you from doing. You can take the rest of the day off and go to the beach or watch some World Cup matches. Thank you, `NSFetchedResultsController`!

"Cache" the ball

As you can probably imagine, grouping teams into sections is not a cheap operation. There's no way to avoid iterating over every team.

It's not a performance problem in this case because there are only 32 teams to consider but imagine what would happen if your data set were much larger. What if your task were to iterate over 3 million census records and separate them by state/province?

"I'd just throw that on a background thread!" might be your first thought. The table view, however, can't populate itself until all sections are available. You might save yourself from blocking the main thread, but you'd still be left looking at a spinner.

There's no denying that this operation is expensive. At a bare minimum, you should only pay the cost once: figure out the section grouping a single time, and reuse your result every time after that.

The authors of `NSFetchedResultsController` thought about this problem and came up with a solution: caching. You don't have to do much to turn it on.

Head back to `viewDidLoad` and make the following modification to the fetched results controller initialization, adding a value to the `cacheName` parameter:

```
fetchedResultsController =
  NSFetchedResultsController(fetchRequest: fetchRequest,
    managedObjectContext: coreDataStack.context,
    sectionNameKeyPath: "qualifyingZone",
    cacheName: "worldCup")
```

You specify a cache name to turn on `NSFetchedResultsController`'s on-disk section cache. That's all you need to do! Keep in mind that this section cache is completely separate from Core Data's persistent store, where you persist the teams.

> **Note:** `NSFetchedResultsController`'s section cache is very sensitive to changes in its fetch request. As you can imagine, any changes—such as a different entity description or different sort descriptors—would give you a completely different set of fetched objects, invalidating the cache completely. If you make changes like this, you must delete the existing cache using `deleteCacheWithName:` or use a different cache name.

Build and run the application a few times. The second launch should be a *little* bit faster than the first. This is not the author's power of suggestion (psst, say "fast" five times in a row); it is `NSFetchedResultsController`'s cache system at work!

On the second launch, `NSFetchedResultsController` reads directly from your cache. This saves a round trip to Core Data's persistent store, as well as the time needed to compute those sections. Hooray!

> Note: You'll learn about measuring performance and seeing if your code changes really did make things faster in Chapter 9, "Measuring and Boosting Performance".

In your own apps, consider using `NSFetchedResultsController`'s cache if you're grouping results into sections and either have a very large data set or are targeting older devices.

Monitoring changes

This chapter has already covered two of the three main benefits of using `NSFetchedResultsController`: sections and caching. The third and last benefit is somewhat of a double-edged sword: it is powerful but also easy to misuse.

Earlier in the chapter, when you implemented the tap to increment the number of wins, you added a line of code to reload the table view to show the updated score. This was a brute force solution, but it worked.

Sure, you could have reloaded only the selected cell by being smart about the `UITableView` API, but that wouldn't have solved the root problem.

Not to get too philosophical, but the root problem is *change*. Something changed in the underlying data and you had to be explicit about reloading the user interface. Imagine for a moment what a second version of the World Cup app would look like.

Maybe there's a detail screen for every team where you can change the score. Maybe the app calls an API endpoint and gets new score information from the web service. It would be your job to refresh the table view *for every code path* that updates the underlying data.

Doing it explicitly is error-prone, not to mention a little boring. Isn't there a better way? Yes, there is. Once again, fetched results controller comes to the rescue.

`NSFetchedResultsController` can listen for changes in its result set and notify its delegate, `NSFetchedResultsControllerDelegate`. You can use this delegate to refresh the table view as needed any time the underlying data changes.

What does it mean that a fetched results controller can monitor changes in its "result set"? It means that it can monitor changes in all objects, old and new, that it *would* have fetched, in addition to objects it has already fetched. This distinction will become clearer later in this section.

Let's see this in practice. Make the following change to the class declaration:

```
class ViewController: UIViewController,
NSFetchedResultsControllerDelegate {
```

This simply tells the compiler that the `ViewController` class will implement some of the fetched results controller's delegate method.

Now go back to `viewDidLoad` and set the view controller as the fetched results controller's delegate.

Add the following line of code after you initialize the fetched results controller:

```
fetchedResultsController.delegate = self
```

That's all you need to start monitoring changes! Of course, the next step is to do something when those change reports come in. You'll do that next.

> **Note:** A fetched results controller can only monitor changes made via the managed object context specified in its initializer. If you create a separate `NSManagedObjectContext` somewhere else in your app and start making changes there, your delegate method won't run until those changes have been saved and merged with the fetched results controller's context.

Responding to changes

First, remove the `reloadData` call from `tableView(_:didSelectRowAtIndexPath:)`. As mentioned before, this was the brute force approach that you're now going to replace.

`NSFetchedResultsControllerDelegate` has four methods that come in varying degrees of granularity. To start out, implement the broadest delegate method, the one that says: "Hey, something just changed!"

Add the following new method:

```
func controllerDidChangeContent(controller:
  NSFetchedResultsController) {
    tableView.reloadData()
}
```

The change may seem small, but implementing this method means that any change whatsoever, no matter the source, will refresh the table view.

Build and run the application. Verify that the table view's cells still update correctly by tapping on a few cells:

The score labels update as before, but this reveals another problem. If you tap around enough times, you might get into a state where teams within a qualifying zone are not ranked by number of wins. For example, in the previous screenshot, you can see Cameroon below Algeria. However, Cameroon has 16 wins and Algeria 6. Also, when the cells do move around, it's pretty jumpy, almost as if you were completely reloading the table every time something changed. :]

Maintaining the relative order of the table view's cells would require you to write some logic to determine when cells need to be reordered, then calling the appropriate `UITableView` APIs to make it happen. Fortunately, you don't have to do any of that—a common theme in this chapter!

The fetched results controller delegate can tell you if something needs to be moved, inserted or deleted due to a change in the fetched results controller's result set.

Replace the implementation of `controllerDidChangeContent` that you just added with the following three delegate methods to see this in action:

```
func controllerWillChangeContent(controller:
  NSFetchedResultsController!) {
    tableView.beginUpdates()
}

func controller(controller: NSFetchedResultsController,
  didChangeObject anObject: AnyObject,
```

```
    atIndexPath indexPath: NSIndexPath!,
    forChangeType type: NSFetchedResultsChangeType,
    newIndexPath: NSIndexPath!) {
      switch type {
      case .Insert:
        tableView.insertRowsAtIndexPaths([newIndexPath],
          withRowAnimation: .Automatic)
      case .Delete:
        tableView.deleteRowsAtIndexPaths([indexPath],
          withRowAnimation: .Automatic)
      case .Update:
        let cell = tableView.cellForRowAtIndexPath(indexPath)
          as TeamCell
        configureCell(cell, indexPath: indexPath)
      case .Move:
        tableView.deleteRowsAtIndexPaths([indexPath],
          withRowAnimation: .Automatic)
        tableView.insertRowsAtIndexPaths([newIndexPath],
          withRowAnimation: .Automatic)
      default:
        break
      }
  }

  func controllerDidChangeContent(controller:
    NSFetchedResultsController!) {
      tableView.endUpdates()
  }
```

Whew! That's a wall of code. Fortunately, it's mostly boilerplate and easy to understand. Let's briefly go over all three methods you just added or modified:

- **controllerWillChangeContent:** This delegate method notifies you that changes are about to occur. You ready your table view using `beginUpdates()`.
- **controller(_:didChangeObject...):** This method is quite a mouthful. And with good reason—it tells you exactly what objects changed, what the type of change was (insertion, deletion, update or reordering) and what the affected index paths are.

  This middle method is the proverbial glue that synchronizes your table view with Core Data. No matter how much the underlying data changes, your table view will stay true to what's going on in the persistent store.
- **controllerDidChangeContent:** The delegate method you had originally implemented to refresh the UI turned out to be the third of three delegate methods that notify you of changes. Rather than refresh the table view, you just need to call `endUpdates()` to apply the changes.

> **Note:** What you end up doing with the change notifications depends on your individual app. The implementation you see above is an example Apple provided in the `NSFetchedResultsControllerDelegate` documentation. Note that the order and nature of the methods ties in very neatly to the "begin updates-make changes-end updates" pattern used to update table views. This is not a coincidence!

Build and run to see your work in action. Right off the bat, each qualifying zone lists teams by the number of wins. Tap on different countries a few times. You'll see the cells animate smoothly to maintain this order.

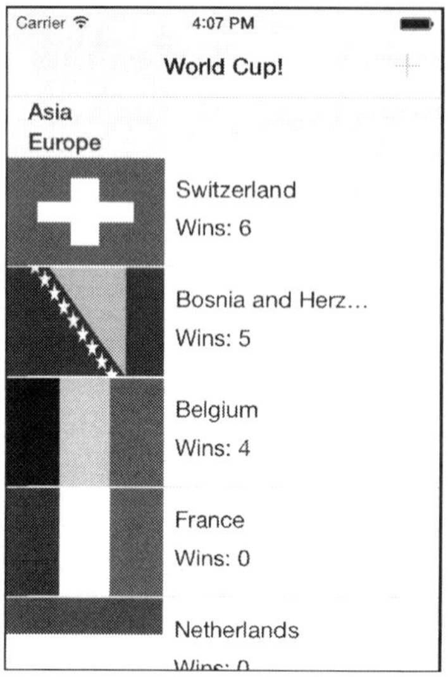

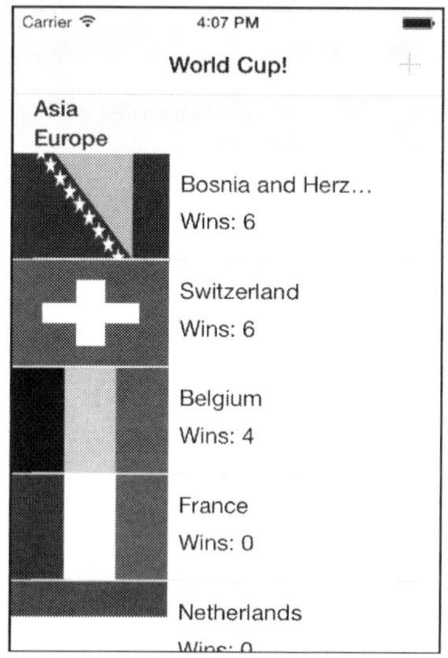

For example, in the first screenshot, Switzerland leads Europe with 6 wins. Tapping on Bosnia & Herzegovina brings *their* score to 6 and moves the cell on top of Switzerland with a nice animation. This is the fetched results controller delegate in action!

There is one more delegate method in `NSFetchedResultsControllerDelegate`. Add it to the class:

```
func controller(controller: NSFetchedResultsController,
  didChangeSection sectionInfo: NSFetchedResultsSectionInfo,
  atIndex sectionIndex: Int,
  forChangeType type: NSFetchedResultsChangeType) {

    let indexSet = NSIndexSet(index: sectionIndex)
```

```
    switch type {
    case .Insert:
      tableView.insertSections(indexSet,
        withRowAnimation: .Automatic)
    case .Delete:
      tableView.deleteSections(indexSet,
        withRowAnimation: .Automatic)
    default :
      break
    }
}
```

This delegate method is similar to `didChangeObject`... but notifies you of changes to sections rather than to individual objects. Here, you handle the cases where changes in the underlying data trigger the creation or deletion of an entire section.

Take a moment and think about what kind of change would trigger these notifications. Maybe if a new team entered the World Cup from a completely new qualifying zone, the fetched results controller would pick up on the uniqueness of this value and notify its delegate about the new section.

This would never happen in a standard-issue World Cup. Once the 32 qualifying teams are in the system, there's no way to add a new team. Or is there?

Inserting an underdog

For the sake of demonstrating what happens to the table view when there's an insertion in the result set, let's assume there *is* a way to add a new team.

If you were paying close attention, you may have noticed the "+" bar button item on the top-right. It's been disabled all this time. Perhaps the World Cup has a secret backdoor entrance!

Let's implement this now. Add the following method to the class in **ViewController.swift**:

```
override func motionEnded(motion: UIEventSubtype,
  withEvent event: UIEvent) {

    if motion == .MotionShake {
      addButton.enabled = true
    }
}
```

You override `motionEnded` so that shaking the device enables the "+" bar button item. This will be your secret way in. The `addButton` property held a reference to this bar button item all along!

Next, add the following method below `motionEnded`:

```
@IBAction func addTeam(sender: AnyObject) {
  var alert = UIAlertController(title: "Secret Team",
    message: "Add a new team",
    preferredStyle: UIAlertControllerStyle.Alert)

  alert.addTextFieldWithConfigurationHandler {
    (textField: UITextField!) in
    textField.placeholder = "Team Name"
  }
  alert.addTextFieldWithConfigurationHandler {
    (textField: UITextField!) in
    textField.placeholder = "Qualifying Zone"
  }

  alert.addAction(UIAlertAction(title: "Save",
    style: .Default, handler: { (action: UIAlertAction!) in
      println("Saved")

    let nameTextField = alert.textFields![0] as UITextField
    let zoneTextField = alert.textFields![1] as UITextField

    let team =
     NSEntityDescription.insertNewObjectForEntityForName("Team",
     inManagedObjectContext: self.coreDataStack.context) as Team

    team.teamName = nameTextField.text
    team.qualifyingZone = zoneTextField.text
    team.imageName = "wenderland-flag"

    self.coreDataStack.saveContext()
  }))

  alert.addAction(UIAlertAction(title: "Cancel",
    style: .Default, handler: { (action: UIAlertAction!) in
      println("Cancel")
  }))

  presentViewController(alert, animated: true, completion: nil)
}
```

This is a fairly long, but simple to understand method. When the user taps the Add button, it presents an alert view prompting the user to enter a new team.

The alert view has two text fields: one for entering a team name and another for entering the qualifying zone. Tapping "Save" commits the change and inserts the new team into Core Data's persistent store.

The action is already connected in the storyboard, so there's nothing more for you to do.

Build and run the app one more time. If you're running on a device, shake it. If you're running on the Simulator, press **Command+Control+Z** to simulate a shake event.

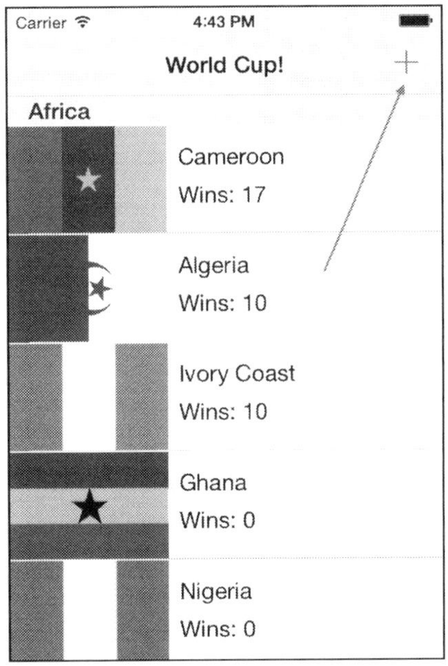

Open sesame! After much negotiation, both parties decided to "shake on it" and the Add button is now active! The World Cup is officially accepting one new team.

Scroll down the table to the end of the European qualifying zone and the beginning of the North, Central America & Caribbean qualifying zone, as shown below. You'll see why in a moment.

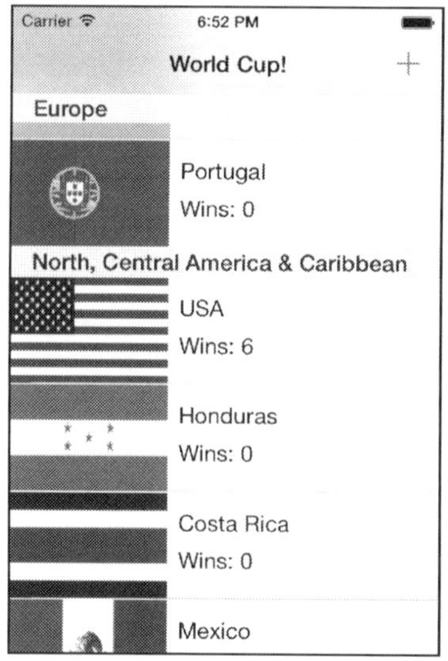

Before moving on, take a few seconds to take this in. You're going to change history by adding another team to the World Cup. Are you ready?

Tap the "+" button on the top right. You'll be greeted by an alert view asking for the new team's details:

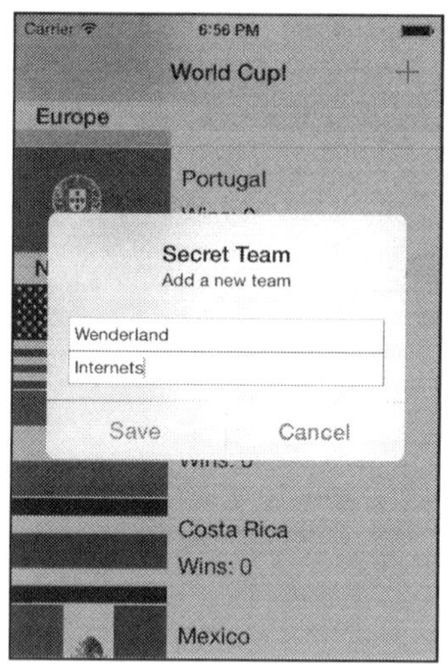

Enter the fictitious (yet thriving) nation of **Wenderland** as the new team. Type **Internets** for qualifying zone and tap **Save**. After a quick animation, your user interface should look like the following:

Since "Internets" is a new value for the fetched results controller's `sectionNameKeyPath`, this operation created both a new section and added a new team to the fetched results controller result set. That handles the data side of things.

Additionally, since you implemented the fetched results controller delegate methods appropriately, the table view responded by inserting a new section with one new row.

That's the beauty of `NSFetchedResultsControllerDelegate`. You can set it once and forget it. The underlying data source and your table view will always be synchronized.

As for how the Wenderland flag made it into the app: Hey, we're developers! We need to plan for all kinds of possibilities. ;]

Where to go from here?

You've seen how powerful and useful `NSFetchedResultsController` can be, and you've learned how well it works together with a table view. Table views are so common in iOS apps and you've seen first hand how the fetched results controller can save you a lot of time and code!

With some adaptation to the delegate methods, you can also use a fetched results controller to drive a collection view—the main difference being that collection views don't bracket their updates with begin and end calls, so it's necessary to store up the changes and apply them all in a batch at the end.

There are a few things you should bear in mind before using fetched results controllers in other contexts. They're not designed as general Core Data monitoring tools—there are other notifications or techniques that probably do the job better. Be mindful of how you implement the fetched results controller delegate methods. Even the slightest change in the underlying data will fire those change notifications, so avoid performing any expensive operations that you're not comfortable performing over and over.

It's not every day that a single class gets an entire chapter in a book; that honor is reserved for the select few. `NSFetchedResultsController` is one of them. As you've seen in this chapter, the reason this class exists is to save you time.

`NSFetchedResultsController` is important for another reason: it fills a gap that iOS developers have faced compared to their OS X developer counterparts. OS X has Cocoa bindings, which provide a way to tightly couple a view with its underlying data model. Sound familiar?

If you ever find yourself writing complex logic to compute sections or breaking a sweat trying to get your table view to play nicely with Core Data says, think back to this chapter!

Chapter 6: Versioning and Migration

By Saul Mora

You've seen how to design your data model and `NSManagedObject` subclasses in your Core Data apps. During app development, thorough testing can help iron out the data model well before shipping. However, changes in app usage, design or features after an app's release will inevitably lead to changes in the data model. What do you do then?

You can't predict the future, but with Core Data, you can *migrate* toward the future with every new release of your app. The migration process will update data created with a previous version of the data model to match the current data model.

This chapter discusses the many aspects of Core Data migrations by walking you through the evolution of a note-taking app's data model. You'll start with a simple app with only a single entity in its data model. As you add more features and data to the app, the migrations you do in this chapter will become progressively more complex.

Let the journey begin!

When to migrate

When is a migration necessary? The easiest answer to this common question is "when you need to make changes to the data model."

However, there are some cases in which you can avoid a migration. If an app is using Core Data merely as an offline cache, then when you update the app, you can simply delete and rebuild the data store. This is only possible if the source of truth for your user's data isn't in the data store. In all other cases, you'll need to safeguard your user's data.

That said, any time it's impossible to implement a design change or feature request without changing the data model, you'll need to create a new version of the data model and provide a migration path.

The migration process

When you initialize a Core Data stack, one of the steps involved is adding a store to the persistent store coordinator. When you encounter this step, Core Data does a few things prior to adding the store to the coordinator.

First, Core Data analyzes the store's model version. Next, it compares this version to the coordinator's configured data model. If the store's model version and the coordinator's model version don't match, then Core Data will perform a migration, when enabled.

> **Note:** If migrations aren't enabled, and the store is incompatible with the model, Core Data will simply not attach the store to the coordinator and specify an error with an appropriate reason code.

To start the migration process, Core Data needs the original data model and the destination model. It uses these two versions to load or create a mapping model for the migration, which it uses to convert data in the original store to data that it can store in the new store. Once Core Data determines the mapping model, the migration process can start in earnest.

Migrations happen in three steps:

1. First, Core Data copies over all the objects from one data store to the next.
2. Next, Core Data connects and relates all the objects according to the relationship mapping.
3. Enforce any data validations in the destination model. Core Data disables destination model validations during the data copy.

You might ask, "If something goes wrong, what happens to the original source data store?" With nearly all types of Core Data migrations, nothing happens to the original store unless the migration completes without error. Only when a migration is successful, will Core Data remove the original data store.

Types of migrations

In my own experience using Core Data, I've found there are a few more migration variants than the simple distinction between lightweight and heavyweight. Below, I've provided the more subtle variants of migration names, but these names are not official categories by any means. I'll start with the least complex form of migration and end with the most complex form.

Lightweight migrations

A lightweight migration is Apple's term for the migration with the least amount of work involved on your part. Simply enable a couple of flags when setting up a Core Data stack, and the migration happens automatically. There are some limitations on how much you can change the data model, but because of the small amount of work required to enable this option, it is the ideal setting.

Manual migrations

Manual migrations involve a little more work on your part. You need to specify how to map the old set of data onto the new set, but you get the benefit of a more explicit **mapping model** file to configure. Setting up a mapping model in Xcode is much like setting up a data model, with similar GUI tools and some automation.

Custom manual migrations

This is level 3 of the migration complexity index. You still use a mapping model, but add to that custom code with the ability to also specify custom transformation logic on data. In this case, custom entity transformation logic involves creating an `NSEntityMigrationPolicy` subclass and performing custom transformations there.

Fully manual migrations

Fully manual migrations are for those times when even specifying custom transformation logic isn't enough to fully migrate data from one model version to another. In this case, custom version detection logic and custom handling of the migration process are necessary. In this chapter, you'll use set up a fully manual migration to update data across non-sequential versions, such as jumping from version 1 to 4.

Throughout this chapter, you'll learn about each of these migration types and when to use them. Let's get started!

Getting started

Included with the resources for this book is a starter project called **UnCloudNotes**. Find the starter project and open it in Xcode.

> **Note**: We've called the app **UnCloudNotes** as a teaser for Chapter 7, "Syncing with iCloud." In that chapter, you'll change **UnCloudNotes** to **CloudNotes**, and modify it so that it syncs its Core Data store to multiple devices using iCloud.

Build and run the app in the iPhone simulator. You'll see an empty list of notes:

Tap the plus (+) button in the top-right corner to add a new note. Add a title (there is default text in the note body to make the process faster) and tap **Create** to save the new note to the data store. Repeat this a few times so that you have some sample data to migrate.

Back in Xcode, open the **UnCloudNotesDatamodel.xcdatamodeld** file to show the entity modeling tool in Xcode. The data model is simple—just one entity, a **Note**, with a few attributes.

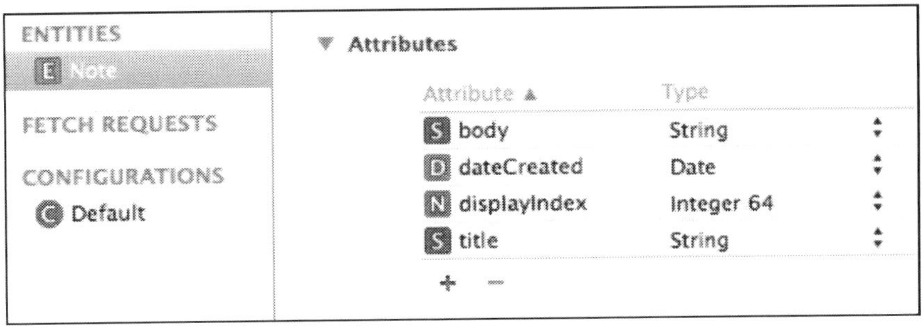

You're going to add a new feature to the app: the ability to attach a photo to a note. The data model doesn't have any place to persist this kind of information, so you'll need to add a place in the data model to hold onto the photo. But you already added a few test notes in the app—how can you change the model without breaking the existing notes? It's time for your first migration!

A lightweight migration

With the entity modeler open, open the **Editor** menu and select **Add Model Version...**. Call the new version **UnCloudNotesDataModel v2** and select **UnCloudNotesDataModel** in the "Based on Model" field. Xcode will now create a copy of the data model.

> **Note:** You can give this file any name you want. The sequential v2, v3, v4, et cetera naming helps you tell the versions apart easily.

This step will create a second version of the data model, but you still need to tell Xcode to use the new version as the current model. In the File Inspector pane on the right, find the option toward the bottom called **Model Version**.

Change that selection to match the name of the new data model, **UnCloudNotesDataModel v2**:

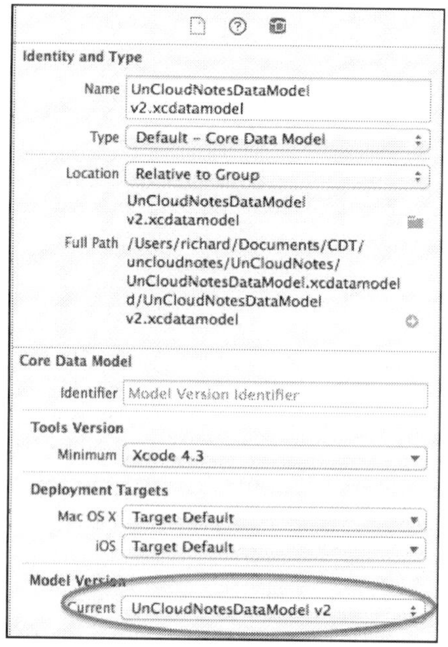

Once you've made that change, notice in the project navigator that the little green check mark icon has moved from the previous data model to the v2 data model:

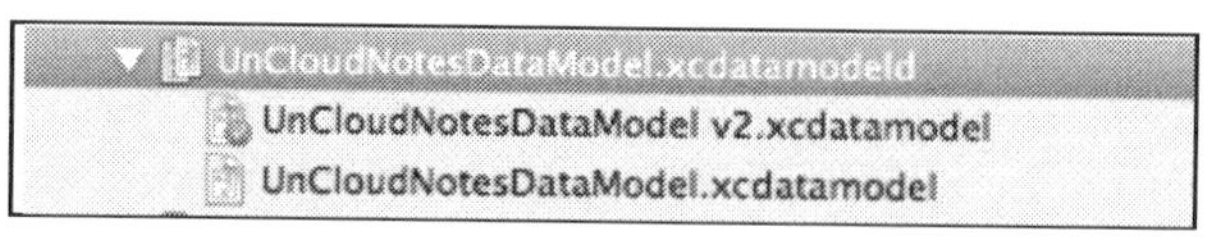

Core Data will load the ticked version when setting up the stack. The older version is there to support migration—it's hard to migrate to a new model without knowing the old one!

Make sure you have the v2 data model selected and add an image attribute to the **Note** entity. Set the attribute's name to **image** and the attribute's type to **Transformable**.

Since this attribute is going to contain the actual binary bits of the image, you'll use a custom `NSValueTransformer` to convert from binary bits to a `UIImage` and back again. Just such a transformer has been provided for you as `ImageTransformer`. In the **Value Transformer Name** field in the Data Model Inspector on the right of the screen, enter **UnCloudNotes.ImageTransformer**.

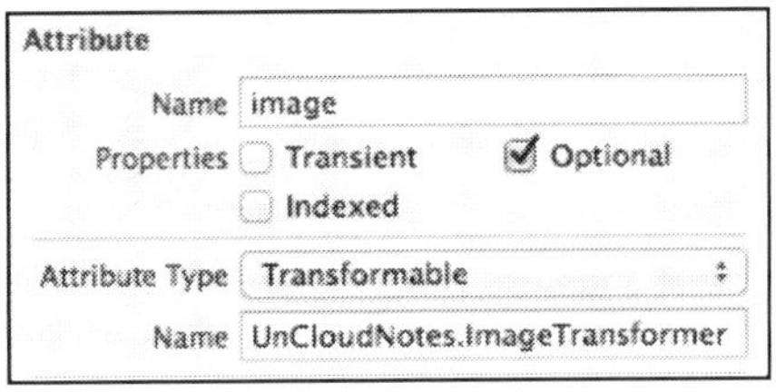

The new model is now ready for some code! Open **Note.swift** and add a property to match the new attribute:

```
@NSManaged var image: UIImage?
```

Build and run, and you'll see your notes have disappeared! In the Xcode console, you'll see some error text related to the `CoreDataStack` object:

```
context: <NSManagedObjectContext: 0x7a96c8f0>
modelName: UnCloudNotesDataModelmodel: [Note: <c393d6c8 d5e65f5a
bb5e4394 eb6ce54c a99e724d bdb64072 ed2e99dd 99e77ba0>]
coordinator: <NSPersistentStoreCoordinator: 0x7a973310>
storeURL:
file:///Users/YOURNAME/Library/Developer/CoreSimulator/Devices/A24A4E6
8-D616-4F63-8946-
652164EE5E53/data/Containers/Data/Application/9921B2DD-D0FD-4330-90F9-
A2F44CC9899A/Library/Application%20Support/UnCloudNotes.sqlite
store: nil
```

The store file is still around (`storeURL` in the log above), but since it's incompatible with the new v2 model, Core Data couldn't attach it to the persistent store, so `store` is still `nil`.

Core Data can automatically update your store if all you've done is add a new property like this. These are called **lightweight migrations**.

Enabling lightweight migrations

To enable lightweight migrations, you need to set two flags on initialization. The stack in this app lives in an object imaginatively titled `CoreDataStack`, which you'll modify to do this.

Open **CoreDataStack.swift** and add a property to the class:

```
var options: NSDictionary?
```

Right now, you're setting up the persistent store with no options for default behavior. You'll use the `options` dictionary to set the necessary flags.

Next, update the initializer to match the following:

```
init(modelName: String, storeName: String,
 options: NSDictionary? = nil) {
  self.modelName = modelName
  self.storeName = storeName
  self.options = options
}
```

In setting the default value of `options` to `nil`, the old method signature remains valid and you have the additional choice of passing in the options dictionary.

Find the `coordinator` computed property and change the initialization of the persistent store as follows:

```
store = coordinator.addPersistentStoreWithType(
  NSSQLiteStoreType,
  configuration: nil,
  URL: storeURL,
  options: self.options,
  error: nil)
```

There's just a small change here to pass in the extra options when creating the stack.

Open **NotesListViewController.swift** and change the `CoreDataStack` lazy initialization statement to use the lightweight migration options:

```
lazy var stack : CoreDataStack = CoreDataStack(
  modelName:"UnCloudNotesDataModel",
  storeName:"UnCloudNotes",
  options:[NSMigratePersistentStoresAutomaticallyOption: true,
           NSInferMappingModelAutomaticallyOption: true])
```

The `NSMigratePersistentStoresAutomaticallyOption` is what tells Core Data (the `NSPersistentStoreCoordinator`, actually) to start a migration if the persistent store model isn't compatible with the current data model. Core Data will handle all the details, from finding the source model to creating the destination store file, and all the steps in between.

The `NSInferMappingModelAutomaticallyOption` is the other half of what makes a lightweight migration possible. Every migration requires a mapping model. Here's an analogy: If you're traveling from a known place on Earth to somewhere unknown, you'll want a map to tell you where to go. The mapping model is that guide.

It just so happens that Core Data can infer a mapping model in many cases. That is, Core Data can automatically look at the differences in two data models and create a mapping model between them. For entities and attributes that are identical between model versions, this is a straightforward data pass through mapping. For other changes, just follow a few simple rules for Core Data to create a mapping model. In the new model, changes must fit an obvious migration pattern, such as:

1. Deleting entities, attributes or relationships;
2. Renaming entities, attributes or relationships using the `renamingIdentifier`;
3. Adding a new, optional attribute;
4. Adding a new, required attribute with a default value;
5. Changing an optional attribute to non-optional and specifying a default value;
6. Changing a non-optional attribute to optional;
7. Changing the entity hierarchy;
8. Adding a new parent entity and moving attributes up or down the hierarchy;
9. Changing a relationship from to-one to to-many;
10. Changing a relationship from non-ordered to-many to ordered to-many (and vice versa).

> **Note**: Check out Apple's documentation for more information on how Core Data infers a lightweight migration mapping:
> https://developer.apple.com/library/Mac/DOCUMENTATION/Cocoa/Conceptual/CoreDataVersioning/Articles/vmLightweightMigration.html

As you can see from this list, Core Data can detect, and more importantly, automatically react to, a wide variety of common changes between data models. As a rule of thumb, all migrations, if necessary, should start as lightweight migrations and only move to more complex mappings when the need arises.

As for the migration from UnCloudNotes to UnCloudNotes v2, the image property has a default value of `nil` since it's an optional property. This means Core Data can easily migrate the old data store to a new one, since this change follows item 3 in the list of lightweight migration patterns.

Build and run, and your old notes have returned! Core Data has migrated the data store automatically using an inferred mapping model.

The non-`nil` value for the `store:` entry in the logs is a nice confirmation that the migration actually happened and that there's now an `NSPersistentStore` object representing the store.

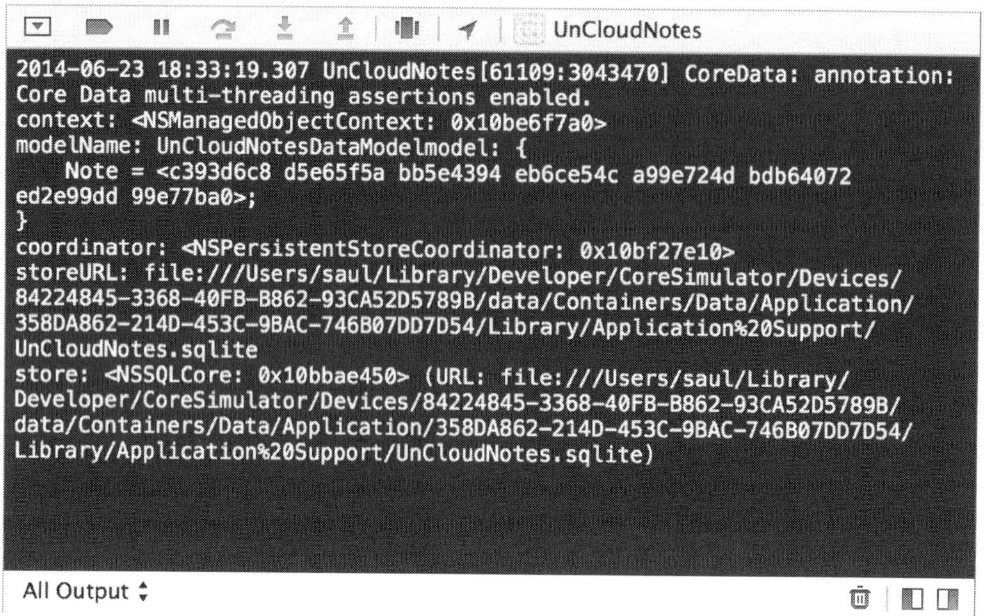

Congratulations—you've completed your first data migration!

Image attachments

Now that data is migrated, you need to update the UI to allow image attachments to new notes. Luckily, most of this work has been done for you, so you can quickly get to the interesting part. :]

Open **Main.storyboard** and go to the **Create Note** scene. Just underneath, you'll see a **Create Note With Images** scene that includes the interface to attach an image.

The Create Note scene is attached to a navigation controller with a root view controller relationship. **Control-drag** from the navigation controller to the **Create Note With Images** scene and select the **root view controller relationship** segue. This will disconnect the old Create Note scene and connect the new, image-powered one instead:

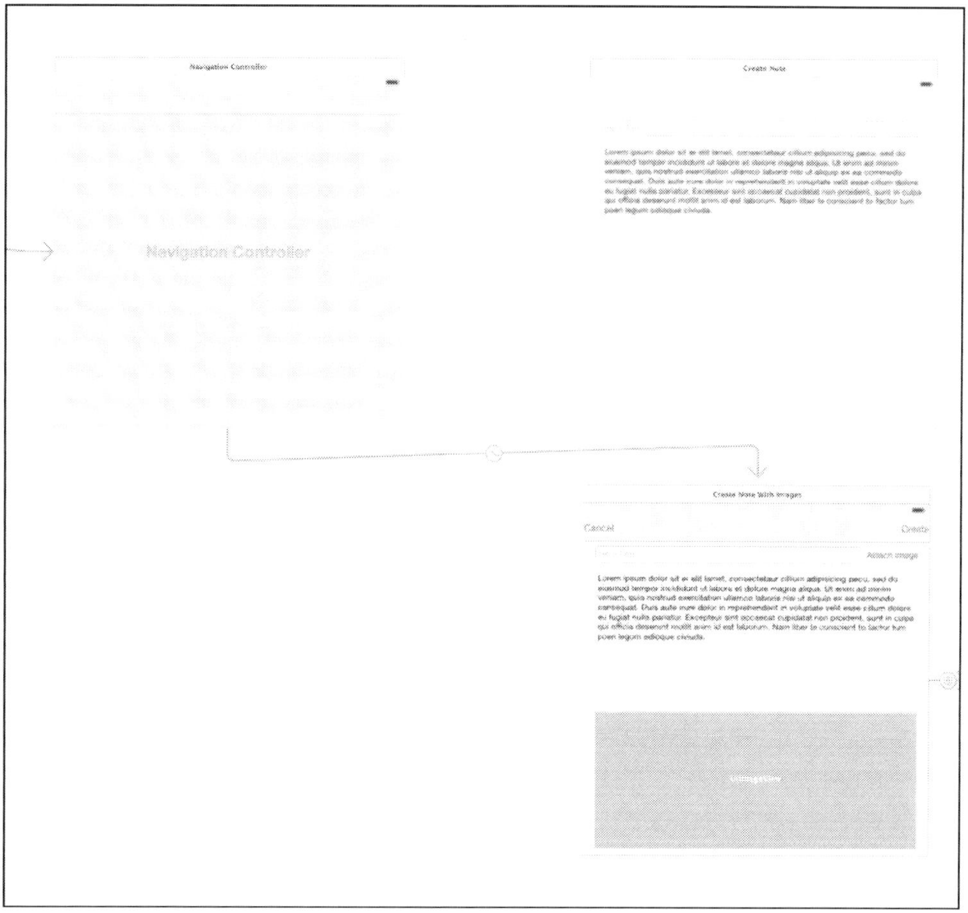

Open **AttachPhotoViewController.swift** and add the following method to the class:

```
func imagePickerController(picker: UIImagePickerController,
 didFinishPickingMediaWithInfo info: NSDictionary) {
  if let note = note {
    note.image = info[UIImagePickerControllerOriginalImage] as?
UIImage
  }
  self.navigationController?.popViewControllerAnimated(true)
}
```

This will populate the new image property of the note once the user selects something from the standard image picker.

Open **CreateNoteViewController.swift** and replace `viewDidAppear` with the following:

```
override func viewDidAppear(animated: Bool) {
  super.viewDidAppear(animated)
  if let image = _note?.image {
    attachedPhoto.image = image
    view.endEditing(true)
  } else {
    titleField.becomeFirstResponder()
  }
}
```

This implementation will display the new image if the user has added one.

Next, open **NotesListViewController.swift** and update `tableView(_:cellForRowAtIndexPath)` with the following:

```
override func tableView(tableView: UITableView,
cellForRowAtIndexPath indexPath: NSIndexPath) -> UITableViewCell
{
  let note = notes.fetchedObjects![indexPath.row] as Note
  var identifier = "NoteCell"
  if note.image != nil {
    identifier = "NoteCellImage"
  }
  var cell =
tableView.dequeueReusableCellWithIdentifier(identifier,
forIndexPath: indexPath) as NoteTableViewCell;
  cell.note = notes.fetchedObjects![indexPath.row] as? Note
  return cell
}
```

This will set the correct cell identifier based on whether an image is present in the note. If there is an image, you also need to populate the image view in the cell. Open **NoteTableViewCell.swift** and add the following lines after the code that sets the creation date label's text in `updateNoteInfo()`:

```
if let image = note?.image {
  noteImage.image = image
}
```

Build and run, and choose to add a new note:

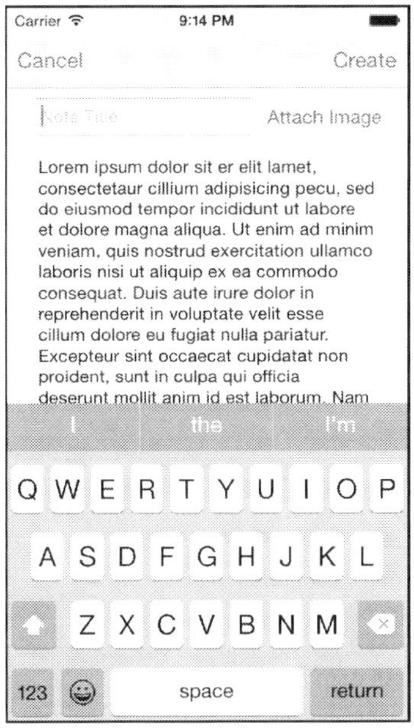

Tap the **Attach Image** button to add an image to the note. Choose an image and you'll see it in your new note:

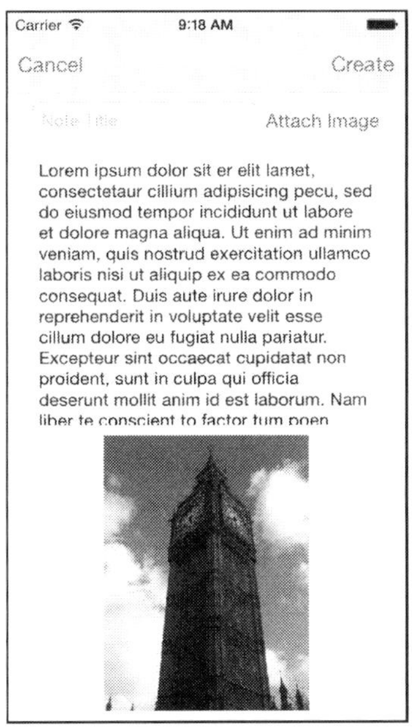

The app uses a standard `UIImagePickerController` to add photos as attachments to notes.

> **Note:** To add your own images to the Simulator's photo album, drag an image file onto the open Simulator window. Thankfully, the iOS 8 Simulator now comes with a library of photos ready for your use. :]
>
> If you're using a device, go to **AttachPhotoViewController.swift** and set the `sourceType` attribute on the image picker controller to `.Camera` to take photos with the device camera. The existing code uses the photo album, since there is no camera in the Simulator.

Add a couple of sample notes with photos, since in the next section you'll be using sample data from this state of the project to move forward with a slightly more complex migration.

> **Note:** At this point, you might want to make a copy of the v2 source code into a different folder to come back to later. Or if you're using source control, set a tag here so you can come back to this point.

A manual migration

The next step in the evolution of this data model is to move from attaching only a single image to a note to allowing the user to attach multiple images. The note entity will stay, and you'll need a new entity for an image. Since a note can have many images, there will be a to-many relationship.

Splitting one entity into two isn't exactly on the list of things lightweight migrations can support. It's time to level up to a custom manual migration!

The first step in every migration is to create a new model version. As before, select the **UnCloudNotesDataModel.xcdatamodeld** file and from the **Editor** menu item, select **Add Model Version...**. Name this model **UnCloudNotesDataModel v3** and base it on the v2 data model. Set the new model version as the default model and open it in Xcode to start making the necessary changes.

First, you'll add a new entity to the new data model. In the lower-left corner, click the **Add Entity** button. Rename this entity **Attachment**. Select the entity and in the Data Model inspector pane, set the **Class** to **UnCloudNotes.Attachment**.

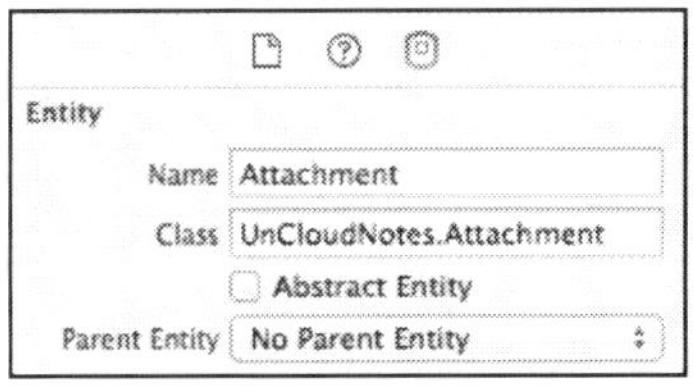

Create two attributes in the Attachment entity. Add an attribute named **image** of type **Transformable**, with the value transformer set to **UnCloudNotes.ImageTransformer**. This is the same as the image attribute you added to the Note entity earlier. Add a second attribute called **dateCreated** and make it a **Date** type.

Next, add a relationship to the Attachment entity to relate it to its Note. Set the relationship name to **note** and its destination to **Note**.

Select the **Note** entity and delete the **image** attribute. Finally, create a to-many relationship from the **Note** entity to the **Attachment** entity. Name the relationship **attachments**, set the destination to **Attachment** and select the **note** relationship you just created as the inverse.

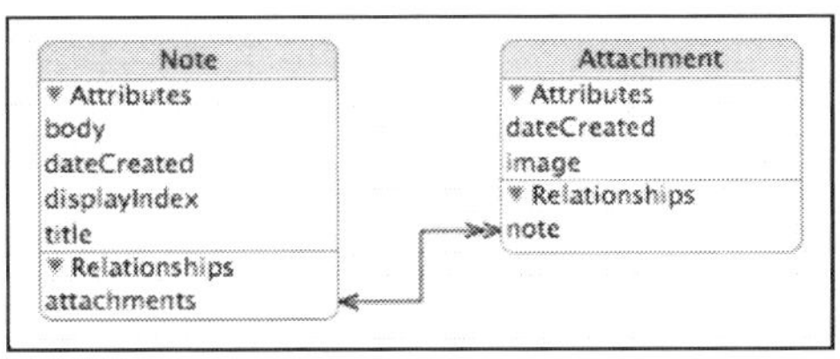

The data model is now ready for migration!

Mapping models

With lightweight migrations, Core Data can automatically determine the steps to take to move from one model version to another when the changes are simple. When the changes aren't as simple, you can manually set up the steps to migrate from one model version to another with a **mapping model**.

It's important that before creating a mapping model, you complete and finalize your target model. You've finished the changes to the v3 data model, and you know that lightweight migration isn't going to do the job. To create a mapping model, open the **File** menu in Xcode and select **New\File**. Navigate to the **iOS\Core Data** section and select **Mapping Model**:

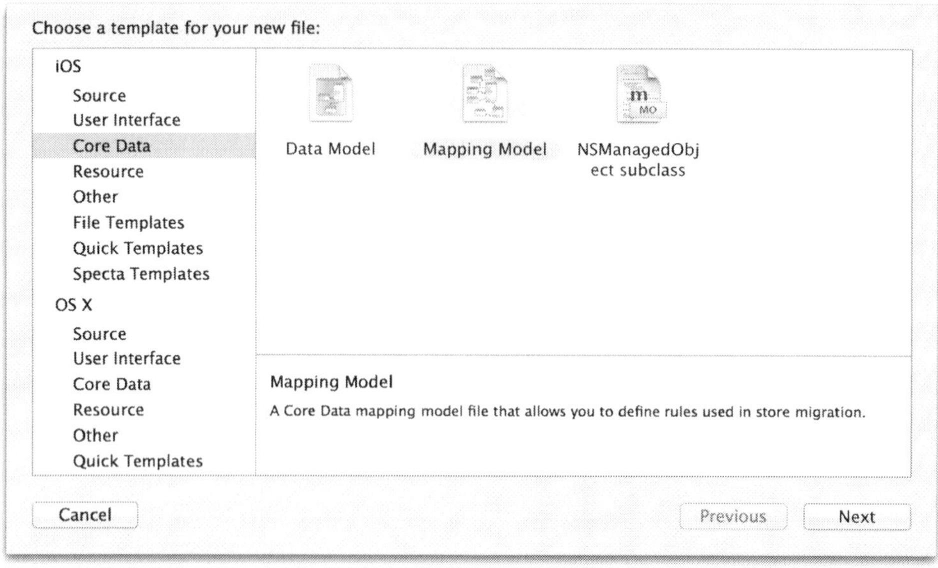

Click **Next**, select the v2 data model as the source model and select the v3 data model as the target model.

Name the new file **UnCloudNotesMappingModel_v2_to_v3**. The file naming convention I typically use is the data model name along with the source version and destination version. As an application collects more and more mapping models over time, this file naming convention makes it easier to distinguish between files and the order in which they have changed over time.

Open **UnCloudNotesMappingModel_v2_to_v3.xcmappingmodel**. Luckily, the mapping model doesn't start completely from scratch—Xcode examines the source and target models and infers as much as it can, so you're starting out with a mapping model that consists of the basics.

Attribute mapping

There are two mappings, one named **NoteToNote** and another simply named **Attachment**. NoteToNote describes how to migrate the v2 Note entity to the v3 Note entity.

Select **NoteToNote** and you'll see two sections: **Attribute Mappings** and **Relationship Mappings**.

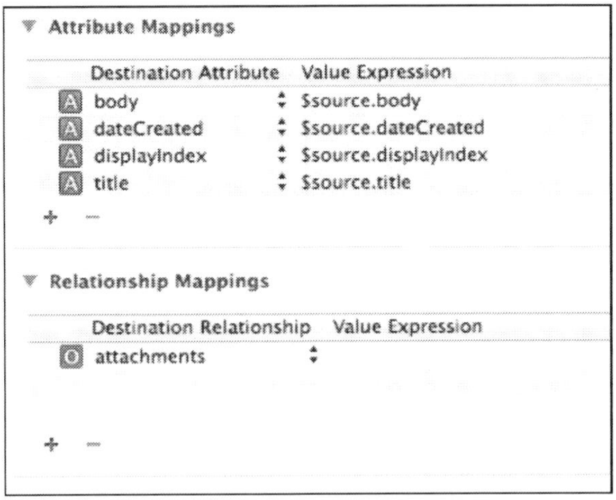

The attributes mappings here are fairly straightforward. Notice the value expressions with the pattern `$source`. The `$source` is a special token for the mapping model editor, representing a reference to the source instance. Remember, with Core Data, you're not dealing with rows and columns in a database. Instead, you're dealing with objects, their attributes and classes.

In this case, the values for `body`, `dateCreated`, `displayIndex` and `title` will be transferred directly from the source. Those are the easy cases!

The attachments relationship is new, so Xcode couldn't fill in anything from the source. You'll get to that shortly.

Select the **Attachment** mapping and make sure the Utilities panel on the right is open. Select the last tab in the Utilities panel to open the **Entity Mapping** inspector:

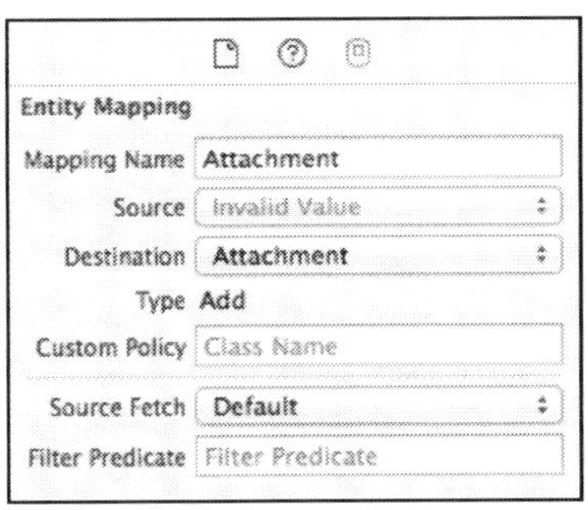

Change the **Mapping Name** to **NoteToAttachment**. This mapping name convention (also used by default Core Data mappings) indicates that data for the new Attachment entity will come from Note. Select **Note** as the source entity in the drop-down list. Once you select the source entity, Xcode will try to resolve the mappings automatically based on the names of the attributes of the source and destination entities. In this case, Xcode will fill in the `dateCreated` and `image` mappings for you:

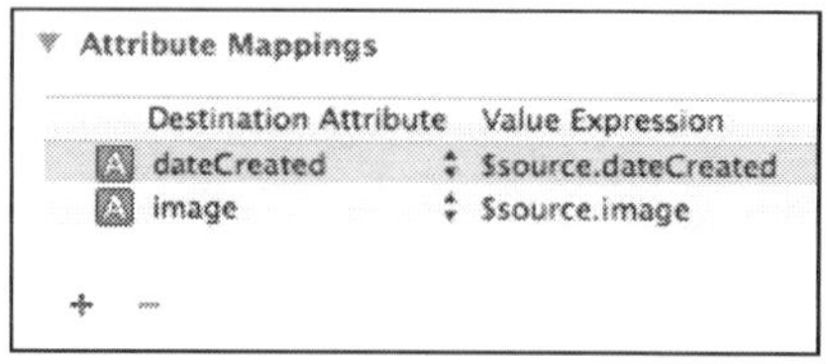

Xcode is being helpful again; it just needs a small nudge from you specifying the source entity. Since the attribute names match, Xcode will fill in the value expressions for you. What does it mean to map data from Note entities to Attachment entities? Think of this as saying, "For each Note, make an Attachment and copy the `image` and `dateCreated` attributes across."

This mapping will create an Attachment for every Note, but you really only want an Attachment if there was an image attached to the note. Make sure the **NoteToAttachment** entity mapping is selected and in the inspector, set the **Filter Predicate** field to **image != nil**. This will ensure the Attachment mapping will only happen when there is an image present in the source.

Relationship mapping

The migration is able to copy the images from Notes to Attachments, but as of yet, there's no relationship linking the Note to the Attachment. The next step to get that behavior is to add a relationship mapping.

In the **NoteToAttachment** mapping, you'll see a relationship mapping called **note**. Like the relationship mapping you saw in NoteToNote, the value expression is empty since Xcode doesn't know how to automatically migrate the relationship.

Select the attachment relationship row in the list of relationships so that the Inspector changes to reflect the properties of the relationship mapping. In the **Source Fetch** field, select **Auto Generate Value Expression**. Enter **$source** in the **Key Path** field and select **NoteToNote** from the **Mapping Name** field.

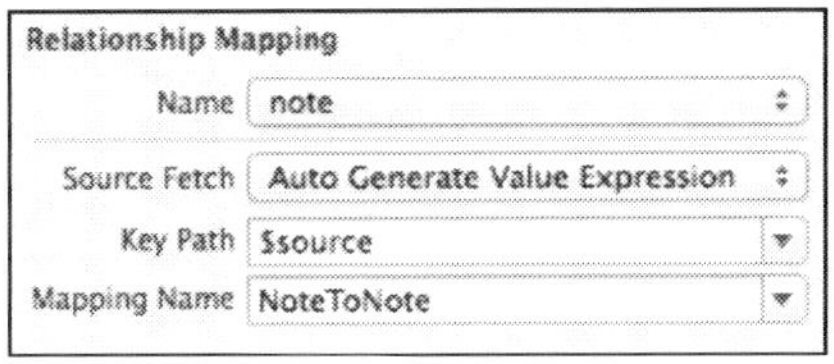

This should generate a value expression that looks like this:

```
FUNCTION($manager,
  "destinationInstancesForEntityMappingNamed:sourceInstances:",
  "NoteToNote", $source)
```

The `FUNCTION` statement resembles the `objc_msgSend` syntax. That is, the first argument is the object instance, the second argument is the selector and any further arguments are passed into that method as parameters.

So really, the mapping model is calling a method on the `$manager` object. The `$manager` token is a special reference to the `NSMigrationManager` object that is handling the migration process.

> **Note:** Using `FUNCTION` expressions still relies on some knowledge of Objective-C syntax. It might be some time until Apple gets around to revamping Core Data 100% to Swift! :]

Core Data creates the migration manager during the migration. The migration manager keeps track of which source objects are associated with which destination objects. The method `destinationInstancesForEntityMappingNamed:sourceInstances:` will look up the destination instances for a source object. The expression above is saying "set the note relationship to whatever the `$source` object for this mapping gets migrated to by the `NoteToNote` mapping," which in this case will be the Note entity in the new data store.

You've completed your custom mapping! You now have a mapping that is configured to split a single entity into two and relate the proper data objects together.

Persistent store and entity classes

Before running this migration, you need to update the Core Data setup code to use this mapping model and not try to infer one on its own. Open

NotesListViewController.swift and find the `CoreDataStack` property initializer near the top of the class. Change the options dictionary to match the following:

```
options:[NSMigratePersistentStoresAutomaticallyOption:true,
        NSInferMappingModelAutomaticallyOption:false]
```

By setting `NSInferMappingModelAutomaticallyOption` to `false`, you've ensured that the persistent store coordinator will now use the new mapping model to migrate the store. Yes, that's all the code you need to change; there is no new code!

What will happen here is that Core Data will look for the mapping model files in the default or main bundle when it's told not to infer or generate one. Since the mapping model knows the source and destination versions of the model, Core Data will use that information to determine which mapping model to use to perform a migration. It really is as simple as changing a single option to use the custom mapping model.

The code in the app also needs updating—you're not working with the image property on a note any more, but with multiple attachments.

Create a new Swift file called **Attachment** and implement the managed object subclass:

```
import Foundation
import UIKit
import CoreData

class Attachment: NSManagedObject {
  @NSManaged var dateCreated: NSDate
  @NSManaged var image: UIImage?
  @NSManaged var note: Note
}
```

Open **Note.swift** and delete the **image** property. Replace it with a property for the `attachments` relationship:

```
@NSManaged var attachments: NSSet
```

The rest of your app is still depending on an `image` property, so you'll get a compile error if you try to build the app. Add the following computed property and helper method to the `Note` class:

```
var image : UIImage? {
  if let image = self.latestAttachment()?.image {
    return image
  }
  return nil
```

```
}

func latestAttachment() -> Attachment? {
  var attachmentsToSort = attachments.allObjects as [Attachment]
  if attachmentsToSort.count == 0 {
    return nil
  }

  attachmentsToSort.sort {
    let date1 = $0.dateCreated.timeIntervalSinceReferenceDate
    let date2 = $1.dateCreated.timeIntervalSinceReferenceDate
    return date1 > date2
  }

  return attachmentsToSort[0]
}
```

This implementation uses a computed property, which gets the image from the latest attachment. If there are several attachments, `latestAttachment()` will, as its name suggests, grab the latest one and return it.

Next, open **AttachPhotoViewController.swift** to update it to create a new Attachment object when the user chooses an image. Add the Core Data import to the top of the file:

```
import CoreData
```

Replace the image picker delegate method with the following:

```
func imagePickerController(picker: UIImagePickerController,
didFinishPickingMediaWithInfo info: NSDictionary) {
    if let note = note {
      let attachment =
NSEntityDescription.insertNewObjectForEntityForName("Attachment"
, inManagedObjectContext: note.managedObjectContext) as
Attachment
      attachment.dateCreated = NSDate()
      attachment.image =
info[UIImagePickerControllerOriginalImage] as? UIImage
      attachment.note = note
    }
    navigationController?.popViewControllerAnimated(true)
}
```

Build and run the app, and you'll notice that not a whole lot has changed on the surface! However, if you still see your notes and images as before, that means the mapping model worked; under the covers, Core Data has updated the underlying schema of the SQLite store to reflect the changes in the v3 data model.

> **Note**: Again, you might want to make a copy of the v3 source code into a different folder to come back to later. Or if you're using source control, set a tag here so you can come back to this point.

A complex mapping model

The higher-ups have thought of a new feature for UnCloudNotes, so you know what that means: It's time to migrate the data model once again! This time, they've decided that supporting only image attachments isn't enough. They want future versions of the app to support videos, audio files or really add any kind of attachment that makes sense.

You make the decision to have a base entity called **Attachment** and a subclass called **ImageAttachment**. This will enable each attachment type to have its own useful information. Images could have attributes for a caption, image size, compression level, file size, et cetera. Later, you can add more subclasses for other attachment types.

While new images will grab this information prior to saving, you'll need to extract that information from current images during the migration. You'll need to use either CoreImage or the ImageIO libraries. These are data transformations that Core Data definitely doesn't support out of the box, which makes a custom manual migration the proper tool for the job.

As usual, the first step in any data migration is to select the data model file in Xcode and select **Editor\Add Model Version...**. This time, create version 4 of the data model called **UnCloudNotesDataModel v4**. Don't forget to set the current version of the data model to v4 in the Xcode Inspector.

Open the v4 data model and add a new entity named **ImageAttachment**. Set the class to **UnCloudNotes.ImageAttachment**. Make the following changes to ImageAttachment:

- Set the **Parent Entity** to **Attachment**.
- Add a String attribute named **caption**.
- Add a Float attribute named **width**.

- Add a Float attribute name **height**,Add a Transformable attribute named **image**. Set the Value Transformer Name to **UnCloudNotes.ImageTransformer**.

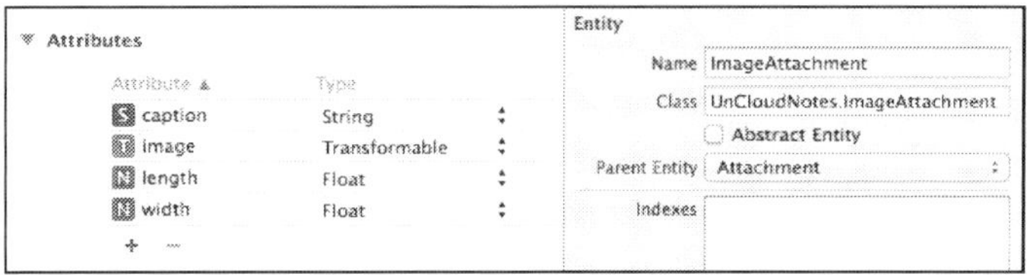

Having a parent entity is like being a subclass, which means ImageAttachment will inherit the attributes of Attachment. When you set up the managed object subclass later, you'll see this inheritance made explicit in the code.

Now that the image is stored in ImageAttachment, you can remove it from Attachment. Select the **Attachment** entity and delete the **image** property.

That should do it for the new data model. Once you've finished, your version 4 data model should look like this:

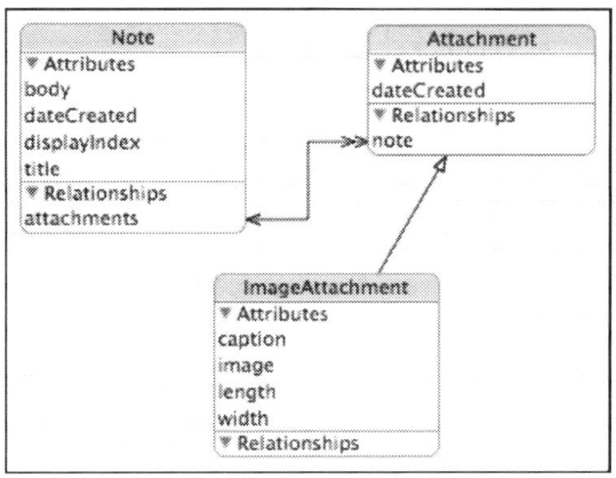

Mapping model

In the Xcode menu, choose **File\New File** and select the **iOS\Core Data\Mapping Model** template. Select version 3 as the source model and version 4 as the target, and name the file **UnCloudNotesMappingModel_v3_to_v4.**

Open the new mapping model in Xcode and you'll see that Xcode has again helpfully filled in a few mappings for you.

Starting with the **NoteToNote** mapping, Xcode has directly copied the source entities from the source store to the target with no conversion or transformation. The default Xcode values for this simple data migration are good to go, as-is!

Select the **AttachmentToAttachment** mapping. Xcode has also detected some common attributes in the source and target entities and generated mappings. However, you want to *convert* Attachment entities to ImageAttachment entities. What Xcode has created here will map Attachment to Attachment, which isn't necessary. Delete this mapping.

Now select the **ImageAttachment** mapping and rename it to **AttachmentToImageAttachment** to describe what it will do more accurately.

This mapping has no source entity since this is a completely new entity. In the inspector, change the source entity to be **Attachment**. Now that it knows the source, Xcode will fill in a few of the value expressions for you.

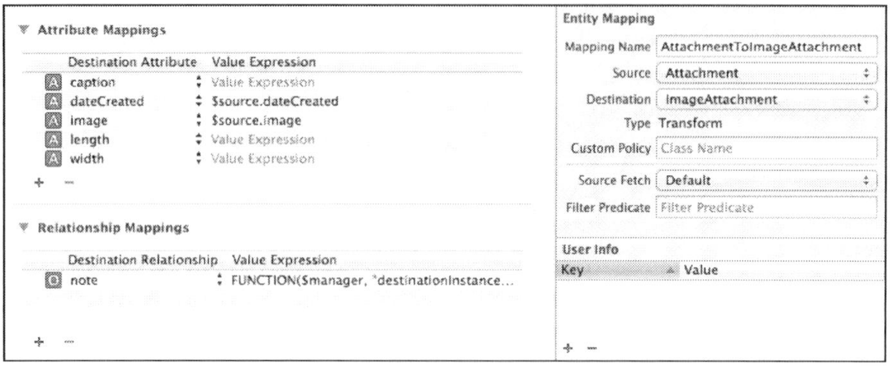

For the remaining attributes, you'll need to write some code. This is where you need image processing and custom code beyond simple `FUNCTION` expressions!

Custom migration policies

To move beyond `FUNCTION` expressions in the mapping model, you can subclass `NSEntityMigrationPolicy` directly. This lets you write Swift code to handle the migration, instance by instance, so you can call on any framework or library available to the rest of your app.

Add a new Swift file to the project called **AttachmentToImageAttachmentMigrationPolicyV3toV4** and replace its contents with the following starter code:

```
import CoreData
import UIKit
```

```
class AttachmentToImageAttachmentMigrationPolicyV3toV4:
NSEntityMigrationPolicy {

}
```

This naming convention should look familiar to you, as it's noting that this is a custom migration policy and is for transforming data from Attachments in model version 3 to ImageAttachments in model version 4.

Back in the v3-to-v4 mapping model file, select the **AttachmentToImageAttachment** entity mapping. In the Entity Mapping Inspector, fill in the **Custom Policy** field with the class name you just created, **UnCloudNotes.AttachmentToImageAttachmentMigrationPolicyV3toV4**.

Now, when Core Data runs this migration, it will create an instance of your custom migration policy when it needs to perform a data migration for that specific set of data. That's your chance to run any custom transformation code to do what's needed to extract image information during migration! Now, it's time to add some custom logic to the custom entity mapping policy.

Open **AttachmentToImageAttachmentMigrationPolicyV3toV4.swift** and add the method to perform the migration:

```
override func createDestinationInstancesForSourceInstance(
 sInstance: NSManagedObject,
 entityMapping mapping: NSEntityMapping,
 manager: NSMigrationManager, error: NSErrorPointer) -> Bool {
  // 1
  let newAttachment =
NSEntityDescription.insertNewObjectForEntityForName(
    "ImageAttachment",
    inManagedObjectContext: manager.destinationContext)
    as NSManagedObject

  // 2
  for propertyMapping in mapping.attributeMappings
   as [NSPropertyMapping]! {
    let destinationName = propertyMapping.name!
    if let valueExpression = propertyMapping.valueExpression {
      let context: NSMutableDictionary = ["source": sInstance]
      let destinationValue: AnyObject =
        valueExpression.expressionValueWithObject(sInstance,
        context: context)
      newAttachment.setValue(destinationValue,
        forKey: destinationName)
    }
```

```
    }
    // 3
    if let image = sInstance.valueForKey("image") as? UIImage {
      newAttachment.setValue(image.size.width, forKey: "width")
      newAttachment.setValue(image.size.height, forKey: "height")
    }
    // 4
    let body = sInstance.valueForKeyPath("note.body") as NSString
    newAttachment.setValue(body.substringToIndex(80),
      forKey: "caption")
    // 5
    manager.associateSourceInstance(sInstance,
      withDestinationInstance: newAttachment,
      forEntityMapping: mapping)
    // 6
    return true
  }
```

This method is an override of the default `NSEntityMigrationPolicy` implementation. Overriding this method is the way the migration manager creates instances of destination entities. That is, an instance of the source object is the first parameter, and, when overridden, it's up to the developer to create the destination instance and associate it properly to the migration manager.

Here's what's going on, step by step:

1. First, you create an instance of the new destination object. The migration manager has two Core Data stacks—one to read from the source and one to write to the destination—so you need to be sure to use the destination context here.

2. Even though this is a custom manual migration, most of the attribute migrations should be performed using the expressions you defined in the mapping model. To do this, you loop through each attribute mapping from the `entityMapping` parameter, apply the value expression to the source instance and set the result to the new destination object.

3. Next, you try to get an instance of the image. If it exists, then you grab its width and height to populate the data in the new object.

4. For the caption, you simply grab the note's body text and take the first 80 characters.

5. The migration manager needs to know the connection between the source object, the newly created destination object and the mapping. Failing to call this method at the end of a custom migration will result in missing data in the destination store.

6. Finally, the return value tells the migration manager that everything went well.

That's it for the custom migration code! Core Data will pick up the mapping model when it detects a v3 data store on launch, and apply it to migrate it to the new data model version. Since you added the custom `NSEntityMigrationPolicy` subclass and linked to it in the mapping model, Core Data will call through to your code automatically.

You just need to wrap up the changes to the new entity subclasses. Open **Attachment.swift** and remove the **image** property.

Next, create a new Swift file called **ImageAttachment** and replace its contents with the following:

```
import UIKit
import CoreData

class ImageAttachment: Attachment {
  @NSManaged var image: UIImage?
  @NSManaged var width: CGFloat
  @NSManaged var height: CGFloat
  @NSManaged var caption: NSString
}
```

There are several places in the app that reference `Attachment` that you now need to change to reference `ImageAttachment`.

Open **Note.swift** and change the first two lines of `latestAttachment()` so that they reference `ImageAttachment` instead:

```
func latestAttachment() -> ImageAttachment? {
  var attachmentsToSort = attachments.allObjects as
[ImageAttachment]
```

Finally, open **AttachPhotoViewController.swift** and find `imagePickerController(_:didFinishPickingMediaWithInfo:)`. Change the line that sets up `attachment` so that it uses `ImageAttachment` instead:

```
let attachment =
  NSEntityDescription.insertNewObjectForEntityForName(
  "ImageAttachment",
  inManagedObjectContext: note.managedObjectContext)
  as ImageAttachment
```

Now build and run UnCloudNotes, and the data should migrate properly. Again, your notes will be there, images and all, but you're now future-proof and ready to add video, audio and anything else!

Migrating non-sequential versions

Thus far, you've walked through a series of data migrations in order. You've migrated the data from version 1 to 2 to 3 to 4, in sequence. Inevitably, in the real world of App Store launches, a user might skip an update and need to go from version 2 to 4, for example. What happens then?

When Core Data performs a migration, its intention is to perform only a single migration. In this hypothetical scenario, Core Data would look for a mapping model that goes from version 2 to 4; if one didn't exist, Core Data would infer one, if you tell it to. Otherwise the migration will fail, and Core Data will report an error when attempting to attach the store to the persistent store coordinator.

How can you handle this scenario? You could provide multiple mapping models, but as your app grows, you'd need to provide an inordinate number of these: from v1 to v4, v1 to v3, v2 to v4, et cetera. You would spend more time on mapping models than on the app itself!

The solution to this scenario is to implement a fully custom migration sequence. You already know that the migration from version 2 to 3 works; to go from 2 to 4, it will work well if you manually migrate the store from 2 to 3 and then from 3 to 4. This step-by-step migration means you'll prevent Core Data from looking for a direct 2 to 4 or even a 1 to 4 migration.

A self-aware stack

To begin implementing this solution, you'll want to create a separate "migration manager" class. The responsibility of this class will be to provide a properly migrated Core Data stack, when asked. That is, this class will have a stack property and will return an instance of `CoreDataStack`, as UnCloudNotes uses throughout, which has run through all the migrations necessary to be useful for the app.

First, create a new Swift file called **DataMigrationManager**. Open the file and replace its contents with the following:

```
import Foundation
import CoreData

class DataMigrationManager {
  let storeName: String
  let modelName: String
```

```
  var options: NSDictionary?
  var stack: CoreDataStack

  init(storeNamed: String, modelNamed: String) {
    self.storeName = storeNamed
    self.modelName = modelNamed
  }
}
```

You'll keep track of the store name and model name with two properties. There is also an optional options dictionary property for use when performing the final adding of the store. As seen from previous migrations, this options dictionary will become more important when you finally get to the step where you add a persistent store to a coordinator.

Next, open **NotesListViewController.swift** and replace the stack lazy initialization code with the following:

```
lazy var stack : CoreDataStack = {
  let manager = DataMigrationManager(
    storeNamed:"UnCloudNotes",
    modelNamed:"UnCloudNotesDataModel")
  return manager.stack
}()
```

First of all, you only want the stack to be "initialized" once, so the lazy attribute takes care of that. Second, the initialization is actually handled by the `DataMigrationManager`, so the stack used will be the one returned from the migration manager.

Now to the harder part: How do you figure out if the store needs migrations? And if it does, how do you figure out where to start? To do this, you're going to need helper methods. At the bottom of **DataMigrationManager.swift**, add an extension on `NSManagedObjectModel`:

```
extension NSManagedObjectModel {
  class func modelVersionsForName(name: String)
   -> [NSManagedObjectModel] {
    let urls = NSBundle.mainBundle().
      URLsForResourcesWithExtension(
       "mom", subdirectory:"\(name).momd") as [NSURL]
    return urls.map
      { url in NSManagedObjectModel(contentsOfURL:url)! }
  }
```

```
    class func uncloudNotesModelNamed(name: String)
    -> NSManagedObjectModel {
      let modelURL = NSBundle.mainBundle().URLForResource(name,
        withExtension:"mom",
        subdirectory:"UnCloudNotesDataModel.momd")
      return NSManagedObjectModel(contentsOfURL: modelURL!)!
    }
  }
```

The first method will return all model versions for a given name. The second method will return a specific instance of `NSManagedObjectModel`. Usually, Core Data will give you the most recent data model version, but this method will let you dig inside for a specific version.

> **Note:** When Xcode compiles your app into its app bundle, it will also compile your data models. The app bundle will have at its root a .momd folder that contains .mom files. MOM or Managed Object Model files are the compiled versions of .xcdatamodel files. You'll have a .mom for each data model version.

To use this method, add the following method inside the class extension:

```
class func version1() -> NSManagedObjectModel {
  return uncloudNotesModelNamed("UnCloudNotesDataModel")
}
```

This method will return the first version of the data model. That takes care of *getting* the model, but what about checking the version of a model? Add the following method to the class extension:

```
func isVersion1() -> Bool {
  return self == self.dynamicType.version1()
}
```

You'll be able to call this method to check whether it is from version 1 when you have a `NSManagedObjectModel` instance.

Next, add similar methods for versions 2 to 4 to the class extension:

```
class func version2() -> NSManagedObjectModel {
  return uncloudNotesModelNamed("UnCloudNotesDataModel v2")
}
func isVersion2() -> Bool {
  return self == self.dynamicType.version2()
```

```
}
class func version3() -> NSManagedObjectModel {
  return uncloudNotesModelNamed("UnCloudNotesDataModel v3")
}
func isVersion3() -> Bool {
  return self == self.dynamicType.version3()
}
class func version4() -> NSManagedObjectModel {
  return uncloudNotesModelNamed("UnCloudNotesDataModel v4")
}
func isVersion4() -> Bool {
  return self == self.dynamicType.version4()
}
```

To get the == comparison to work on two `NSManagedObjectModel` objects, add an operator overload to the file. You'll need to add this outside of the class extension, right in the global scope:

```
func ==(firstModel:NSManagedObjectModel,
otherModel:NSManagedObjectModel) -> Bool {
  let myEntities = firstModel.entitiesByName as NSDictionary
  let otherEntities = otherModel.entitiesByName as NSDictionary

  return myEntities.isEqualToDictionary(otherEntities)
}
```

The idea here is simple: two `NSManagedObjectModel` objects are identical if they have the same collection of entities, with the same version hashes.

Go back to the `DataMigrationManager` class declaration part of the file and add these two helper methods:

```
func storeIsCompatibleWith(Model model:NSManagedObjectModel)
 -> Bool {
  let storeMetadata = metadataForStoreAtURL(storeURL)

  return model.isConfiguration(nil,
    compatibleWithStoreMetadata:storeMetadata)
}

func metadataForStoreAtURL(storeURL:NSURL) -> NSDictionary! {
  var error : NSError?
  let metadata =
NSPersistentStoreCoordinator.metadataForPersistentStoreOfType(
    NSSQLiteStoreType, URL: storeURL, error: &error)
  if metadata == nil {
    println(error)
```

```
    }
    return metadata
  }
```

The first method is a simple convenience wrapper to determine whether the persistent store is compatible with a given model. The second method helps by retrieving the metadata for the store.

Next, add the following computed properties to the class:

```
lazy var storeURL : NSURL = {
  var storePaths = NSSearchPathForDirectoriesInDomains(
    .ApplicationSupportDirectory, .UserDomainMask, true)
  let storePath = storePaths[0] as String
  return NSURL.fileURLWithPath(
    storePath.stringByAppendingPathComponent(
      self.storeName + ".sqlite"))!
}()

lazy var storeModel : NSManagedObjectModel? = {
  for model in NSManagedObjectModel
   .modelVersionsForName(self.modelName) {
    if self.storeIsCompatibleWith(Model:model) {
      println("Store \(self.storeURL) is compatible with model
\(model.versionIdentifiers)")
      return model
    }
  }

  println("Unable to determine storeModel")
  return nil
}()
```

These properties will allow you to access the current store URL and model. As it turns out, there is no method in the CoreData API to ask a store for its model version. Instead, the easiest solution is brute force. Since you've already created helper methods to check if a store is compatible with a particular model, you'll simply need to iterate through all the available models until you find one that works with the store.

Next, you need your migration manger remember the current model version. Add a property to the class, as follows:

```
lazy var currentModel: NSManagedObjectModel = {
  // Let core data tell us which model is the current model
  let modelURL = NSBundle.mainBundle().URLForResource(
    self.modelName, withExtension:"momd")
```

```
    let model = NSManagedObjectModel(contentsOfURL: modelURL!)!
    return model
  }()
```

The `currentModel` property is lazy, so you load it only once since it should return the same thing every time. Core Data will, by default, return the "current" data model when loading the model using the `.momd` folder URL, and return a properly initialized `NSManagedObjectModel`.

Of course, if the model you have isn't the current model, that's the time to run the migration! Add a starter method to the class (which you'll fill in later), as follows:

```
  func performMigration() {
  }
```

Now, head up to the `stack` property you added earlier. Change that definition to the following:

```
  var stack: CoreDataStack {
    if !storeIsCompatibleWith(Model: currentModel) {
      performMigration()
    }

    return CoreDataStack(modelName: modelName,
      storeName: storeName, options: options)
  }
```

In the end, the computed property will return a `CoreDataStack` instance. Before it does so, it checks if the store specified in the initialization is compatible with what Core Data determines to be the current version of the data model. If the store can't be loaded with the current model, then it needs to be migrated.

You now have a self-aware Core Data stack that can tell you what version it is! Build the project to make sure everything compiles. The next step is to add the custom migration logic.

The self-migrating stack

Now it's time to start building out the migration logic. Add the big method that does the heavy lifting:

```
  func migrateStoreAt(URL storeURL:NSURL,
    fromModel from:NSManagedObjectModel,
    toModel to:NSManagedObjectModel,
```

```
    mappingModel:NSMappingModel? = nil) {
    // 1
    let migrationManager = NSMigrationManager(sourceModel: from,
      destinationModel:to)

    // 2
    var migrationMappingModel : NSMappingModel
    if let mappingModel = mappingModel {
      migrationMappingModel = mappingModel
    } else {
      var error : NSError?
      migrationMappingModel = NSMappingModel.
        inferredMappingModelForSourceModel(
         from, destinationModel: to, error: &error)!
    }
    // 3
    let destinationURL = storeURL.URLByDeletingLastPathComponent
    let destinationName = storeURL.lastPathComponent + "~" + "1"
    let destination =
  destinationURL!.URLByAppendingPathComponent(destinationName)

    println("From Model: \(from.versionIdentifiers)")
    println("To Model: \(to.versionIdentifiers)")
    println("Migrating store \(storeURL) to \(destination)")
    println("Mapping model: \(mappingModel)")
    // 4
    var error : NSError?
    let success =
      migrationManager.migrateStoreFromURL(storeURL,
      type:NSSQLiteStoreType,
      options:nil,
      withMappingModel:mappingModel,
      toDestinationURL:destination,
      destinationType:NSSQLiteStoreType,
      destinationOptions:nil,
      error:&error)
    // 5
    if success {
      println("Migration Completed Successfully")
      var error : NSError?
      let fileManager = NSFileManager.defaultManager()
      fileManager.removeItemAtURL(storeURL, error: &error)
      fileManager.moveItemAtURL(destination, toURL:
        storeURL, error:&error)
    } else {
      NSLog("Error migrating \(error)")
    }
  }
```

This method takes the store URL, a source model, destination model and an optional mapping model. If you need to do a lightweight migration, you can pass `nil` or simply skip the final parameter.

Here's what's going on, step by step:

1. First, you create an instance of the migration manager.
2. If a mapping model was passed in to the method, then you use that. Otherwise, you create an inferred mapping model.
3. Since migrations will create a second data store and migrate data, instance-by-instance, from the original to the new file, the destination URL must be a different file. Now, the example code in this section will create a `destinationURL` that is the same folder as the original and a file concatenated with "~1". The destination URL can be in a temp folder or anywhere your app has access to write files.
4. Here's where you put the migration manager to work! You've already set it up with the source and destination models, so you simply need to add the mapping model and the two URLs to the mix.
5. Given the result, you can print a success or error message to the console. In the success case, you perform a bit of cleanup, too. In this case, it's enough to remove the old store and replace it with the new store.

Now it's simply a matter of calling that method with the right parameters. Remember your empty implementation of `performMigration`? It's time to fill that in. Add the following lines to that method:

```
if !currentModel.isVersion4() {
  fatalError("Can only handle migrations to version 4!")
}
```

You know the most recent version of the model, so this code bails out and kills the app if the current model is anything other than version 4. This is a little extreme—in your own apps, you might want to continue the migration anyway—but doing it this way will definitely remind you to think about migrations if you ever add another data model version to your app!

Add the next bit of code to the end of `performMigration`:

```
if let storeModel = self.storeModel {
  if storeModel.isVersion1() {
    options =
      [NSMigratePersistentStoresAutomaticallyOption: true,
```

```
        NSInferMappingModelAutomaticallyOption: true]
  } else {
    options =
      [NSMigratePersistentStoresAutomaticallyOption: true,
       NSInferMappingModelAutomaticallyOption: false]
  }

  if storeModel.isVersion1() {
    let destinationModel = NSManagedObjectModel.version2()

    migrateStoreAt(URL: storeURL,
      fromModel: storeModel,
      toModel: destinationModel)

    performMigration()
  } else if storeModel.isVersion2() {
    let destinationModel = NSManagedObjectModel.version3()
    let mappingModel = NSMappingModel(fromBundles: nil,
          forSourceModel: storeModel,
          destinationModel: destinationModel)

    migrateStoreAt(URL:storeURL,
      fromModel:storeModel,
      toModel:destinationModel,
      mappingModel: mappingModel)

    performMigration()
  } else if storeModel.isVersion3() {
    let destinationModel = NSManagedObjectModel.version4()
    let mappingModel = NSMappingModel(fromBundles: nil,
          forSourceModel: storeModel,
          destinationModel: destinationModel)

    migrateStoreAt(URL:storeURL,
      fromModel:storeModel,
      toModel:destinationModel,
      mappingModel: mappingModel)
  }
}
```

The steps are similar, no matter which version you start from:

- **Set up the options dictionary.** Remember, the version 1 model used a simple lightweight migration, while the others used mapping model files. You need to have different options dictionaries to account for this.
- **Set the destination model to the correct model version.** Remember, you're only going "up" one version at a time, so from 1 to 2 and from 2 to 3.

- **For version 2 and above, also load the mapping model.**
- **Finally, call migrateStoreAt(URL:fromModel:toModel:mappingModel:)**, which you wrote at the start of this section.

Note that if you're starting from version 1 or 2, there's a recursive call to `performMigration()` at the end. That will trigger another run to continue the sequence; once you're at version 3 and run the migration to get to version 4, there is no more recursive call. You can imagine adding to this method as you add more data model versions to continue the automatic sequence of migrations.

Testing sequential migrations

Testing this type of migration can be a little complicated, since you need to go back in time and run previous versions of the app to generate data to migrate. If you saved copies of the app project along the way, then great! Otherwise, you'll find previous versions of the project in the resources bundled with the book.

First, make sure you make a copy of the project as it is right now—that's the final project!

Here are the general steps you'll need to take to test each migration:

1. Delete the app from the Simulator to clear out the data store.
2. Open version 2 of the app (so you can at least see some pictures!), and build and run.
3. Create some test notes.
4. Quit the app from Xcode and close the project.
5. Open the final version of the app, and build and run.

At that point, you should see some console output with the migration status. Note that the migration will happen prior to the app presenting onscreen.

```
Store file:///Users/gth/Library/Developer/CoreSimulator/Devices/AB207049-DC2A-4EF9-A3F3-629417192CA6/data/Containers/Data/
Application/0A9BA27B-BEC0-471F-A8D5-1EAA561CFBF5/Library/Application%20Support/UnCloudNotes.sqlite is compatible with
model {(
    v2
)}
From Model: {(
    v2
)}
To Model: {(
    v3
)}
Migrating store file:///Users/gth/Library/Developer/CoreSimulator/Devices/AB207049-DC2A-4EF9-A3F3-629417192CA6/data/
Containers/Data/Application/0A9BA27B-BEC0-471F-A8D5-1EAA561CFBF5/Library/Application%20Support/UnCloudNotes.sqlite to
file:///Users/gth/Library/Developer/CoreSimulator/Devices/AB207049-DC2A-4EF9-A3F3-629417192CA6/data/Containers/Data/
Application/0A9BA27B-BEC0-471F-A8D5-1EAA561CFBF5/Library/Application%20Support/UnCloudNotes.sqlite~1
Mapping model: Optional((NSMappingModel), entityMappings (
    "(NSEntityMapping), name NoteToAttachment, mappingType 5, sourceEntityName Note, sourceEntityVersionHash <c393d6c8
d5e65f5a bb5e4394 eb6ce54c a99e724d bdb64072 ed2e99dd 99e77ba0>, destinationEntityName Attachment,
destinationEntityVersionHash <0f48166f 6850bb10 f15e1102 859544e2 f343ab0b 8b2e95cf 30d002c5 32af87fc>, attributeMappings
(\n    \"(NSPropertyMapping), name dateCreated, valueExpression $source.dateCreated, userInfo (null)\",\n
\"(NSPropertyMapping), name image, valueExpression $source.image, userInfo (null)\"\n), relationshipMappings (\n
\"(NSPropertyMapping), name note, valueExpression FUNCTION($manager, \\
\"destinationInstancesForEntityMappingNamed:sourceInstances:\\\" , \\\"NoteToNote\\\", $source), userInfo (null)\"\n),
sourceExpression FETCH(FUNCTION($manager, \"fetchRequestForSourceEntityNamed:predicateString:\" , \"Note\", \"image != nil
\"), $manager.sourceContext, NO), entityMigrationPolicyClassName (null), userInfo (null)",
```

You now have an app that will successfully migrate between any combinations of old data versions to the latest version.

Where to go from here?

That was a whole lot of data migration! Migrations can be extremely tricky, as you've no doubt observed in the more complicated forms in this chapter. Before you move on to the next chapter, I want to share a few words of advice from my experience using Core Data migrations.

First, when you decide a data migration is in order, make a reasonable effort to use the simplest migration possible. Migrations can be tricky to test, so you want them to be as simple as possible. And, as you've seen in this chapter, you can go a long way without the need for the most custom of migrations involving code.

Second, make sure to save some data store versions for testing future migrations. You'll thank yourself later. In some cases, real live data will be the only way to break a migration. Sometimes, it may be useful to ask a customer's permission to use their data store for testing a particular problem. Remember to use **extreme care** with customer data and properly secure, anonymize or encrypt the files when they aren't being used during a test.

Core Data migrations are one of the more powerful, and in many cases, useful, aspects of the Core Data framework. Now that you've seen the spectrum of Core Data migrations from lightweight all the way to fully custom manual migrations, you'll be able to tackle data even the most difficult model changes in your own apps.

Chapter 7: Syncing with iCloud

By Saul Mora

Thus far, the tutorials in this book have walked you through Core Data as a locally persistent storage mechanism—that is, Core Data with only a single store on a single device for a single user process. Core Data and its predecessor, EOF (Enterprise Objects Framework), have worked this way since their inception.

However, the world has changed a bit since then. Users have multiple devices and want—even expect!—their data to be synchronized between all of them. This usually happens over what is mystically called "The Cloud."

This chapter covers the steps necessary to sync a Core Data store using Apple's iCloud. You'll update the app from the previous chapter to sync to iCloud and then see how changes make it back and forth between two running copies of the app.

> **Note**: You'll need a paid iOS developer account to set up and test iCloud-enabled apps. Make sure your account is in good standing and that you have your iTunes Connect login information handy before continuing.

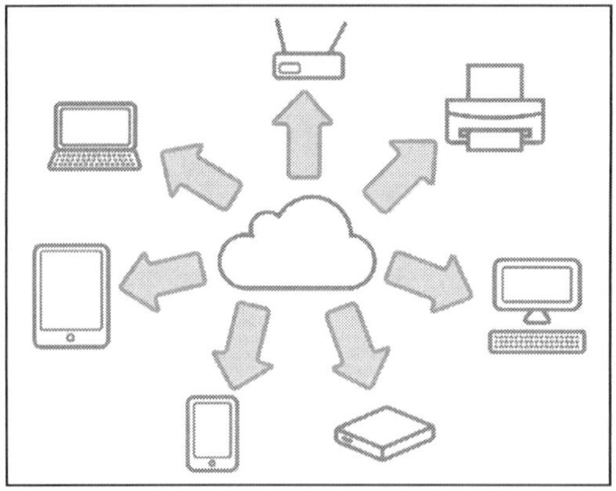

No discussion or tutorial on iCloud is complete without the required diagram showing a cloud. Check that one off the list, and let's get started!

Getting started

iCloud is Apple's method of syncing files and content from one device to all the user's other registered devices. Users will usually sign into iCloud right when they first set up their devices.

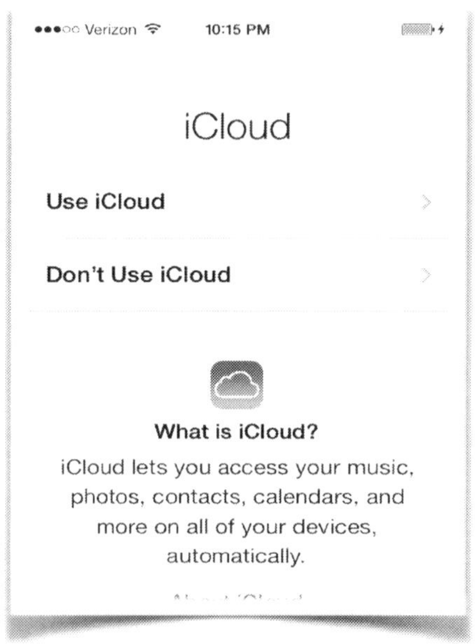

From then on, iCloud takes care of everything for the user. When it syncs, it "just works" and the user is happy.

As developers, we simply need to detect if iCloud is enabled on the device and turn on support for it in our apps. There are no logins or passwords to deal with. And since Apple is managing the iCloud services as well, there are no servers to worry about.

Using iCloud means not having to worry (too much) about scheduling syncing or how it works—which means less code for you to write. With iCloud, you don't care how or when data is syncing between devices, just that syncing happens, eventually.

The downside

While iCloud works well for the key-value store and document sharing, its relationship with Core Data got off to a shaky start. But fear not! Apple has been listening to developer feedback and has improved the API for Core Data's iCloud integration, making it more reliable.

iCloud is Apple-only, so you won't be able to use it if you ever plan to release an Android or Windows Phone version of your app. However, you could say the same thing about Core Data itself. If you're sticking with OS X and iOS devices and you're already using Core Data, you're well on your way to cloud syncing!

CloudNotes

In the previous chapter, you learned the essentials of Core Data migrations by upgrading an app called UnCloudNotes. Going forward, this app will cloud syncing, and thus the first step in your journey to using Core Data with iCloud is to rename the project from UnCloudNotes to **CloudNotes**.

You'll find a fully-renamed version of the project in the resources bundled with this book. Open the **CloudNotes** starter project, which should be familiar to you from the previous chapter, and prepare to get your head in the cloud!

> **Note:** Swift apps are namespaced, so renaming a project isn't trivial—you'll also need to change any instances of the module name in the storyboards, data models, mapping models and so forth. In the starter project, this has been done for you.

Enabling iCloud

iCloud syncs your Core Data store using **ubiquity containers**. The term ubiquity is appropriate, since it means "found everywhere." Ubiquity containers are stored in a special place in your application sandbox that iOS manages for you. You might have asked `NSFileManager` for your app's Documents directory before; for iCloud, you'll ask for a ubiquity container URL.

Core Data saves your app's data to the ubiquity container URL in the same way it would save a URL pointing to the Documents directory. The difference is that the iCloud background process will see changes to files in this special URL and begin uploading the contents to the cloud. You have no control over when or how often this happens—it's all managed by the operating system.

Each time you save data to a SQLite store, transaction logs contain the data changes in these "atomic" commits. The term atomic here means all the changes in the log are valid, or none of them are. So we can be sure that applying changes from one log to the next, there is no data inconsistency, at least at the SQLite level. When using iCloud with Core Data SQLite based stores, it is the syncing of these transaction logs across the cloud, rather than the data store itself, that actually transfer data from one device to another. This is a far safer method of merging database changes than trying to merge the database files since the logs are replayed in the same order they were created.

When the London Bridge was moved from spanning the river Thames in London to span a portion of the Colorado River in Lake Havasu City, Arizona, it was dismantled, brick by brick. Each brick was numbered and the order logged properly as the bridge was taken apart. It was then rebuilt in the correct order using the brick numbers as the guide. The transaction logs and their contents are the bricks that are rebuilt on other users' devices.

To set up a ubiquity container for CloudNotes, you need to modify the app's capabilities. In Xcode, select the **CloudNotes** project file and then the **CloudNotes** target. From there, select the **Capabilities** tab at the top, and you should see the screen below:

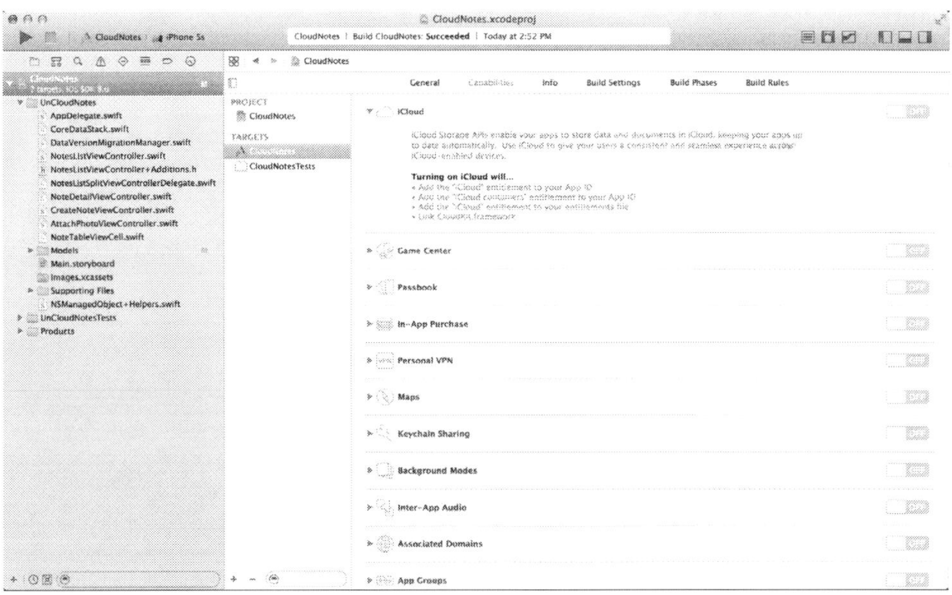

To enable iCloud in your app, simply click the switch next to the iCloud details at the top of the list. You may be asked to log into the Apple Developer Portal through an Xcode dialog. You may also be asked to select a team.

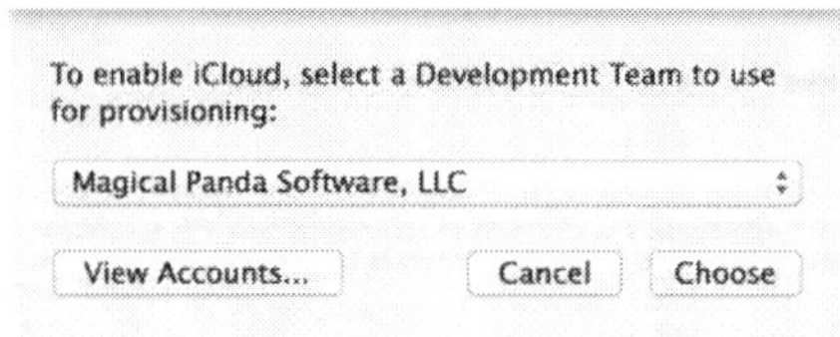

Xcode will then connect to the Developer Portal and provision the server side of things for you. After that setup is complete, uncheck the **Key-value storage** service (if it's checked) and instead select **CloudKit** and **iCloud Documents**.

Once Xcode has completed all its steps, you'll see the name of your ubiquity container in the list of ubiquity containers. In this case, it's set to **iCloud.com.razeware.CloudNotes**.

> **Note:** Xcode may be telling you that an App ID with identifier **iCloud.com.razeware.CloudNotes** is not available. This probably means you're not the first person in the universe to attempt this tutorial and the name is taken!
>
> If that's the case, switch to the **General** tab and amend the bundle identifier to something a little more personal, like **com.razeware.yourname.CloudNotes**. Switch back to **Capabilities** and click the **Fix Issue** button, and you should be all good.

You are free to change this name; however, remember that if you change the container name between versions of your app, previous versions and other applications referencing this container name will no longer be able to sync with the new versions.

You've completed the application setup! That was easy. :] It's time to configure the code to use iCloud to sync data.

The cloud stack

Open **NotesListViewController.swift** and find the `stack` property near the top of the class definition. This is where the app lazily loads the Core Data stack.

Replace the property declaration and initialization code with the following:

```
lazy var stack : CoreDataStack = {
  let options =
   [NSPersistentStoreUbiquitousContentNameKey: "CloudNotes",
    NSMigratePersistentStoresAutomaticallyOption: true,
    NSInferMappingModelAutomaticallyOption: true]
  let stack = CoreDataStack(modelName: "CloudNotesDataModel",
    storeName: "CloudNotes",
    options: options)
  return stack
}()
```

Here, you use the `NSPersistentStoreUbiquitousContentNameKey` value to uniquely identify the persistent store in the cloud and across devices. This means you can have several named "data buckets" in your app's ubiquity container. This would be helpful if, for example, you had an iOS app that only accessed a subset of the data from a Mac app.

Believe it or not, you now have a Core Data app with iCloud syncing enabled! This is far easier than in previous versions of the API, as Apple has essentially taken control of all the error-prone setup previously involved with this process. Don't worry—there are plenty of things to add in the user interface and there are sync operations to test, which will keep you busy for the rest of this chapter!

Core Data is doing a number of things under the hood to enable this capability for you. One of the items Core Data sets up for you is a fallback store. In some instances, circumstances will severely compromise access to iCloud (the "driving through a tunnel" scenario). For Core Data to continue to function for your app during these times, the fallback store is there to hold onto data while iCloud is offline. You don't have to worry about the fallback store at all; Core Data manages it for you entirely.

However, one of the caveats to letting Core Data manage the iCloud mechanism for you is that you can only have a single iCloud persistent store file per account. When it comes to testing your app, it's helpful to have multiple test accounts.

Testing iCloud

Testing applications with iCloud means you have to have the app installed on at least two devices. In the olden days of iOS 5 and 6, iCloud syncing wasn't available on the iOS Simulator, which meant that to test iCloud, developers had to own multiple devices and run their app on each device.

Luckily, Apple has heard our calls, and you can now enable iCloud in your iOS Simulator! This means you only need one device and the Simulator to test iCloud integration.

Fire up CloudNotes right now on the Simulator. Not much has changed. The app launches, but nothing is happening otherwise, especially in regard to data syncing. There are a couple of steps necessary to set up the Simulator for iCloud testing.

If you want to use your regular iCloud account, you can skip ahead to the section called, "Setting up iCloud on the Simulator," below. I suggest continuing with creating and using a test account so as to keep test data separate from your personal data. You'll need to enable iCloud drive on the accounts you use for this tutorial, which you might not want for your personal iCloud account.

Creating a test account

Point Safari or your web browser of choice to https://itunesconnect.apple.com and log in with your Apple developer ID.

From the main menu of the iTunes Connect portal, select **Users and Roles**. You want a test user so select **Sandbox Testers** at the top of the screen, then click the plus (+) button to add a new user. From here, you can fill out the form to create a new test user on the iTunes store.

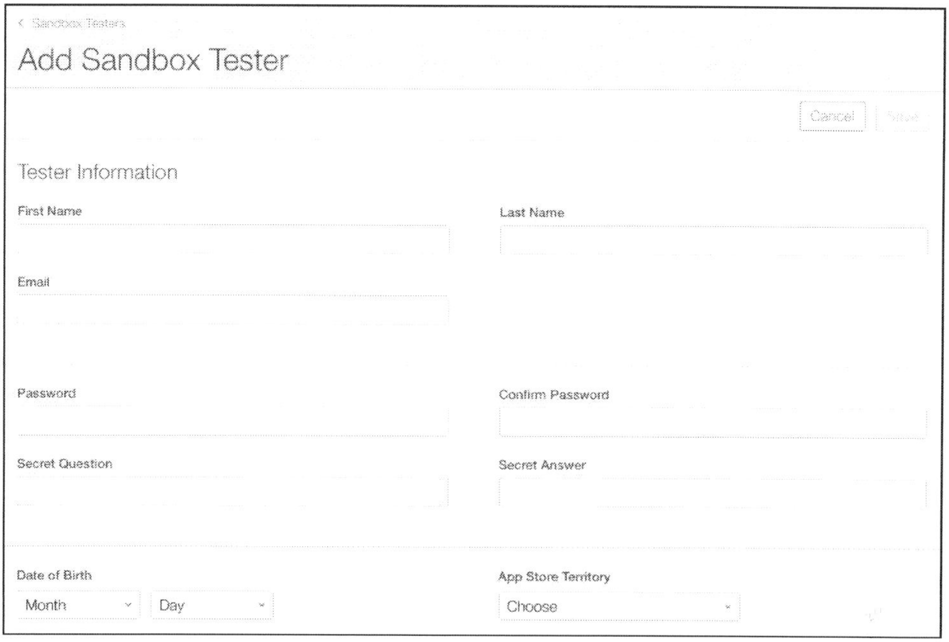

This test user only has access to the sandbox iTunes environment. That is, this user cannot purchase real items from the real iTunes store. Even though this is a test user, you'll still need a valid and unique email account to confirm the user. Apple uses this email account for initial validation, so you won't be able to use your test account until you receive the email and click the acknowledgement link.

> **Note**: You don't have to create a brand new email account, depending on your mail provider. For example, if you use Gmail and your email address is ray.wenderlich@gmail.com, you can add a test address called ray.wenderlich+icloudtest@gmail.com and all emails to that address will still come to your main account.

Now, open the Settings app on both your device and the Simulator and select iCloud. Enter your test account credentials to log into iCloud. You'll need to log into iCloud on your device *first* to activate the account, and then log in on the Simulator.

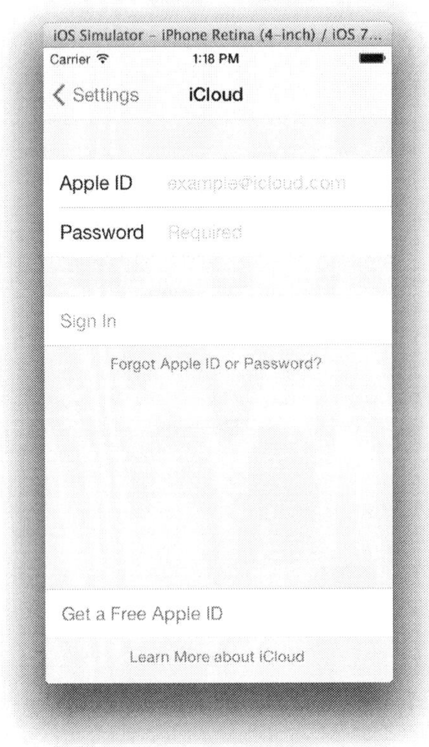

Once you've logged in, make sure iCloud Drive is enabled:

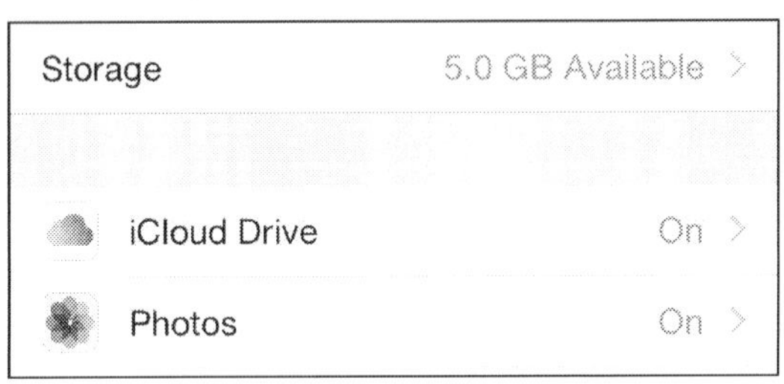

Debugging with the iCloud gauge

Now you can get back to running CloudNotes. First, fire up the CloudNotes app in the Simulator. You should be able to see any notes that you entered previously.

Now, in the same instance of Xcode, change the launch target from iPhone (Simulator) to your device.

After changing the target device, without stopping the instance running in the Simulator, click the **run** button, or press **Cmd+R** for you keyboard shortcut lovers. You'll see the CloudNotes app load and launch on your device, too. It turns out Xcode knows how to run two separate instances of your app against difference devices.

Now, in the Simulator, add a new note and tap **Create** to save it. At this point, iCloud will notice that the user made changes to the ubiquitous container through Core Data. The iCloud background syncing process will then queue the transaction logs to be sent to the cloud.

You can speed things along and force a sync by navigating to **Debug\Trigger iCloud Sync** in the Simulator or switch back to Xcode and select **Debug\iCloud\Trigger Sync in Simulator**. Try these menu options and then keep an eye on the console log for sync-related messages.

Since you've added a new note in the instance running on the Simulator, you'd expect it to show up on the device. However, you might have noticed that doesn't happen. This is a great opportunity to see what iCloud debugging tools are available and nail down the reason data isn't showing up as expected.

Xcode 5 introduced debugging gauges, one of which is the iCloud gauge. This gauge displays and continuously updates several key pieces of information that are useful in debugging iCloud syncing issues.

While the app is running, select the Debug navigator by pressing Command-6. Since CloudNotes is already running it has already registered some information.

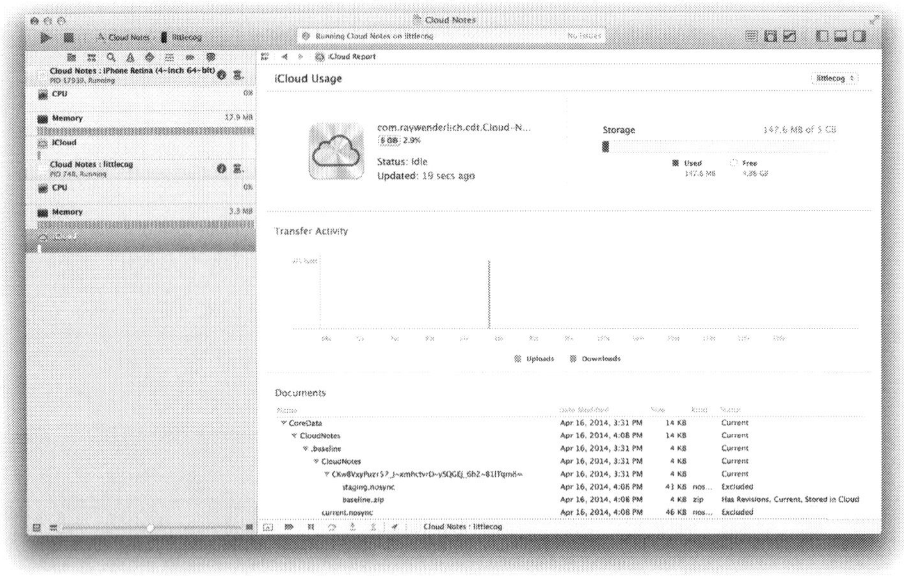

The first thing you may notice if you haven't configured iCloud syncing properly is that the **Status:** label has a message reading *iCloud Not Configured.* It's likely one of the containers or entitlements for your Core Data store was not properly configured. More often, you'll see a status of **Idle** when you're not syncing data.

Also of use is the **Transfer Activity** in the center, a short history of data transferred via iCloud into and out of your app.

Looking at the history shown in the screenshot above, the app did download some data into the device instance of into CloudNotes. So data did come across the wire and was registered by CloudNotes.

> **Note:** At the time of writing, the iOS Simulator doesn't support iCloud gauges, and there is an open bug in Xcode where iCloud Drive-enabled apps don't show activity in the gauges with the iCloud status always showing "disabled."

There's one thing to try before making any code changes. Quit the device instance of CloudNotes and relaunch it, again through Xcode. You'll see an extra note with the proper timestamp.

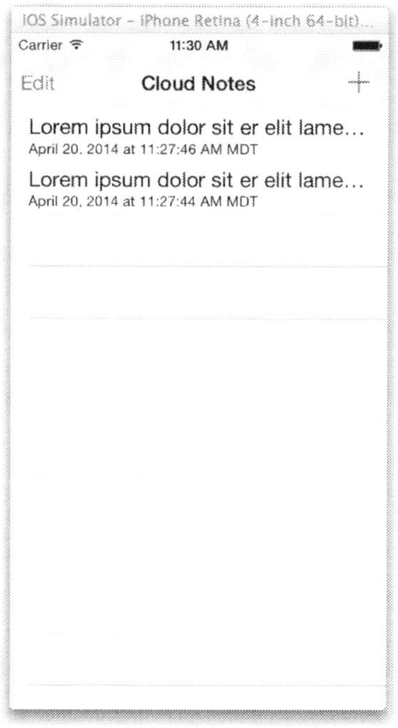

The app did indeed transfer the data and merge it into the data store, yet the data did not show up in the list of notes in the UI. This means the app is not updating the UI when the data model is updated through iCloud.

> **Note**: The sync process can be difficult to debug! Once you have notes in the Simulator, trigger a manual iCloud sync and wait a few moments.
>
> Then, start up the app on your device. You might need to stop and start the app on your device to see the results—the data syncs the first time, and then the table view refreshes the second time.

Now you can summarize the three basic steps to get iCloud working:

1. Enable iCloud and set up the ubiquity containers.
2. Enable iCloud-Core Data syncing with a couple of options when setting up the persistent store.

3. Set up your app to respond to new changes in data that arrive while the app is running.

You've taken care of the first two steps, so it's time to address the final step. Otherwise, your users would need to re-launch the app over and over to see their sync results!

Responding to iCloud changes

The `NotesListViewController` is populating the table view using a `NSFetchedResultsController`. This is a pattern than should be familiar to you by now.

The fetched results controller is connected to the main `NSManagedObjectContext` from the Core Data stack. When iCloud applies updates, it does so at the persistent store level. These changes won't show up in your context unless you merge them in.

Core Data sends out an `NSPersistentStoreDidImportUbiquitousContentChangesNotification` notification informing the app that updates have been applied to the data, and that it's time to refresh any contexts using the modified data.

There will be a little Objective-C-style dynamic dispatch in iCloud, so you need to make sure the Core Data stack will work with that. Open **CoreDataStack.swift** and change the class declaration as follows:

```
@objc class CoreDataStack: Printable {
```

This will ensure the stack can play nicely with dynamic dispatch.

To allow the stack to observe the notifications, add the following code to **CoreDataStack.swift**:

```
var updateContextWithUbiquitousContentUpdates: Bool = false {
  willSet {
    ubiquitousChangesObserver = newValue ?
      NSNotificationCenter.defaultCenter() : nil
  }
}

private var ubiquitousChangesObserver : NSNotificationCenter? {
  didSet {
    oldValue?.removeObserver(self, name:
 NSPersistentStoreDidImportUbiquitousContentChangesNotification,
```

```
        object: coordinator)
      ubiquitousChangesObserver?.addObserver(self,
        selector:
         "persistentStoreDidImportUbiquitousContentChanges:",
        name:
   NSPersistentStoreDidImportUbiquitousContentChangesNotification,
        object:coordinator)
    }
  }
```

updateContextWithUbiquitousContentUpdates is a flag that tells the stack to start or stop listening for the notification. It has a property observer, which sets an internal property to either the default notification center or nil. Using a property observer on *that* property actually starts or stops observing the notification. This might sound complicated, but it takes advantage of a number of Swift features to remove a lot of checking and conditional code.

Next, since this call to addObserver references a selector, that function needs to exist on the CoreDataStack object. Add the following straightforward method:

```
  func persistentStoreDidImportUbiquitousContentChanges(
   notification: NSNotification){
    NSLog("Merging ubiquitous content changes")
    context.performBlock {
      self.context.mergeChangesFromContextDidSaveNotification(
        notification)
    }
  }
```

With this change, enabling iCloud updates to refresh the UI context is as simple as setting the updateContextWithUbiquitousContentUpdates to true. This will come in handy in the NotesListViewController.

Open **NotesListViewController.swift** and tell the Core Data stack to start looking for iCloud changes in viewWillAppear:

```
    override func viewWillAppear(animated: Bool){
      super.viewWillAppear(animated)
      notes.performFetch(nil)
      tableView.reloadData()
      stack.updateContextWithUbiquitousContentUpdates = true
    }
```

As before, build and run CloudNotes on the device as well as in the Simulator. Try adding a note from the Simulator, trigger an iCloud refresh, and the new note should appear on the device within a few moments!

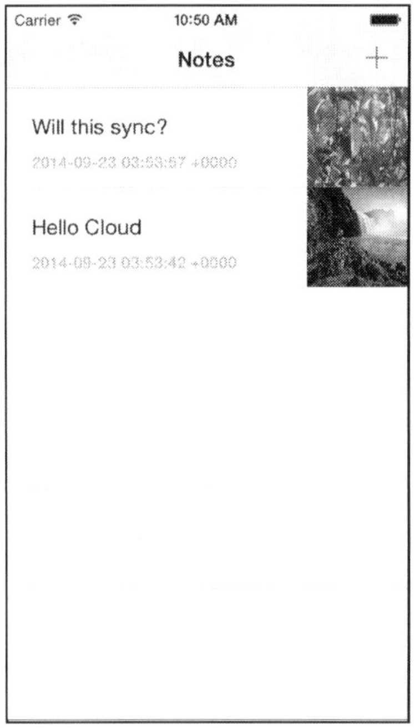

Switching iCloud accounts

On occasion, a user may disable iCloud syncing from his account while your app is running. Or, a user may decide to switch iCloud accounts on her device. What should happen to your app's data when this occurs?

When a user logs out of an account, Core Data will manage the deletion of the underlying fallback data store for you. Since the data always exists in the cloud, the fallback store can be rebuilt using iCloud once the user logs back into her account. Core Data sends two useful notifications when handling iCloud account changes:

- `NSPersistentStoreCoordinatorStoresWillChangeNotification`
- `NSPersistentStoreCoordinatorStoresDidChangeNotification`.

The "will change" notification signals that a persistent store coordinator is adding or removing a persistent store. As such, the notification will contain instances of `NSPersistentStore` objects being added and removed. Core Data sends this notification only for coordinators with iCloud stores configured and running.

Core Data fires the "did change" notification after the persistent stores have been swapped out and the coordinator is ready to supply the new data.

You're going to modify CloudNotes to respond to these notifications to handle changes to iCloud accounts.

When Core Data sends the "will change" notification, the Core Data stack will save any unchanged data to the current store, so the user who is logging out doesn't lose any data. It will then reset the managed object context to clear any of the old objects from memory.

When Core Data sends the "did change" notification, the notes list controller needs to reload its view to either use the newly signed-in account or local storage.

You'll deal with the "will change" notification first. Add the following method to **CoreDataStack.swift** that you will call when Core Data fires the notification:

```
func persistentStoreCoordinatorWillChangeStores(
 notification: NSNotification){
  var error : NSErrorPointer = nil
  if context.hasChanges {
    if context.save(error) == false {
      print("Error saving \(error)")
    }
  }
  context.reset()
}
```

This saves the context and then resets it.

You can consider observing this notification as part of observing ubiquitous content updates in general, so you can simply expand the property observer on `ubiquitousChangesObserver` to include the new notification. Add the following code inside the `didSet` closure:

```
oldValue?.removeObserver(self,
  name:NSPersistentStoreCoordinatorStoresWillChangeNotification,
  object: coordinator)

ubiquitousChangesObserver?.addObserver(self,
  selector: "persistentStoreCoordinatorWillChangeStores",
  name:NSPersistentStoreCoordinatorStoresWillChangeNotification,
  object:coordinator)
```

Now you need to deal with the "did change" notification. In **NotesListViewController.swift**, add the following method, which you'll call when you receive the notification:

```
func persistentStoreCoordinatorDidChangeStores(
 notification:NSNotification){
  notes.performFetch(nil)
}
```

To connect `NotesListViewController` to the notifications, you're going to use the same technique as before: set up an `NSNotificationCenter` property and add and remove observers based on the property. Create a new optional property in **NotesListViewController.swift**:

```
var persistentStoreCoordinatorChangesObserver:
 NSNotificationCenter? {
  didSet {
    oldValue?.removeObserver(self,
 name: NSPersistentStoreCoordinatorStoresDidChangeNotification,
 object: stack.coordinator)

persistentStoreCoordinatorChangesObserver?.addObserver(self,
  selector: "persistentStoreCoordinatorDidChangeStores:",
  name: NSPersistentStoreCoordinatorStoresDidChangeNotification,
  object: stack.coordinator)
  }
}
```

The proper time to connect the `NotesListViewController` to these notifications is when you enable the ubiquitous content change updates on the `CoreDataStack`. Add the following code to the end of `viewWillAppear`:

```
persistentStoreCoordinatorChangesObserver =
  NSNotificationCenter.defaultCenter()
```

Note: You never remove the observers in this project, because the notes list view controller is at the root of the whole application and owns the Core Data stack. If there were a chance either object could be deallocated, you would have to stop observing the notifications. The setup used in this tutorial makes it easy to remove all notifications in one go by setting the flag to `false` or the observer property to `nil`.

Now, build and run CloudNotes in the Simulator. In the Simulator, navigate to the Settings app while CloudNotes is running. In the iCloud setting view, click **Logout**. Depending on the logging you have enabled, you may see some activity in the debug console.

Now, navigate back to CloudNotes and you'll see that there are no notes in the Notes List. Core Data has successfully handled an account logout scenario for you.

Now, log in with another account. CloudNotes will handle this case as well. If this account previously contained data, you'll see data as it comes in from iCloud updates.

It's a neat effect to show users that you haven't lost their data and are indeed populating as it appears in your data store.

Where to go from here?

Core Data's iCloud functionality has come a long way since its initial introduction and first year in the hands of developers. These days, iCloud and Core Data are far easier to use and set up, as well as less prone to unrecoverable errors.

There are many intricacies with cloud syncing, most of which will be specific to your own app. How do you want to handle merging, or migrating existing stores? Check out Apple's *iCloud Programming Guide for Core Data* and especially their "Best Practices" page for more information:
https://developer.apple.com/library/mac/documentation/DataManagement/Conceptual/UsingCoreDataWithiCloudPG/BestPractices/BestPractices.html

iCloud was intended to remove your desktop or laptop computer as the holder of your merged data, replacing these with "the cloud." In this, it has generally succeeded. Cloud syncing is rapidly becoming a necessary feature in most apps, and for Core Data-based apps, it's never been easier to integrate data syncing using iCloud.

Chapter 8: Unit Testing

By Aaron Douglas

Unit testing is a testing method where the goal is to test small pieces (or "units") of software. Rather than test "the app creates a new record when you tap the button" you might break this down into testing the button touch-up event, creating the entity, testing whether the save succeeded, and so on.

Why should you care about unit testing your apps? There are lots of reasons:

- Unit testing helps you work out the architecture and behavior of your app at a very early stage. You can test much of the app's functionality without needing to worry about the UI.
- Unit testing gives you the confidence to add features or refactor, knowing that you haven't broken other parts of the app. If you have existing tests that pass, you can be confident that the tests will fail and give you a warning if you break something later.
- When working on projects with multiple developers, unit tests can help keep you all on the same page and ensure that each developer can make changes independently.
- If you've ever found yourself working on a particular feature of an app and each time you want to check it out, you have to tap through three different screens and enter some data, unit testing is your new best friend. You can run any part of your app's code from a unit test, which is much faster than testing "manually" through the UI.

In this chapter, you'll learn how to use the **XCTest** framework in Xcode to test your Core Data apps. Unit testing Core Data apps isn't as straightforward as it could be, because most of the tests will depend on having a valid Core Data stack. You might not want a mess of test data from the unit tests to interfere with your own manual testing done in the simulator or on device, so you'll learn how to keep the test data separate.

You'll get a good introduction to XCTest in this chapter, but you should have a basic understanding of it already to make the most from this chapter. For more information, check out Apple's documentation (https://developer.apple.com/library/ios/documentation/DeveloperTools/Conceptual/testing_with_xcode/Introduction/Introduction.html) or our book *iOS 7 by Tutorials*, which includes a chapter on XCTest.

Getting started

The sample project you'll work with in this chapter, **CampgroundManager**, is a reservation system to keep track of campground sites, the amenities for each site and the campers themselves.

The app is a work in progress. The concept is a small campground could use this app to manage their campsites and reservations including the schedule and payments. The user interface is extremely basic: It functions but doesn't provide much value. That's OK, because in this tutorial, you're never going to build and run the app!

I've broken down the business logic for the app into small pieces, and you're going to write unit tests to help with the design. As you develop the unit tests and flesh out the business logic, it'll become clearer what work is left to do on the user interface.

The business logic is split up into three distinct classes arranged by subject. There's one for campsites, one for campers and one for reservations, and all have the suffix **Service**. Your tests will focus on these service classes.

Access control

By default, classes in Swift have the internal access level. That means they can only be accessed from within their module. Since the app and the tests are separate targets and separate modules, you normally won't be able access the classes from the app in your tests!

There are two ways around this issue:

1. You can mark classes and methods in your app as `public` to make them visible from the tests.
2. You can add classes to the test target in the File Inspector so they will be compiled in and accessible from the tests.

In the CampgroundManager sample project, the necessary classes and methods in the app target are already marked as `public`. That means you'll just need to `import CampgroundManager` from the tests and you'll be able to access whatever you need.Core Data stack for testing

Since you'll be testing the Core Data parts of the app, the first order of business is getting the Core Data stack set up for testing.

Good unit tests follow the acronym **FIRST**:

- **F**ast: If your tests take too long to run, you won't bother running them.
- **I**solated: Any test should function properly when run on its own or before or after any other test.
- **R**epeatable: You should get the same results every time you run the test against the same codebase.
- **S**elf-verifying: The test itself should report success or failure; you shouldn't have to check the contents of a file or a console log.
- **T**imely: There's some benefit to writing the tests after you've already written the code, particularly if you're writing a new test to cover a new bug. Ideally, though, the tests come first to act as a specification for the functionality you're developing.

CampgroundManager uses Core Data to store data in a database file on disk. That doesn't sound very **I**solated, since the data from one test may be written out to the database and could affect other tests. It doesn't sound very **R**epeatable, either, since data will be building up in the database file each time. You could manually delete and recreate the database file before running each test, but that wouldn't be very **F**ast.

The solution is a modified Core Data stack that uses an **in-memory store** instead of an SQLite-backed store. This will be fast and provide a clean slate every time.

The `CoreDataStack` you've been using in most of this book can support multiple contexts, including a background root/parent context to which the `NSPersistentStoreCoordinator` is connected. When you use `CoreDataStack` for a test, you don't want it to access the SQLite database but rather an in-memory store. Create a new class that subclasses `CoreDataStack` so you can change the store:

1. Right-click **Services** under the **CampgroundManagerTests** group and click **New File**.
2. Select **Swift File** under **iOS/Source**. Click **Next**.
3. Name the file **TestCoreDataStack.swift**. Make sure only the **CampgroundManagerTests** target is selected.
4. Select **No** if prompted to add an Objective-C bridging header.
5. Click **Create**.

Replace the contents of the file with the following:

```
import CampgroundManager
import Foundation
import CoreData

class TestCoreDataStack: CoreDataStack {
  override init() {
    super.init()
    self.persistentStoreCoordinator = {
      var psc: NSPersistentStoreCoordinator? =
      NSPersistentStoreCoordinator(managedObjectModel:
        self.managedObjectModel)
      var error: NSError? = nil

      var ps = psc!.addPersistentStoreWithType(
        NSInMemoryStoreType, configuration: nil,
        URL: nil, options: nil, error: &error)
```

```
      if (ps == nil) {
        abort()
      }

      return psc
      }()

  }
}
```

Notice that this class subclasses `CoreDataStack` and only overrides the default value of a single property: `persistentStoreCoordinator`. Since you are overriding the value in `init()`, the persistent store coordinator from `CoreDataStack` is not used or even instantiated. The persistent store coordinator in `TestCoreDataStack` uses an in-memory store only.

An in-memory store is never persisted to disk, which means you can instantiate the stack, write as much data you want in the test, and poof...when the test ends, the in-memory store gets cleared out automatically.

With the stack in place, it's time to work on your first test!

Your first test

Unit tests require your app to be designed with little pieces in mind. Instead of throwing all of your business logic into one huge view controller, you instead create a class to encapsulate that logic.

In most cases, you'll probably be adding unit tests to an application you've already partially written. In the case of CampgroundManager, I've created the `CamperService`, `CampSiteService` and `ReservationService` classes, but they aren't all feature-complete yet. Let's test the simplest class, `CamperService`.

Begin by creating a new test class:

1. Right-click the **Services** group under the **CampgroundManagerTests** group and click **New File**.
2. Select **Test Case Class**. Click **Next**.
3. Name the class **CamperServiceTests** (subclass of **XCTestCase** should already be selected) and pick **Swift** for the language.

4. Make sure the **CampgroundManagerTests** target checkbox is the only target selected. Click **Create**.

In **CamperServiceTests.swift**, import the app and Core Data frameworks into the test case, along with the other existing import statements:

```
import CampgroundManager
import CoreData
```

Add two properties to the class:

```
var camperService: CamperService!
var coreDataStack: CoreDataStack!
```

These properties will hold references to the `CamperService` instance to test and to the Core Data stack. The properties are implicitly unwrapped optionals, since they'll be initialized in `setUp` rather than in `init`.

Next, replace the implementation of `setUp` with the following:

```
override func setUp() {
  super.setUp()

  coreDataStack = TestCoreDataStack()
  camperService = CamperService(
    managedObjectContext: coreDataStack.mainContext!,
    coreDataStack: coreDataStack)
}
```

`setUp` is called before each test runs, and this is your chance to create any resources required by all unit tests in the class. In this case, you initialize the `camperService` and `coreDataStack` properties.

It's wise to reset your data after every test so that results are repeatable. Using the in-memory store and creating a new context in `setUp` accomplishes this reset for you.

Notice the `CoreDataStack` instance is actually a `TestCoreDataStack` instance. The `CamperService` initialization method takes the context it needs and also an instance of the `CoreDataStack`, since the context save methods are part of that class. You can also use `setUp()` to insert standard test data into the context for use later.

Next, replace `tearDown` with the following implementation:

```
override func tearDown() {
  super.tearDown()
```

```
    camperService = nil
    coreDataStack = nil
  }
```

`tearDown` is the opposite of `setUp`, and is called after each test executes. Here, the method will simply make all the properties `nil`, resetting the `CoreDataStack` after every test.

There's only a single method on `CamperService` at this point, and that is `addCamper(_:phonenumber:)`. Still in **CamperServiceTests.swift**, create a new method to test `addCamper`:

```
  func testAddCamper() {
    let camper = camperService.addCamper("Bacon Lover",
      phoneNumber: "910-543-9000")

    XCTAssertNotNil(camper, "Camper should not be nil")
    XCTAssertTrue(camper?.fullName == "Bacon Lover")
    XCTAssertTrue(camper?.phoneNumber == "910-543-9000")
  }
```

You create a camper with certain properties, then check to confirm that a camper exists with the properties you expect.

Remove the `testExample` and `testPerformanceExample` methods from the class.

It's a simple test, but it ensures that if any logic inside of `addCamper` is modified, the basic operation doesn't change. For example, if you add some new data validation logic to prevent bacon-loving people from reserving campgrounds, `addCamper` might return nil. This test would then fail, alerting you that either you made a mistake in the validation or that the test needs to be updated.

> **Note:** To round out this test case in a real development context, you would want to write unit tests for strange scenarios like `nil` or empty parameters, duplicate camper names and so forth.

Run the unit tests by clicking on the **Product** menu, then selecting **Test** (or type **Command+U**). You should see a green checkmark in Xcode:

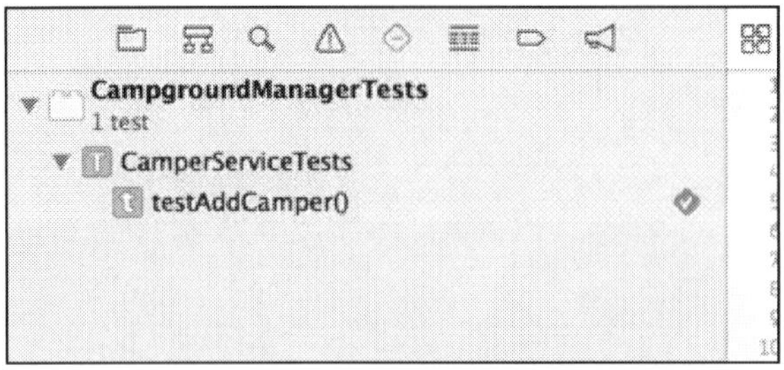

There's your first test! You can imagine this kind of testing is useful for your data models, checking that the attributes were stored correctly.

Also notice how it acts like documentation for people using the API; it's an example of how to call `addCamper` and describes the expected behavior, for example that the method should return a valid object and not nil.

Notice this test creates the object and checks the attributes, but doesn't save anything to the store. This project uses a separate queue context, allowing it to perform saves in the background. However, the test runs straight through so you can't check for the save result with an `XCTAssert` since you can't be sure when the background operation has completed. Of course saving is an important part of Core Data, so how can you test this part of the app?

Asynchronous tests

When using a single managed object context in Core Data, everything runs on the main UI thread. However, this project has a separate private queue context which acts as the root context, allowing saving to be performed on a background thread. The main context exposed by the Core Data stack is a child of this context.

Performing work on the right thread for a context is easy: You simply wrap the work in `performBlockAndWait()` or `performBlock()` to ensure it's executed on the proper thread associated with the context. The former will wait to finish execution of the block before continuing, and the latter will immediately return, queuing the execution on the context.

Testing `performBlock()` executions can be tricky since you need some way to signal to "the outside world" from inside the block about the test status. Luckily, there are new features in `XCTestCase` called **expectations** that help with this.

The example below shows how you might use an expectation to wait for an asynchronous method to complete before finishing the test:

```
let expectation = self.expectationWithDescription("Done!");

someService.callMethodWithCompletionHandler() {
  expectation.fulfill()
}

self.waitForExpectationsWithTimeout(2.0, handler: nil)
```

The key is that something must fulfill or trigger the expectation so the test moves forward. The wait method at the end takes a time parameter (in seconds), so that the test isn't waiting forever and can time out (and fail) in case the expectation is never fulfilled.

In the example provided, you can see `fulfill()` is called explicitly in the completion handler passed in to the tested method. With Core Data saves, it's easier to listen for the `NSManagedObjectDidSaveNotification`, since it happens in a place where you can't call `fulfill()` explicitly.

Add a new method to **CamperServiceTests.swift** to test that the root context is getting saved when a new camper is added:

```
func testRootContextIsSavedAfterAddingCamper() {
  //1
  let expectRoot = self.expectationForNotification(
    NSManagedObjectContextDidSaveNotification,
    object: coreDataStack.rootContext) {
      notification in
      return true
  }

  //2
  let camper = camperService.addCamper("Bacon Lover",
    phoneNumber: "910-543-9000")

  //3
  self.waitForExpectationsWithTimeout(2.0) {
```

```
      error in
      XCTAssertNil(error, "Save did not occur")
    }
  }
```

Here's a breakdown of the code:

1. You create a text expectation linked to a notification. In this case, the expectation is linked to `NSManagedObjectContextDidSaveNotification` from the root context of the Core Data stack. The handler for the notification is simple—it returns `true` since all you care about is that the notification is fired.
2. You add the camper, exactly the same as before.
3. The test waits up to two seconds for the expectation. If there are errors or the timeout passes, the `error` parameter for the handler block will contain a value.

It's important to keep UI-blocking operations such as Core Data saving off the main thread so your app stays responsive. Test expectations are invaluable to make sure these asynchronous operations are covered by unit tests.

You've added tests for existing features in the app; now it's time to add some features yourself. [TODO: Sentence fragment?] Along with the tests too, of course. Or for even more fun: perhaps write the tests first?

Tests first

An important function of CampgroundManager its ability to reserve sites for campers. Before it can accept reservations, the system has to know about all of the campsites at the campground. I created `CampSiteService` to help with adding, deleting and finding campsites.

Open `CampSiteService`, and you'll notice the only method I've implemented is `addCampSite`. There are no unit tests for this method, so start by creating a test case for the service:

1. Right-click **Services** under the **CampgroundManagerTests** group and click **New File**.
2. Select **Test Case Class**. Click **Next**.
3. Name the class **CampSiteServiceTests** (subclass of **XCTestCase** should already be selected) and pick **Swift** for the language.

4. Make sure the **CampgroundManagerTests** target checkbox is the only target selected. Click **Create**.

Replace the contents of the file with the following:

```
import UIKit
import XCTest
import CampgroundManager
import CoreData

class CampSiteServiceTests: XCTestCase {
  var campSiteService: CampSiteService!
  var coreDataStack: CoreDataStack!

  override func setUp() {
    super.setUp()

    coreDataStack = TestCoreDataStack()
    campSiteService = CampSiteService(managedObjectContext:
      coreDataStack.mainContext!, coreDataStack:
      coreDataStack)
  }

  override func tearDown() {
    super.tearDown()

    campSiteService = nil
    coreDataStack = nil
  }
}
```

This looks very similar to the previous test class. As your suite of tests expands and you notice common or repeated code, you can refactor the tests as well as the application code. You can feel safe doing this because the unit tests will fail if you mess anything up! :]

Add a new method to test adding a campsite. This looks and works like the method for testing the creation of a new camper:

```
func testAddCampSite() {
  let campSite = campSiteService.addCampSite(1,
    electricity: true, water: true)

  XCTAssertTrue(campSite.siteNumber == 1,
    "Site number should be 1")
  XCTAssertTrue(campSite.electricity.boolValue,
    "Site should have electricity")
```

```
  XCTAssertTrue(campSite.water.boolValue,
    "Site should have water")
}
```

You also want to check that the context is saved during this method, so add another method to test for that. This method should also look familiar:

```
func testRootContextIsSavedAfterAddingCampsite() {
  let expectRoot = self.expectationForNotification(
    NSManagedObjectContextDidSaveNotification, object:
    coreDataStack.rootContext) {
      notification in
      return true
  }

  var campSite = campSiteService.addCampSite(1,
    electricity: true, water: true)

  self.waitForExpectationsWithTimeout(2.0) {
    error in
    XCTAssertNil(error, "Save did not occur")
  }
}
```

Run the unit tests, and everything should pass. At this point, you should be feeling a bit of paranoia. Maybe these tests are broken and they *always* pass? It's time to do some test-driven development and get the buzz that comes from turning red tests to green!

> **Note:** Test-Driven Development (TDD) is a way of developing an application by writing a test first, then incrementally implementing the feature until the test passes. The code is then refactored for the next feature or improvement.
>
> TDD methodology goes way beyond the scope of this chapter but may be something you'll find useful. The steps you're covering here will help you use TDD if you do decide to follow it.

Add the following methods to **CampSiteServiceTests.swift** to test `getCampSite()`:

```
func testGetCampSiteWithMatchingSiteNumber() {
  campSiteService.addCampSite(1, electricity: true,
    water: true)

let campSite = campSiteService.getCampSite(1)
```

```
    XCTAssertNotNil(campSite, "A campsite should be returned")
  }

  func testGetCampSiteNoMatchingSiteNumber() {
    campSiteService.addCampSite(1, electricity: true,
      water: true)

    let campSite = campSiteService.getCampSite(2)

    XCTAssertNil(campSite, "No campsite should be returned")
  }
```

Both tests use the `addCampSite` method to create a new `CampSite`. You know this method works from your previous test, so there's no need to test it again. The actual tests cover retrieving the `CampSite` by ID and verifying that it is or isn't `nil`.

Think about how this test is much more reliable starting from an empty database for every test. If you weren't using the in-memory store, there could easily be a campsite matching the ID for the second test, which would then fail!

Run the unit tests. The test expecting a `CampSite` fails because you haven't implemented `getCampSite` yet.

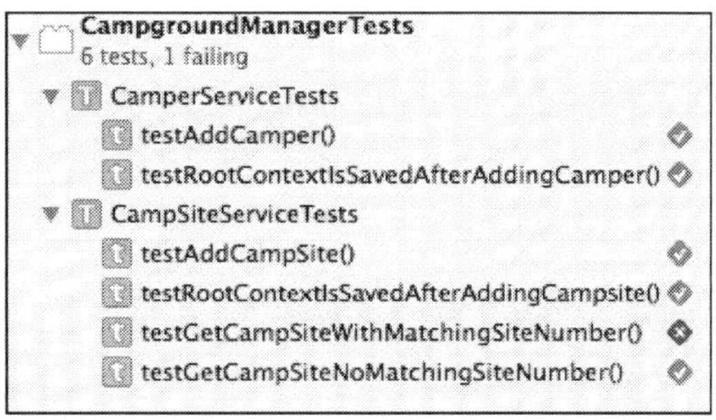

Notice the other unit test expecting no site passes. This is an example of a false positive, because the method always returns `nil`. It's important that you add tests for multiple scenarios for each method to exercise as many code paths as possible.

Implement `getCampSite` in **CampSiteService.swift** with the following code:

```
  public func getCampSite(siteNumber: NSNumber) -> CampSite? {
    let fetchRequest = NSFetchRequest(entityName: "CampSite")
    fetchRequest.predicate = NSPredicate(
      format: "siteNumber == %@", argumentArray: [siteNumber])
    var error: NSError?
```

```
    let results = self.managedObjectContext.executeFetchRequest(
      fetchRequest, error: &error)

    if error != nil || results == nil {
      return nil
    }

    return results!.first as CampSite?
  }
```

Now re-run the unit tests and you should see green check marks. Ah, the sweet satisfaction of success.

> **Note:** The final project for this chapter included in the resources bundled with this book includes unit tests covering multiple scenarios for each method. You can browse through the code there for even more examples.

Validation and refactoring

`ReservationService` will have some of the most complex logic to handle figuring out if a camper is able to reserve a site. The unit tests for `ReservationService` will require every service so far created to test its operation.

Create a new test class as you've done before:

1. Right-click **Services** under the **CampgroundManagerTests** group and click **New File**.
2. Select **Test Case Class**. Click **Next**.
3. Name the class **ReservationServiceTests** (subclass of **XCTestCase** should already be selected) and pick **Swift** for the language.
4. Make sure the **CampgroundManagerTests** target checkbox is the only target selected. Click **Create**.

Replace the contents of the file with the following:

```
import Foundation
import CoreData
import XCTest
import CampgroundManager
```

```
class ReservationServiceTests: XCTestCase {
  var campSiteService: CampSiteService!
  var camperService: CamperService!
  var reservationService: ReservationService!
  var coreDataStack: CoreDataStack!

  override func setUp() {
    super.setUp()
    coreDataStack = TestCoreDataStack()
    camperService = CamperService(managedObjectContext:
      coreDataStack.mainContext!, coreDataStack:
      coreDataStack)
    campSiteService = CampSiteService(managedObjectContext:
      coreDataStack.mainContext!, coreDataStack:
      coreDataStack)
    reservationService = ReservationService(
      managedObjectContext: coreDataStack.mainContext!,
      coreDataStack: coreDataStack)
  }

  override func tearDown() {
    super.tearDown()

    camperService = nil
    campSiteService = nil
    reservationService = nil
    coreDataStack = nil
  }
}
```

This is a slightly longer version of the set up/tear down code you've used in the previous test case classes. Along with setting up the Core Data stack as usual, you're creating a fresh instance of each service in `setUp` for each test.

Add a method to test creating a reservation:

```
func testReserveCampSitePositiveNumberOfDays() {
  let camper = camperService.addCamper("Johnny Appleseed",
    phoneNumber: "408-555-1234")!
  let campSite = campSiteService.addCampSite(15,
    electricity: false, water: false)

  let result = reservationService.reserveCampSite(
    campSite, camper: camper, date: NSDate(), numberOfNights: 5)

  XCTAssertNotNil(result.reservation,
    "Reservation should not be nil")
```

```
  XCTAssertNil(result.error, "No error should be present")
  XCTAssertTrue(result.reservation?.status == "Reserved",
    "Status should be Reserved")
}
```

The unit test creates a camper and campsite, both required to reserve a site. The new part here is using the reservation service to reserve the camp site, linking the camper and camp site together with a date.

The unit test doesn't verify much other than that a `Reservation` object was created and that an `NSError` object wasn't in the returned tuple.

You realize while looking at the `reserveCampSite` call that the number of nights should be at least greater than zero. Add the following unit test to look for that condition:

```
func testReserveCampSiteNegativeNumberOfDays() {
  let camper = camperService.addCamper("Johnny Appleseed",
    phoneNumber: "408-555-1234")!
  let campSite = campSiteService!.addCampSite(15,
    electricity: false, water: false)

  let result = reservationService!.reserveCampSite(campSite,
    camper: camper, date: NSDate(), numberOfNights: -1)

  XCTAssertNotNil(result.reservation,
    "Reservation should not be nil")
  XCTAssertNotNil(result.error, "An error should be present")
  XCTAssertTrue(result.error?.userInfo?["Problem"] as? NSString
    == "Invalid number of days",
    "Error problem should be present")
  XCTAssertTrue(result.reservation?.status == "Invalid",
    "Status should be Invalid")
}
```

Run the unit test, and you'll notice the test fails. Apparently whoever wrote `ReservationService` didn't think to check for this! It's a good thing you caught it here in the test rather than a real user out in the wild – maybe booking a negative number of nights would go as far as to issue a refund!

Tests are a great place for probing your system like this and finding holes in the behavior. As an added benefit, the test provides something like a specification too – the tests is saying you're still expecting a valid non-nil result, but with the error condition set.

Open **ReservationService.swift** and add the check for `numberOfNights` to `reserveCampSite`. Replace the line `reservation.status = "Reserved"` with the following:

```
if numberOfNights <= 0 {
  reservation.status = "Invalid"
  registrationError = NSError(domain: "CampingManager",
   code: 5, userInfo: ["Problem" : "Invalid number of days"])
} else {
  reservation.status = "Reserved"
}
```

Now rerun the tests and see that the negative number of days test passes. You can see how the process continues with refactoring when you want to add additional functionality or validation rules.

Whether you know the details of the code you're testing or if you're treating it like a black box, you can write these kinds of tests against the API to see if behaves as you think. If it does, great! – that means the test will ensure it continues to work like that. If not, you either need to change your test to match what the code does, or change the code to match the test expectation.

Where to go from here?

You've probably heard many times that unit testing your work is key to maintaining a stable software product. While Core Data can help eliminate a lot of error-prone persistence code from your project, it can be a source of logic errors if used incorrectly.

Writing unit tests that can use Core Data will help stabilize your code before it even reaches your users. `XCTestExpectation` is a simplistic yet powerful helper in your quest to test Core Data in an asynchronous manner. Use it wisely.

Challenge: The `CampSiteService` has a number of methods that are not implemented yet, marked with `TODO` comments. Using a TDD approach, write unit tests and then implement the methods to make the tests pass.

Check out the final project included in the resources for this chapter for a sample solution if you get stuck.

Chapter 9: Measuring and Boosting Performance

By Matthew Morey

In many ways, it's a no-brainer: You should strive to optimize the performance of any app you're developing. An app with poor performance will, at best, receive bad reviews and, at worst, become unresponsive and crash.

This is no less true of apps that use Core Data. Luckily, most implementations of Core Data are fast and light already, due to Core Data's built-in optimizations, such as faulting.

However, the flexibility that makes Core Data a great tool can also allow you to use it in ways that negatively impact performance. From poor choices in setting up the data model to inefficient fetching and searching, there are many opportunities for Core Data to slow down your app.

You'll begin the chapter with an app that is a slow-working memory hog. By the end of the chapter, you'll have an app that is light and fast, and you'll know exactly where to look and what to do if you find yourself with you own heavy, sluggish app—and how to avoid that situation in the first place!

Getting started

As with most things, performance is a balance, a balance between memory and speed. Your app's Core Data model objects can exist in two places: in random access memory (RAM) or on disk. Accessing data in RAM is much quicker than accessing data on disk, but devices have much less RAM than disk space.

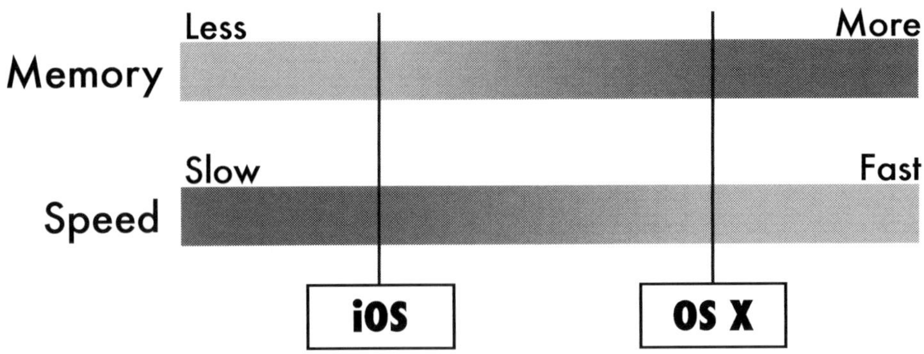

On iOS devices in particular, there is less available RAM and as a result, you can't load as much data. With fewer model objects in RAM, your app's operations will be slower due to frequent slow disk access. If you use too much RAM, your app will receive low memory warnings and the system may even terminate your app!

The more model objects you load into RAM, the faster your app will be, but then your app will be using more RAM. You can minimize RAM usage, but then your app will be slower because more of your model objects are on disk.

The starter project

The starter project, **Employee Directory**, is a tab-bar based app full of employee information. It's like the Contacts app, but for a single fictional company.

Open the starter project for this chapter in the **EmployeeDirectory-Starter** folder and build and run it in Xcode.

The app will take a long time to launch and once it does launch, it will feel sluggish and may even crash as you use it. Rest assured, this is by design!

> **Note:** It's possible the starter project may not even launch on your system. I made the app to be as sluggish as possible while still able to run on most systems, so that the performance improvements you'll make will be easily noticeable.
>
> If the app refuses to work on your system, continue to follow along. The first set of changes you make should enable the app to work on even the slowest devices.

As you can see in the following screenshots, the first tab includes a table view and a custom cell with basic information, such as name and department, for all employees. Tapping on a cell reveals more details for the selected employee, such as start date and remaining vacation days.

Tapping on the profile picture of the employee makes the picture full-screen; tapping anywhere on the full-screen picture dismisses that view.

The startup time of the app is quite long and the initial employee list's scrolling performance could use some work. The app also uses a lot of memory, which you'll measure yourself in the next section.

Measure, change, verify

Instead of guessing where your performance bottlenecks may be, you can save yourself much time and effort by first measuring your app's performance in targeted ways. Xcode provides tools just for this purpose, as you'll see.

Ideally, you would measure, make targeted changes and measure again to validate your changes had the intended impact. You should repeat this measure-change-verify process as many times need to until your app meets all of your performance requirements.

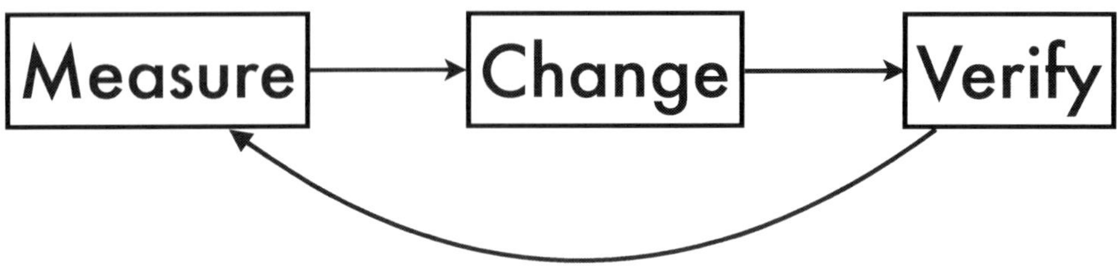

In this chapter, you'll do just that:

- You'll measure performance issues in the provided starter project using Gauges, Instruments and the XCTest framework.
- Next, you'll make changes to the code that will improve the performance of the app.
- Finally, you'll verify that the changes had the intended results by measuring again.

You'll then repeat this cycle until Employee Directory performs like a Core Data champ!

Measuring the problem

Build, run, and wait for the app to launch. Once it does, use the **Memory Report** to view how much RAM the app is using.

To launch the **Memory Report**, first verify the app is running and then perform the following steps:

1. Click on the **Debug navigator** in the left navigator pane.

2. To get more information, expand the **running process**—in this case, **EmployeeDirectory**—by tapping on the arrow.

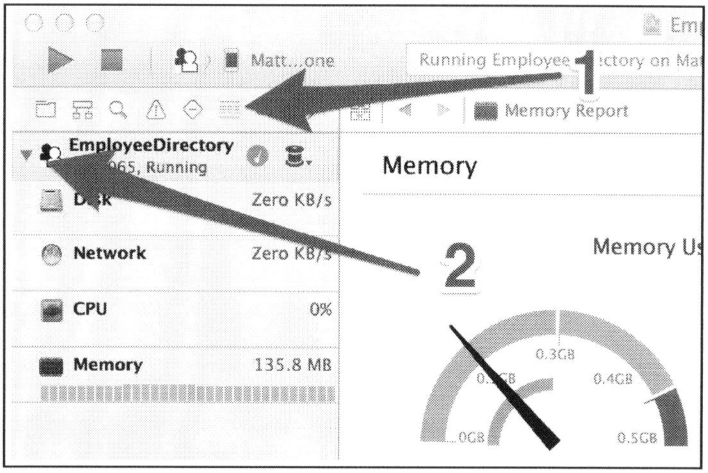

Now, click on the **Memory** row and look at the top half of the memory gauge:

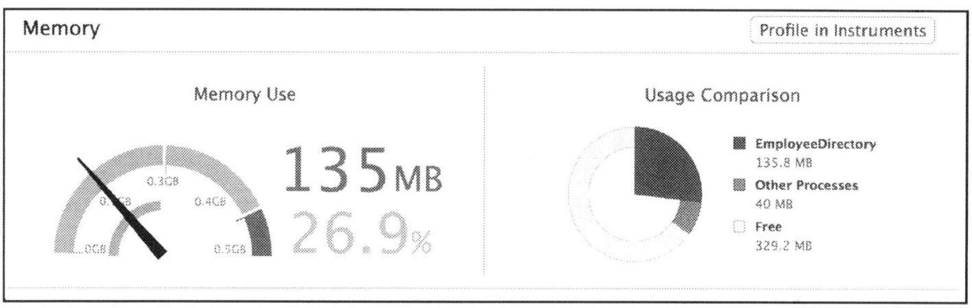

The top half includes a **Memory Use** gauge showing the amount and percentage of memory your app is using. For Employee Directory, you'll see about 135 MB of memory is in use, or about 25% of the available RAM on an iPhone 4S.

The **Usage Comparison** pie chart depicts this chunk of memory as a fraction of the total available memory. It also shows the amount of RAM in use by other processes, as well as the amount of freely available RAM, which in this case is 392.2 MB.

Now look at the bottom half of the Memory Report:

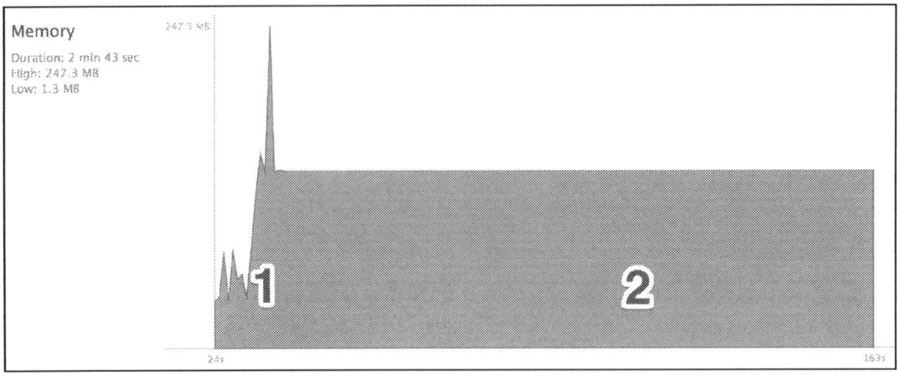

The bottom half consist of a chart that shows RAM usage over time. For Employee Directory, you'll see two distinct areas.

1. Upon first launch, Employee Directory performs an import operation before loading the primary employee list. Ignore these spikes in memory for now.
2. The next area takes place after the import operation, when the employee list is visible. Once the app has fully loaded the list, you can see the memory usage is fairly stable.

> **Note:** If you use a device besides an iPhone 4S, including the iOS Simulator, your memory gauge may not look exactly like these screenshots. The utilization percentages will be based off of the amount of available RAM on your test device, which may not match the RAM available on an iPhone 4S.

There are only 50 employee records in the app so the RAM usage is quite high. It could be something in the data model that's using up so much memory for so few records, so let's start there.

Exploring the data source

In Xcode, open the project navigator and click on **EmployeeDirectory.xcdatamodeld** to view the data model.

The model for the starter project consists of an `Employee` entity with 11 attributes and a `Sale` entity with two attributes.

On the `Employee` entity, the `about`, `address`, `department`, `email`, `guid`, `name` and `phone` attributes are string types; `active` is a Boolean; `picture` is binary data; `startDate` is a date and `vacationDays` is an integer.

`Employee` has a to-many relationship with `Sale`, which contains an `amount` integer attribute and a `date` Date attribute.

On first launch, the app will import sample data from the bundled JSON file **seed.json**. Here's an excerpt of the JSON:


```
{
  "guid": "769adb89-82ad-4b39-be41-d02b89de7b94",
  "active": true,
  "picture": "face10.jpg",
  "name": "Kasey Mcfarland",
  "vacationDays": 2,
  "department": "Marketing",
  "startDate": "1979-09-05",
  "email": "kaseymcfarland@liquicom.com",
  "phone": "+1 (909) 561-2981",
  "address": "201 Lancaster Avenue, West Virginia, 2583",
  "about": "Dolore reprehenderit ... voluptate consectetur.\r\n"
},
```


> Note: You can vary the amount and type of data the app imports from the **seed.json** file by modifying the `amountToImport` and `addSalesRecords` constants located at the top of **AppDelegate.swift**. For now, leave these constants set to their default values.

In terms of performance, the text showing the employee names, departments, email addresses and phone numbers is inconsequential compared to the profile pictures, which are large enough to potentially be impacting the performance of the list.

Now that you've measured the problem and have a baseline for future comparisons, you'll make changes to the data model to reduce the amount of RAM in use.

Making changes to improve performance

The likely culprit to the high memory usage is the employee profile picture. Since the picture is stored as a binary data attribute, Core Data will allocate memory and load the entire picture when you access an employee record. This will happen even if you only need to access the employee's name or email address!

The solution here is to split out the picture into a separate, related record. In theory, you'll be able to access the employee record efficiently, and then take the hit for loading the picture only when you really need it.

To start, open the visual model editor by clicking on **EmployeeDirectory.xcdatamodeld**.

Start by creating an object, or entity, in your model. In the bottom toolbar, click the **Add Entity** plus (+) button to add a new entity.

Name the entity **EmployeePicture**. Then click the entity and make sure the third tab is selected in the Utilities section. Change the class to **EmployeeDirectory.EmployeePicture**; you need to give the full class name with the app's name as the namespace for it to work with Swift.

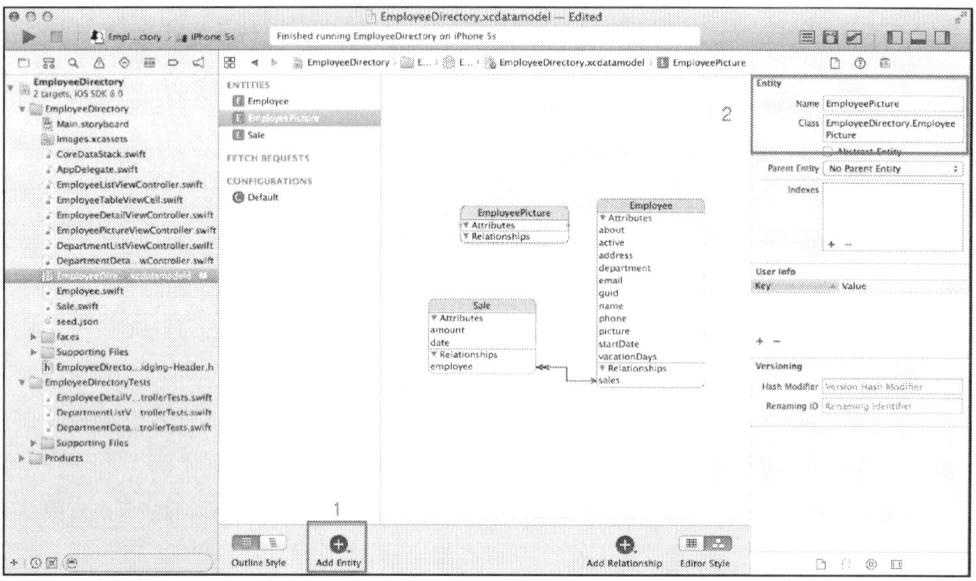

Make sure the **EmployeePicture** entity is selected by clicking on either the entity name in the left panel or the diagram for the entity in the diagram view.

Next, click and hold on the plus (+) button in the lower-right (next to the Editor Style segmented control) and then click **Add Attribute** from the popup. Name the new attribute **picture**.

Finally, in the data model inspector, change the **Attribute Type** to **Binary Data** and check the **Allows External Storage** option.

Your editor should look like this:

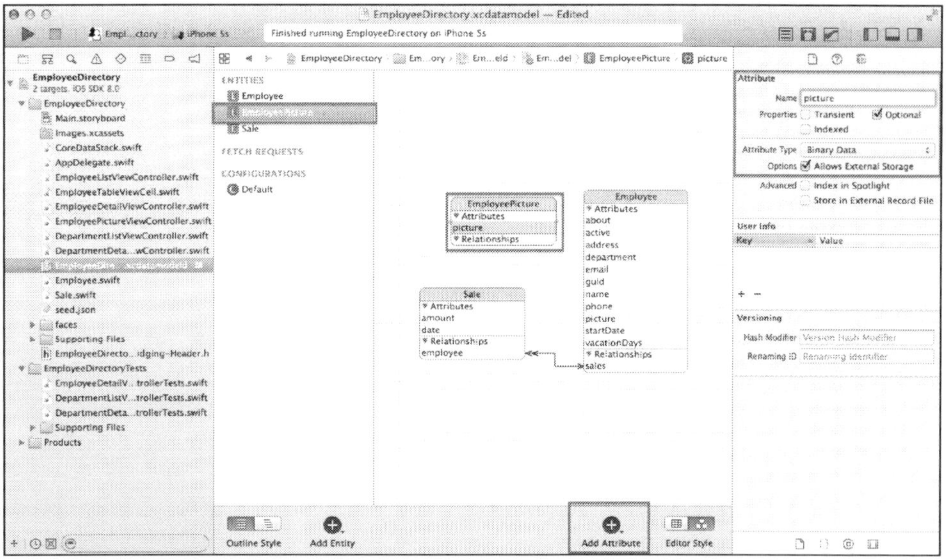

As previously mentioned, binary data attributes are usually stored right in the database. If you check the **Allows External Storage** option, Core Data automatically decides if it's better to save the data to disk as a separate file or leave it in the SQLite database.

Select the Employee entity and rename the **picture** attribute to **pictureThumbnail**. To do so, select the picture attribute in the diagram view and then edit the name in the data model inspector.

You've updated the model so that now, it stores the original picture in a separate entity and stores only a thumbnail version on the main Employee entity. The smaller thumbnail pictures won't require as much RAM when the app fetches Employee entities from Core Data. Once you've finished modifying the rest of the project, you'll get a chance to test this out and verify that the app is using less RAM than before.

You can link the two entities together with a relationship. That way, when the app needs the higher-quality but larger picture, it can still retrieve it, via a relationship.

Select the **Employee** entity and click and hold the plus (+) button in the lower right. This time, select **Add Relationship**. Name the relationship **picture**, set the destination as **EmployeePicture** and finally, set the **Delete Rule** to **Cascade**.

Core Data relationships should always go both ways, so now add a corresponding relationship. Select the **EmployeePicture** entity and add a new relationship. Name the new relationship **employee**, set the **Destination** to **Employee** and finally, set the **Inverse** to **picture**.

Your model should now look like this:

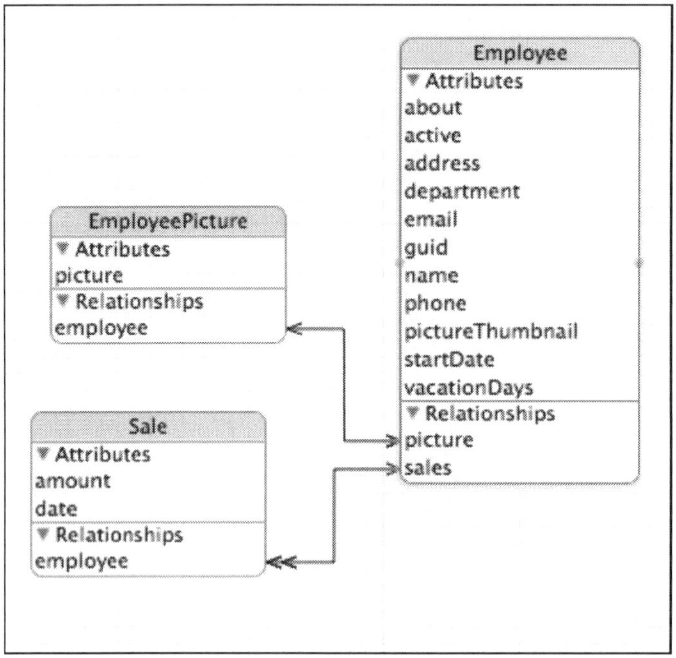

Now that you've finished making changes to the model, you need to create an `NSManagedObject` subclass for the new `EmployeePicture` entity. This subclass will let you access the new entity from code.

Right-click on the **EmployeeDirectory** group folder and select **New File**. Select the **Cocoa Touch Class** template and click **Next**. Name the class **EmployeePicture** and make it a subclass of **NSManagedObject**. Make sure that **Swift** is selected for the **Language**, click **Next** and finally click **Create**.

Select **EmployeePicture.swift** from the project navigator and replace the automatically generated code with the following code:

```
import Foundation
import CoreData

class EmployeePicture: NSManagedObject {
  @NSManaged var picture: NSData
  @NSManaged var employee: EmployeeDirectory.Employee
}
```

This is a very simple class with just two properties. The first, `picture`, matches the single attribute on the `EmployeePicture` entity you just created in the visual data model editor. The second property, `employee`, matches the relationship you created on the `EmployeePicture` entity.

> **Note:** You could also have Xcode create the `EmployeePicture` class automatically. To add a new class this way, go to **Editor\Create NSManagedObject Subclass...**, select the data model and then the **EmployeePicture** entity in the next two dialog boxes. Select **Swift** as the language option in the final box. If you're asked, say **No** to creating an Objective-C bridging header. Click **Create** to save the file.

Next, select the **Employee.swift** file from the project navigator and update the code to make use of the new `pictureThumbnail` attribute and `picture` relationship. Rename the `picture` variable to `pictureThumbnail` and add a new variable named `picture` that is of type `EmployeeDirectory.EmployeePicture`. Your file will now look like this:

```
import Foundation
import CoreData

public class Employee: NSManagedObject {
  @NSManaged var startDate: NSDate
  @NSManaged var about: String
  @NSManaged var active: NSNumber
  @NSManaged var address: String
  @NSManaged var department: String
  @NSManaged var email: String
  @NSManaged var guid: String
  @NSManaged var name: String
  @NSManaged var phone: String
  @NSManaged var pictureThumbnail: NSData
  @NSManaged var picture: EmployeeDirectory.EmployeePicture
  @NSManaged var vacationDays: NSNumber
  @NSManaged var sales : NSSet
}
```

Next, you need to update the rest of the app to make use of the new entities and attributes.

Open **EmployeeListViewController.swift** and find the following lines of code in `tableView(_:cellForRowAtIndexPath:)`. It should be easy to find, as it will have an error marker next to it!

```
cell.pictureImageView.image = UIImage(data: employee.picture)
```

This code sets the picture on the cell in the employee list. Now that the full picture is held in a separate entity, you should use the newly added `pictureThumbnail` attribute. Update the file to match the following code:

```
cell.pictureImageView.image =
  UIImage(data: employee.pictureThumbnail)
```

Now open **EmployeeDetailViewController.swift** and find the following code within `configureView()`. Again, it should be showing an error:

```
if let imageView = headShotImageView {
  let image = UIImage(data: employee.picture)
  imageView.image = image
}
```

Just like you did in EmployeeListViewController.swift, you need to update the picture being set. Like the cell picture, the employee detail view will only have a small picture and therefore only needs the thumbnail version. Update the code to look like the following:

```
if let imageView = headShotImageView {
  let image = UIImage(data: employee.pictureThumbnail)
  imageView.image = image
}
```

Open **EmployeePictureViewController.swift** and find the following code in `configureView()`:

```
if let imageView = employeePictureImageView {
  imageView.image = UIImage(data: employee.picture)
}
```

This time, you want to use the high-quality version of the picture, since the image will be shown full-screen.

Update the file to use the `picture` relationship you created on the `Employee` entity to access the high-quality version of the picture:

```
if let imageView = employeePictureImageView {
  imageView.image = UIImage(data: employee.picture.picture)
}
```

There's one more thing to do before you build and run. Open **AppDelegate.swift** and find the following line of code in `importJSONSeedData()`:

```
employee.picture = pictureData!
```

Now that you have a separate entity for storing the high-quality picture, you need to update this line of code to set the `pictureThumbnail` attribute and the `picture` relationship. Replace the line above with the following:

```
employee.pictureThumbnail =
  imageDataScaledToHeight(pictureData, height: 120)

let employeePictureEntity =
  NSEntityDescription.entityForName("EmployeePicture",
    inManagedObjectContext: coreDataStack.context)
let pictureObject =
  EmployeePicture(entity: employeePictureEntity!,
    insertIntoManagedObjectContext: coreDataStack.context)
pictureObject.picture = pictureData

employee.picture = pictureObject
```

First, you use `imageDataScaledToHeight` to set the `pictureThumbnail` to a smaller version of the original picture. Next, you create a new `picture` entity using the `EmployeePicture` entity description.

You set the `picture` attributed on the new `EmployeePicture` entity to the `pictureData` constant. Finally, you set the `picture` relationship on the `employee` entity to the just-created `picture` entity.

Note: `imageDataScaledToHeight` takes in image data, resizes it to the passed-in height and sets the quality to 80% before returning the new image data.

If you have an app that needs pictures and retrieves data via a network call, you should make sure that the API doesn't already include smaller thumbnail versions of the pictures. There's a small performance cost associated with converting images on the fly like this.

It's time to build and run! Give it a go. You should see exactly what you saw before:

The app should work as before, and you might even notice a small performance difference because of the thumbnails. But the main reason for this change was to improve memory usage.

Verify the changes

Now that you've made all the necessary changes to the project, it's time to see if you actually improved the app.

While the app is running, use the **Memory Report** to view how much RAM the app is using. This time only about 41 MB of RAM or 8.2% of total RAM is being used.

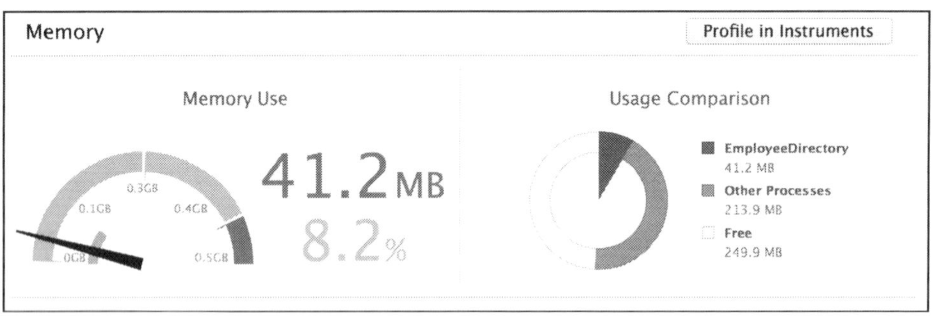

Now look at the bottom half of the report. Like last time, the initial spike is from the import operation and you can ignore it. The flat area is much lower this time.

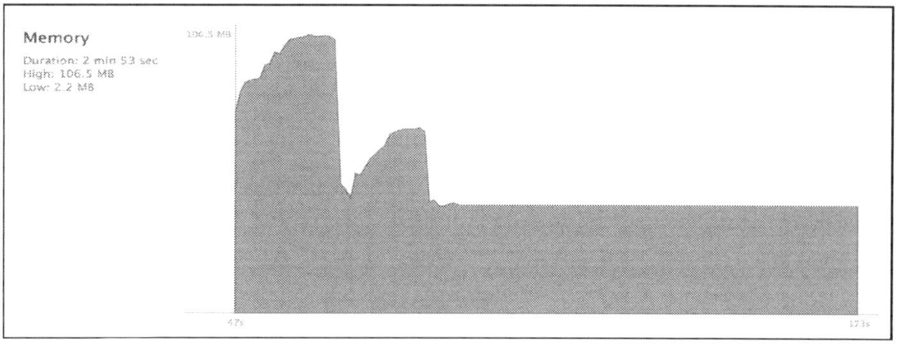

Congratulations, you've reduced this app's RAM usage by making adjustments to its data model!

First, you **measured** the app's performance using the Memory Report tool. Next, you made **changes** to the way Core Data stores and accesses the app's data. Finally, you **verified** that the changes improved the app's performance.

Fetching and performance

Core Data is the keeper of your app's data. Anytime you want to access the data, you have to retrieve it with a fetch request.

For example, when the app loads the employee list, it needs to perform a fetch.

But each trip to the persistent store incurs overhead. You don't want to fetch more data than you need—just enough so that you aren't constantly going back to the disk. Remember, disk access is much slower than RAM access.

For maximum performance, you need to strike a balance between the number of objects you fetch at any given time and the usefulness of having many records taking up valuable space in RAM.

The startup time of the app is a little slow, suggesting something is going on with the initial fetch.

Fetch batch size

Core Data fetch requests include the `fetchBatchSize` property, which makes it easy to fetch just enough data but not too much.

If you don't set a batch size, Core Data uses the default value of 0, which disables batching.

Setting a non-zero positive batch size enables you to limit the amount of data returned to the batch size. As the app needs more data, Core Data automatically performs more batch operations.

If you were to search the source code of the Employee Directory app, you wouldn't see any calls to `fetchBatchSize`. That indicates another potential area for improvement!

Let's see if there are any places you could use a batch size to improve the app's performance. I probably don't have to tell you there are!

Measuring the problem

You'll use the **Instruments** tool to analyze where fetching is occurring in your app.

First, select one of the iPhone simulator targets and then from Xcode's menu bar, select **Product** and then **Profile** (or press ⌘I). This will build the app and launch **Instruments**.

> **Note:** You can only use the Instruments Core Data template with the Simulator, as the template requires the DTrace tool which is not available on real iOS devices.

A selection window like the following will greet you:

Select the **Core Data** template and click **Choose**. This will launch the Instruments window. If this is the first time you've launched Instruments, you might be asked for your password to authorize Instruments to analyze running processes—don't worry, it's safe to enter your password in this dialog.

Once Instruments has launched, click on the **Record** button in the top-left of the window:

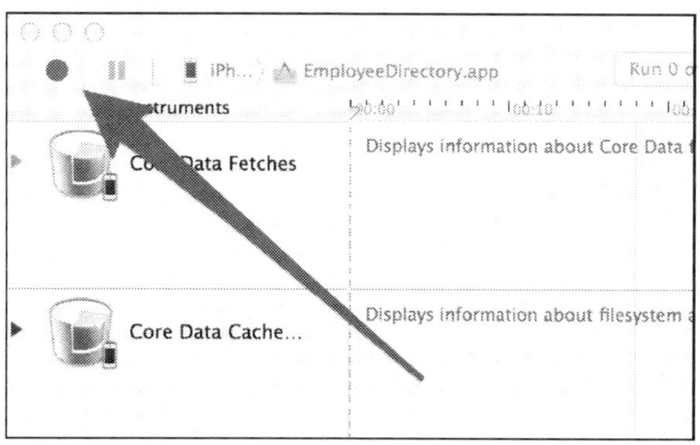

Once Employee Directory has launched, scroll up and down the employee list for about 20 seconds and then click on the **Stop** button that has appeared in place of the Record button.

Click on the **Core Data Fetches** tool. The Instruments window should now look like this:

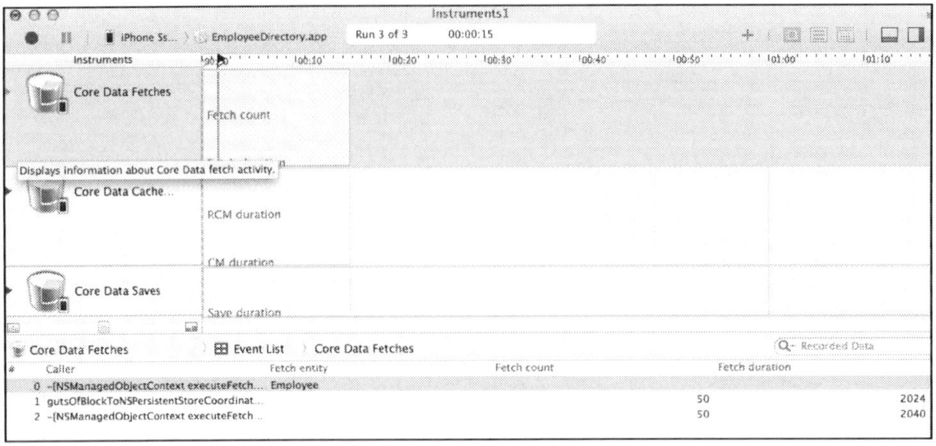

The default Core Data template includes the following tools to help you tune and monitor performance:

- **Core Data Fetches Instrument:** Captures fetch count and duration of fetch operations. This will help you balance the number of fetch requests versus the size of each request.
- **Core Data Cache Misses Instrument:** Captures information about fault events that result in cache misses. This can help diagnose performance in low-memory situations.
- **Core Data Saves Instrument:** Captures information on managed object context save events. Writing data out to disk can be a performance and battery hit, so this instrument can help you determine whether you should batch things into one big save rather than many small ones.

Since you clicked on the **Core Data Fetches** tool, the details section at the bottom of the Instruments window shows more information about each fetch that occurred.

Each of the three rows corresponds to the same line of code in the app. The first two rows are private Core Data calls that are generated by lines of code in the app, so you can ignore them.

Pay attention to the last row, though. This row includes the Objective-C versions of the **caller**, **fetch count** and **fetch duration** in microseconds.

Employee Directory imports 50 employees. Since the fetch count shows 50, the app is fetching all employees from Core Data at the same time. That's not very efficient!

The Core Data Fetches tool corroborates your experience that the fetch is slow and is easily noticeable, as you can see it takes about 2,000 microseconds (2 seconds). The app has to complete this fetch before it makes the table view visible and ready for user interaction.

> **Note:** Depending on your Mac, the numbers onscreen (and the thickness of the bars) might not match those shown in these screenshots. Faster Macs will have quicker fetches. Don't worry—what's important is the change in time you'll see after you modify the project.

Changes to improve performance

Open **EmployeeListViewController.swift** and find the following line of code in `employeeFetchRequest(department:)`:

```
let fetchRequest = NSFetchRequest(entityName: "Employee")
```

This code creates a fetch request using the `Employee` entity. You haven't set a batch size, so it defaults to 0, which means no batching.

Now set the batch size on the fetch request to 10, like so:

```
let fetchRequest = NSFetchRequest(entityName: "Employee")
fetchRequest.fetchBatchSize = 10
```

How do you come up with an optimal batch size? A good rule of thumb is to set the batch size to about double the number of items that appear onscreen at any given time. The employee list shows three to five employees onscreen at once, so 10 is a reasonable batch size.

Verify the changes

Now that you've made the necessary change to the project, it's once again time to see if you've actually improved the app.

To test this fix, first build and run the app and make sure it still works. Next launch Instruments again (from Xcode, select **Product** and then **Profile**, or press ⌘I) and repeat the steps you followed previously. Remember to scroll up and down the employee list for about **20 seconds** before clicking the **Stop** button in Instruments.

> **Note:** To use the latest code, make sure you launch the app from Xcode, which triggers a build, rather than just hitting the red button in Instruments.

This time, the Core Data Instrument should look like this:

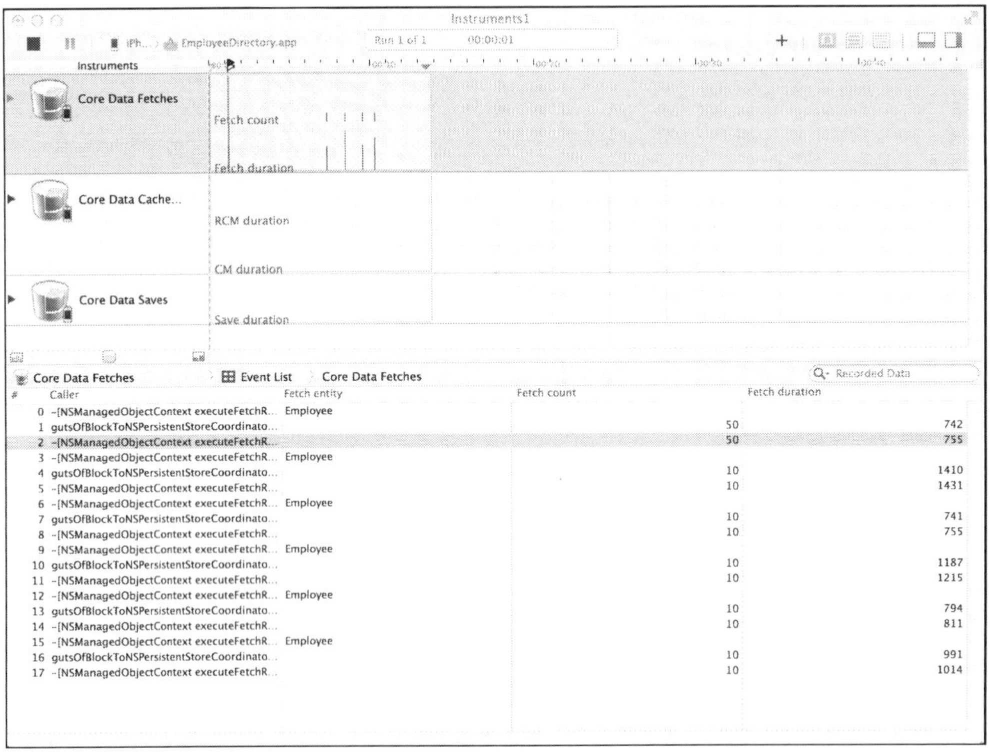

Now there are multiple fetches, and the initial fetch is faster!

Examine the detail section more closely.

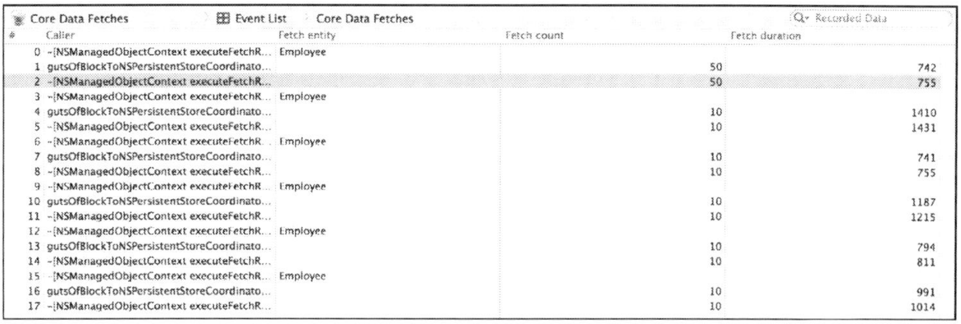

Core Data Fetches | Event List > Core Data Fetches | Recorded Data

#	Caller	Fetch entity	Fetch count	Fetch duration
0	-[NSManagedObjectContext executeFetchR...	Employee		
1	gutsOfBlockToNSPersistentStoreCoordinato...		50	742
2	-[NSManagedObjectContext executeFetchR...		50	755
3	-[NSManagedObjectContext executeFetchR...	Employee		
4	gutsOfBlockToNSPersistentStoreCoordinato...		10	1410
5	-[NSManagedObjectContext executeFetchR...		10	1431
6	-[NSManagedObjectContext executeFetchR...	Employee		
7	gutsOfBlockToNSPersistentStoreCoordinato...		10	741
8	-[NSManagedObjectContext executeFetchR...		10	755
9	-[NSManagedObjectContext executeFetchR...	Employee		
10	gutsOfBlockToNSPersistentStoreCoordinato...		10	1187
11	-[NSManagedObjectContext executeFetchR...		10	1215
12	-[NSManagedObjectContext executeFetchR...	Employee		
13	gutsOfBlockToNSPersistentStoreCoordinato...		10	794
14	-[NSManagedObjectContext executeFetchR...		10	811
15	-[NSManagedObjectContext executeFetchR...	Employee		
16	gutsOfBlockToNSPersistentStoreCoordinato...		10	991
17	-[NSManagedObjectContext executeFetchR...		10	1014

Again, instead of a single fetch, you see multiple quicker fetches.

The first fetch looks like the original fetch, as it is fetching all 50 employees. The difference is that this time, it's only fetching the count instead of the full objects, and thus the fetch duration is much quicker. Core Data is doing this automatically now that you've set a batch size on the request.

Originally this fetch took over 2,000 microseconds, and now it only takes 755 microseconds on my system.

After the first fetch, you can see numerous fetches with fetch counts of 10. These fetches are happening because you set the batch size to 10. As you scroll through the employee list, new entities are fetched only when they are needed.

You've cut the time of the initial fetch down to almost a third of the original, and the subsequent fetches are much smaller and faster. Congratulations, you have increased the speed of your app again!

Advanced fetching

Fetch requests use **predicates** to limit the amount of data returned. As mentioned above, for optimal performance, you should limit the amount of data you fetch to the minimum needed: the more data you fetch, the longer the fetch will take.

Fetch Predicate Performance

When performing fetches, you should limit the amount of data returned to the minimum needed. You can limit your fetch requests by using predicates.

If your fetch request requires a compound predicate, you can make it more efficient by putting the more restrictive predicate first. If your predicate contains string comparisons, this is especially true.

For example, a predicate with a format of `"(active == YES) AND (name CONTAINS[cd] %@)"` would likely be more efficient than `"(name CONTAINS[cd] %@) AND (active == YES)"`.

Please consult Apple's Predicate Programming Guide for more predicate performance optimizations.

Build and run Employee Directory, and select the second tab labeled **Departments**. This tab shows a listing of departments and the number of employees in each department. Tapping a department cell takes the user to a list of the employees in the selected department.

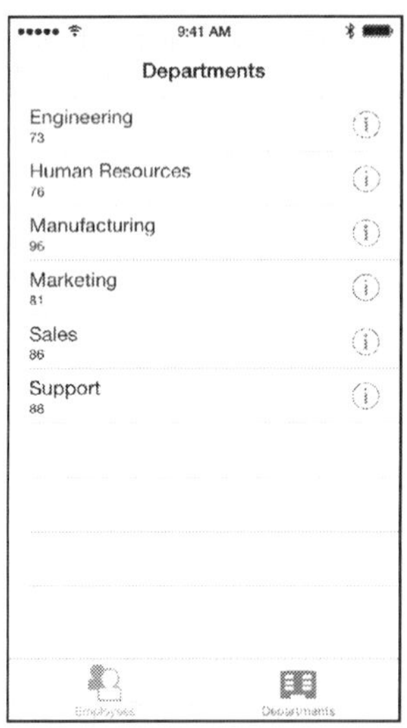

Tapping on the detail disclosure, also known as the information icon, in each department cell will show the total employees, active employees and a breakdown of employees' available vacations days.

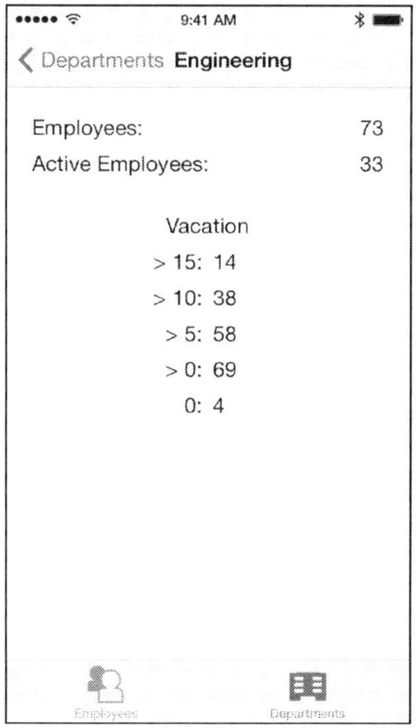

The first screen simply lists the departments and the number of employees per department. There's not too much data here, but there could still be performance issues lurking here. Let's find out.

Measure the problem

Instead of Instruments, you'll use the **XCTest framework** to measure the performance of the department list screen. XCTest is usually used for unit tests, but there are some new performance testing tools available as of Xcode 6.

> Note: For more information on unit tests and Core Data, check out Chapter 8, "Unit Testing"

First, familiarize yourself with how the app creates the department list screen. Open **DepartmentListViewController.swift** and find the following code in `totalEmployeesPerDepartment`.

```
//1
let fetchRequest = NSFetchRequest(entityName: "Employee")
var error: NSError? = nil
var fetchResults =
  coreDataStack.context.executeFetchRequest(fetchRequest,
   error: &error)
if fetchResults {

  //2
  var uniqueDepartments = [String:Int]()
  for object in fetchResults {

    let employee = object as Employee

    if let employeeDepartmentCount =
      uniqueDepartments[employee.department] {

        uniqueDepartments[employee.department] =
          employeeDepartmentCount + 1

    } else {
      uniqueDepartments[employee.department] = 1
    }
  }

  //3
  var results = [[String:String]]()
  for (department, headCount) in uniqueDepartments {

    let departmentDictionary:[String:String] =
      ["department":department,
       "headCount":String(headCount)]

    results.append(departmentDictionary)
  }

  return results
} else {
  println("ERROR: \(error?.localizedDescription)")
  return [[String:String]]()
}
```

This code does the following:

1. It creates a fetch request with the `Employee` entity and then fetches all employees.
2. It iterates though the employees and builds a dictionary, where the key is the department name and the value is the number of employees in that department.
3. It builds an array of dictionaries with the required information for the department list screen.

How could you measure the performance of this code?

Open **DepartmentListViewControllerTests.swift** (notice the **Tests** suffix in the filename) and add the following code after the `tearDown` function:

```
func testTotalEmployeesPerDepartment() {
  measureMetrics([XCTPerformanceMetric_WallClockTime],
    automaticallyStartMeasuring: false) {
    let departmentList = DepartmentListViewController()
    departmentList.coreDataStack = CoreDataStack()
    self.startMeasuring()
    let items = departmentList.totalEmployeesPerDepartment()
    self.stopMeasuring()
  }
}
```

This function uses `measureMetrics` to see how long code takes to execute.

You have to set up a new Core Data stack each time so that you aren't just taking advantage of Core Data's excellent caching to make the subsequent test runs really fast!

Inside the block, you first create a `DepartmentListViewController` and give it a `CoreDataStack`. Then, you call `totalEmployeesPerDepartment` to retrieve the number of employees per department.

Now you need to run this test. From Xcode's menu bar, select **Product** and then **Test**, or press ⌘U. This will build the app and run the tests.

Once the tests have finished running, Xcode will look like this:

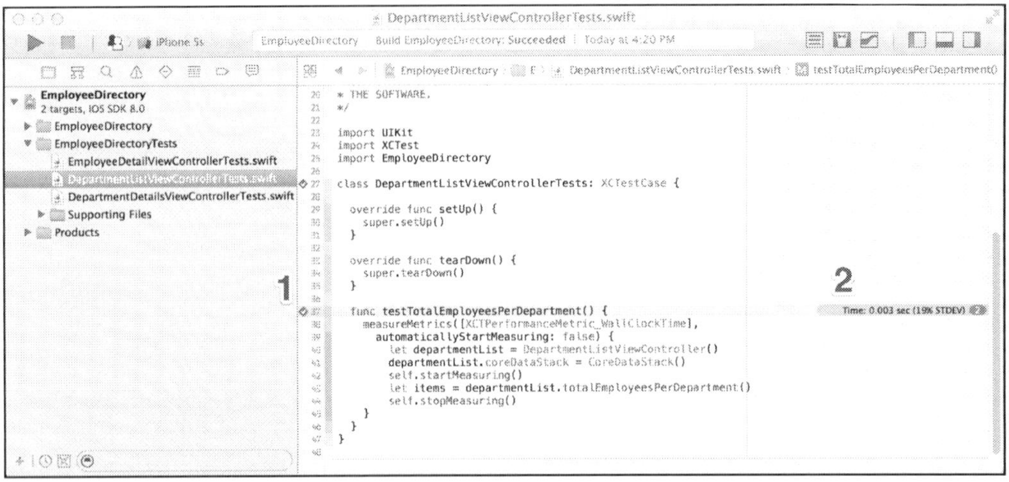

Notice two new things:

1. There's a green checkmark next to `testTotalEmployeesPerDepartment`. That means the test ran and passed.

2. There's a message on the right side with the amount of time the test took.

On my iPhone 4S test device used for the above screenshot, the test took **0.067 seconds** to perform the `totalEmployeesPerDepartment` operation. These results might seem good but there is still room for improvement.

> **Note:** These screenshots where generated with an iPhone 4S. You might get somewhat different test results, depending on your test device. Don't worry—what's important is the change in time you'll see after you modify the project.

Changes to improve performance

The current implementation of `totalEmployeesPerDepartment` uses a fetch request to iterate through all employee records. Remember the very first optimization in this chapter, where you split out the full-size photo into a separate entity? There's a similar issue here: Core Data loads the entire employee record, but all you really need is a *count* of employees by department.

It would be more efficient to somehow group the records by department and just get a count; you don't need the details like employee names and photo thumbnails!

Open **DepartmentListViewController.swift** and add the following code to the class:

```
public func totalEmployeesPerDepartmentFast()
  -> [[String:String]] {

  //1
  let expressionDescription = NSExpressionDescription()
  expressionDescription.name = "headCount"

  //2
  expressionDescription.expression =
    NSExpression(forFunction: "count:",
      arguments:[NSExpression(forKeyPath: "department")])

  //3
  let fetchRequest = NSFetchRequest(entityName: "Employee")
  fetchRequest.propertiesToFetch =
    ["department", expressionDescription]
  fetchRequest.propertiesToGroupBy = ["department"]
  fetchRequest.resultType = .DictionaryResultType

  //4
  var error: NSError? = nil
  if let fetchResults =
    coreDataStack.context.executeFetchRequest(fetchRequest,
      error: &error) {
    return fetchResults as [[String:String]]
  } else {
    println("ERROR: \(error?.localizedDescription)")
    return [[String:String]]()
  }
}
```

This code still uses a fetch request to populate the department list screen, but it also takes advantage of an `NSExpression`. Here's how it works:

1. You create an `NSExpressionDescription` and name it `headCount`.
2. You create an `NSExpression` with the `count:` function for the `department` attribute.
3. You create a fetch request with the `Employee` entity. This time, the fetch request should only fetch the minimum required properties by using `propertiesToFetch`. You only need the department attribute and a calculated property made by the

expression created earlier. The fetch request also groups the results by the `department` attribute. You're not interested in the managed object, so the fetch request return type is `DictionaryResultType`. This will return an array of dictionaries, each containing a department name and an employee count—just what you need!

4. You execute the fetch request.

Now find the following line of code in `viewDidLoad`:

```
items = totalEmployeesPerDepartment()
```

This line of code uses the old and slow function to populate the department list screen. Replace it by calling the function you just created:

```
items = totalEmployeesPerDepartmentFast()
```

Now the app is populating the table view data source for the department list screen with the faster `NSExpression`-backed fetch request.

> **Note:** NSExpression is a powerful API, yet it is seldom used, at least directly. When you create predicates with comparison operations, you may not know it, but you're actually using expressions.
>
> There are many pre-built statistical and arithmetical expressions available in NSExpression, including `average`, `sum`, `count`, `min`, `max`, `median`, `mode` and `stddev`. Consult the NSExpression documentation for a comprehensive overview.

Verify the changes

Now that you've made all the necessary changes to the project, it's once again time to see if you've improved the app.

Open **DepartmentListViewControllerTests.swift** and add a new function to test the `totalEmployeesPerDepartmentFast` function you just created.

```
func testTotalEmployeesPerDepartmentFast() {
  measureMetrics([XCTPerformanceMetric_WallClockTime],
automaticallyStartMeasuring: false, forBlock:{
    let departmentList = DepartmentListViewController()
    departmentList.coreDataStack = CoreDataStack()
```

```
      self.startMeasuring()
      let items =
        departmentList.totalEmployeesPerDepartmentFast()
      self.stopMeasuring()
    })
  }
```

Like before, this test uses `measureMetrics` to see how long a particular function is taking, in this case `totalEmployeesPerDepartmentFast`.

Now you need to run this test. From Xcode's menu bar, select **Product** and then **Test**, or press ⌘U. This will build the app and run the tests.

Once the tests have finished running, Xcode will look like this:

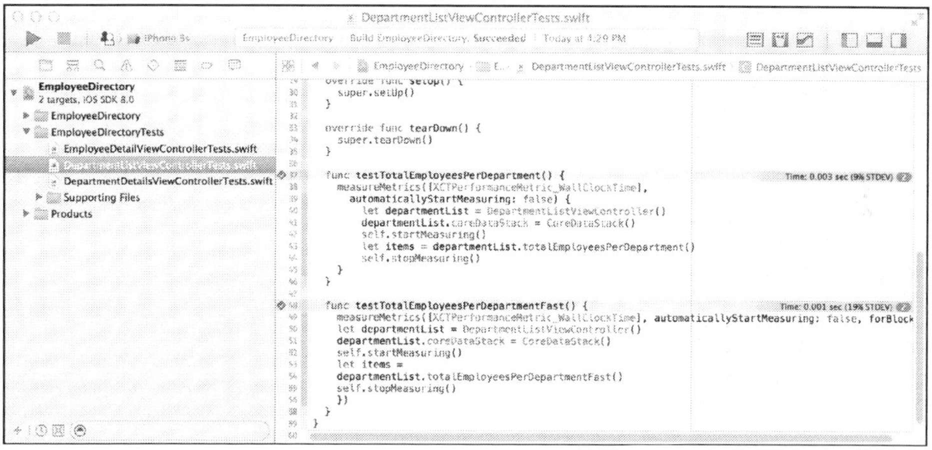

This time, you'll see two messages with total execution time, one next to each test function.

> **Note:** If you don't see the time messages, you can view the details of each individual test run in the logs generated during the test. From Xcode's menu bar, select **View**, **Debug Area**, and then **Show Debug Area**.

As you can see, the new function, `totalEmployeesPerDepartmentFast`, took 0.042 seconds to complete. That's much faster than the 0.070 seconds used by the original function, `totalEmployeesPerDepartment`. You've increased the speed of this fetch by about 40%!

Fetching counts

As you've already seen, it's often not important what your Core Data objects contain. Some screens simply need the counts of objects with certain attributes.

For example, the employee detail screen shows the total number of sales an employee has made since they've been with the company.

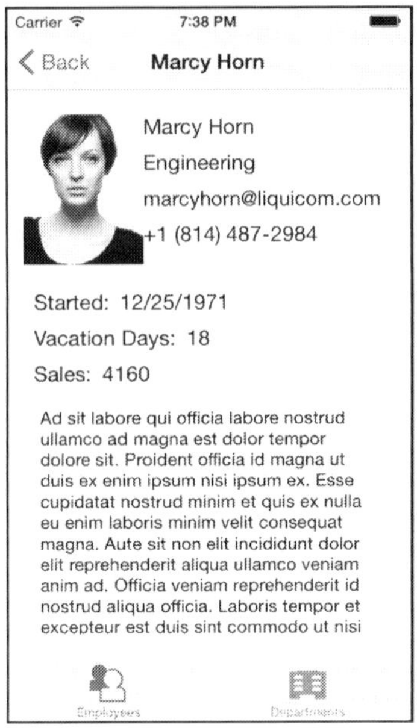

For the purposes of this app, you don't care about the content of each individual sale—for example, the date of the sale or the name of the purchaser—just how many there are.

Measure the problem

You'll use XCTest again to measure the performance of the employee detail screen.

Open **EmployeeDetailViewController.swift** and find `salesCountForEmployee(employee:)`.

```
public func salesCountForEmployee(employee:Employee) -> String {
  let fetchRequest = NSFetchRequest(entityName: "Sale")
  let predicate =
    NSPredicate(format: "employee == %@", employee)
  fetchRequest.predicate = predicate
  var error : NSError?
  let context = employee.managedObjectContext
```

```
    let results =
      context.executeFetchRequest(fetchRequest, error: &error)

    if results == nil {
      println("Error: \(error?.localizedDescription)")
      return "0"
    }

    return "\(results.count)"

  }
```

This code fetches all sales for a given employee and then returns the count of the returned array.

Fetching the full sale object just to see how many sales exist for a given employee is probably wasteful. This might be another opportunity to boost performance!

Let's measure the problem before attempting to fix it.

Open **EmployeeDetailViewControllerTests.swift** and find `testCountSales`.

```
  func testCountSales() {
    self.measureMetrics([XCTPerformanceMetric_WallClockTime],
      automaticallyStartMeasuring: false, forBlock: {
      let employee = self.getEmployee()
      let employeeDetails = EmployeeDetailViewController()
      self.startMeasuring()
      let sales =
        employeeDetails.salesCountForEmployee(employee)
      self.stopMeasuring()
    })
  }
```

Like the previous example, this function is using `measureMetrics` to see how long a single function takes to run. The test gets an employee from a convenience method, creates an `EmployeeDetailViewController`, begins measuring and then calls the method in question.

Run this test. From Xcode's menu bar, select **Product** and then **Test**, or press ⌘U. This will build the app and run the test.

Once the test has finished running, you'll see a time next to this test method, as before.

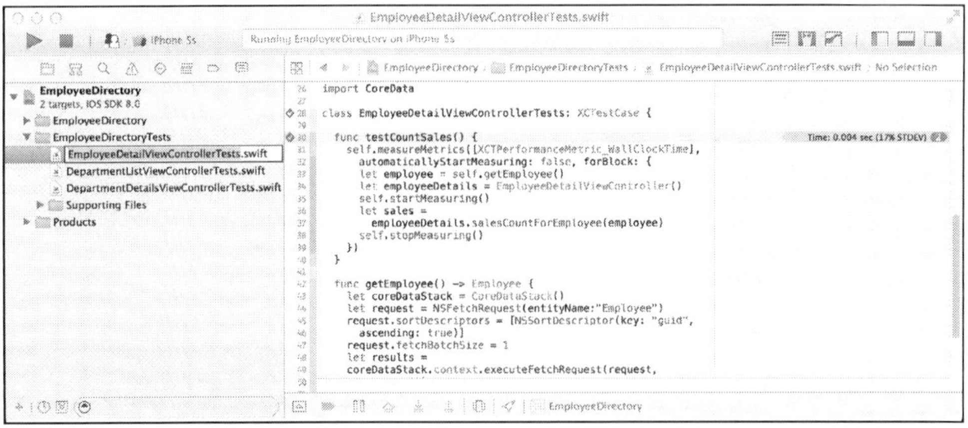

The performance is not too bad, there is room for improvement.

Changes to improve performance

In the previous example, you used NSExpression to group the data and provide a count of employees by department instead of returning the actual records themselves. This time you need to do the same thing, retrieve a count without getting all the actual records.

Open **EmployeeDetailViewController.swift** and add the following code to the class.

```
public func salesCountForEmployeeFast(employee:Employee) ->
String {
  let fetchRequest = NSFetchRequest(entityName: "Sale")
  let predicate =
  NSPredicate(format: "employee == %@", employee)
  fetchRequest.predicate = predicate
  var error : NSError?
  let context = employee.managedObjectContext!
  let results =
    context.countForFetchRequest(fetchRequest, error: &error)

  return "\(results)"
}
```

This code is very similar to the function you reviewed in the last section. The primary difference is that instead of calling `executeFetchRequest`, you are now calling `countForFetchRequest`.

Find the following line of code in `configureView()`:

```
label.text = salesCountForEmployee(employee)
```

This line of code uses the old sales count function to populate the label on the department details screen. Replace it by calling the function you just created:

```
label.text = salesCountForEmployeeFast(employee)
```

Verify the changes

Now that you've made the necessary changes to the project, it's once again time to see if you've improved the app.

Open **EmployeeDetailViewControllerTests.swift** and add a new function to test the `totalEmployeesFast` function you just created.

```
func testCountSalesFast() {
  self.measureMetrics([XCTPerformanceMetric_WallClockTime],
    automaticallyStartMeasuring: false, forBlock: {
    let employee = self.getEmployee()
    let employeeDetails = EmployeeDetailViewController()
    self.startMeasuring()
    let sales =
      employeeDetails.salesCountForEmployeeFast(employee)
    self.stopMeasuring()
  })
}
```

This test is identical to the previous one, except it uses the new and, with any luck, faster function.

Run this test. From Xcode's menu bar, select **Product** and then **Test**, or press ⌘U. This will build the app and run the test.

You'll see another performance improvement!

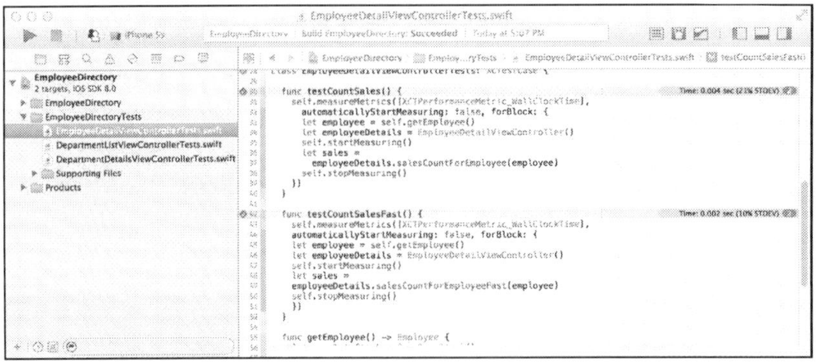

Using relationships

The code above is fast, but the faster method still seems like a lot of work. You have to create a fetch request, create a predicate, get a reference to the context, execute the fetch request and get the results out.

The Employee entity has a `sales` property, which holds an `NSSet` of the sales. Open **EmployeeDetailViewController.swift** and add another new method:

```
public func salesCountForEmployeeSimple(employee:Employee) ->
String {
  return "\(employee.sales.count)"
}
```

Doesn't that look better? By using the `sales` relationship on the Employee entity the code is much simpler and easier to comprehend.

Update the view controller and tests to use this method instead, following the same pattern as above. How's the performance now?

Challenge: Using the techniques you just learned, try to improve the performance of the `DepartmentDetailsViewController`. Don't forget to write tests to measure the before and after execution times.

Hint: There are many methods that provide counts rather than the full records – these can probably be optimized somehow to avoid loading the contents of the records.

Where to go from here?

If you followed this chapter all the way through, you've turned a slow, memory hog of an app into a light and fast app. The final project for this chapter is in the **EmployeeDirectory-Final** folder.

When optimizing the sample app's performance, you followed the measure, change and verify process to avoid unnecessary work. You learned how to use the Memory Report, Instruments and XCTest tools to take measurements.

Along the way, you learned how to improve your data model by putting large BLOBs in separate entities and by letting Core Data decide if data should be stored externally.

You also learned how to improve fetching performance by setting batch sizes and taking advantage of the NSExpression API.

As with most things, performance is a balance between memory and speed. When using Core Data in your apps, always keep this balance in mind. With the measurement tools and some of the techniques in this book, you're well on the way to measuring, improving, and verifying performance in your own apps!

Chapter 10: Multiple Managed Object Contexts

By Matthew Morey

A managed object context is an in-memory scratchpad that you use to work with your managed objects. In Chapter 3, "The Core Data Stack," you learned how the managed object context fits in with the other classes in the Core Data stack.

Most apps need but a single managed object context. A single managed object context with a main queue, the default behavior, is simple to manage and understand. Apps with multiple managed object contexts are harder to debug. For that reason, you should avoid them, if possible.

That being said, certain situations do warrant the use of more than one managed object context. For example, long-running tasks such as exporting data will block the main thread of apps that use only a single main-queue managed object context, causing the UI to stutter.

In other situations, such as when temporarily editing user data, it's helpful to treat a managed object context as a set of changes that the app can just throw away if it no longer needs them. Using child contexts makes this possible.

In this chapter, you'll learn about multiple managed object contexts by taking a journaling app for surfers and improving it in several ways by adding multiple contexts.

> **Note:** If common Core Data phrases such as managed object subclass and persistent store coordinator don't ring any bells, or if you're unsure what a Core Data stack is supposed to do, you may want to read or reread the first three chapters of this book before proceeding. This chapter covers advanced topics and assumes you already know the basics.

Getting started

This chapter's starter project is a simple journal app for surfers. After each surf session, a surfer can use the app to create a new journal entry that records marine parameters, such as swell height or period, and rate the session from 1 to 5. Dude, if you're not fond of hanging ten and getting barreled, no worries, brah. Just replace the surfing terminology with your favorite hobby of choice!

Introducing Surf Journal

Go to this chapter's files and find the **SurfJournal** starter project. Open the project, then build and run the app.

On startup, the application lists all previous surf session journal entries. Tapping on a row in the list brings up the detail view of a surf session with the ability to make edits.

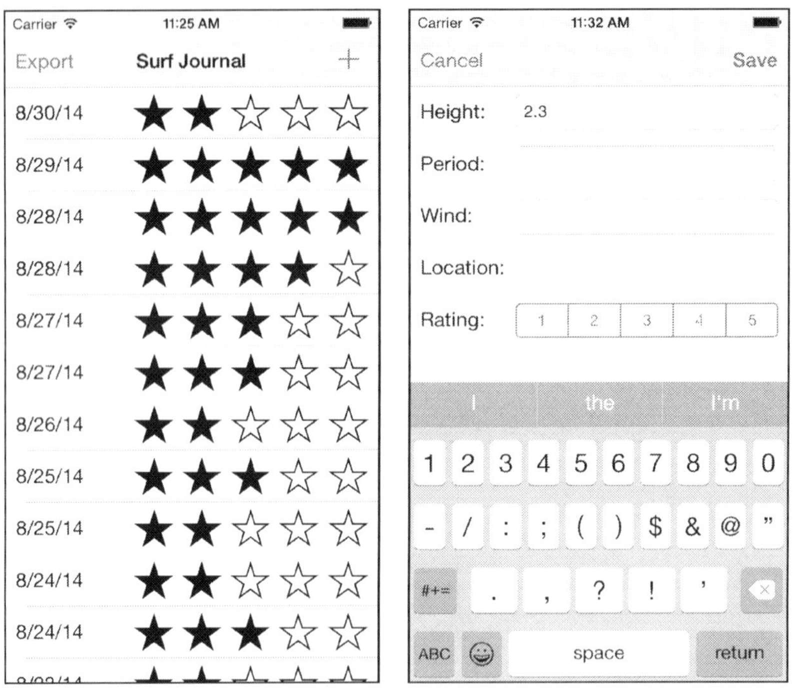

As you can see, the sample app works and has data. Tapping the Export button on the top-left exports the data to a comma-separated values (CSV) file. Tapping the plus (+)

button on the top-right adds a new journal entry. Tapping a row in the list opens the entry in edit mode, letting you make changes or view the details of a surf session.

Although the sample project appears simple, it actually does a lot and will serve as a good base to add multi-context support. First, make sure you have a good understanding of the various classes in the project.

Open the project navigator and take a look at the full list of files in the starter project:

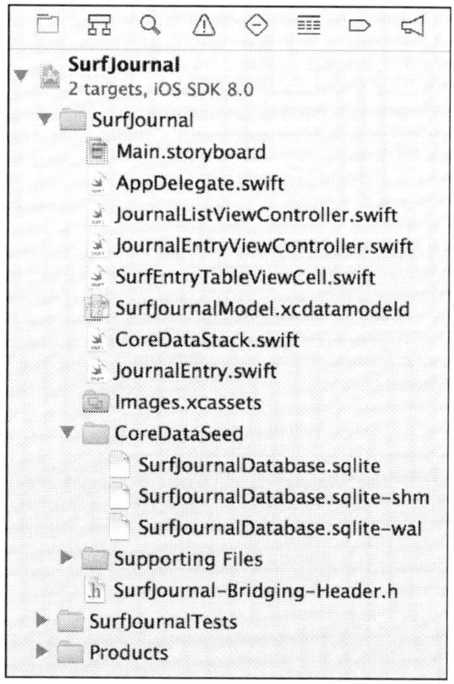

Before jumping into the code, let's briefly go over what each class does for you out of the box. If you've completed the earlier chapters, you should find most of these classes familiar.

- **AppDelegate**: On first launch, the app delegate creates the Core Data stack and sets the `coreDataStack` property on the primary view controller **JournalListViewController**.
- **CoreDataStack**: As in previous chapters, this object contains the cadre of Core Data objects known as the "stack": the context, the model, the persistent store and the persistent store coordinator. Unlike in previous chapters, this time the stack installs a

database that already has data in it on first launch. No need to worry about this just yet; you'll see how it works shortly.

- **JournalListViewController**: The sample project is a one-page table-based application. This file represents that table. If you're curious about its UI elements, head over to **Main.storyboard**. There's a table embedded in a navigation controller and a single prototype cell of type **SurfEntryTableViewCell**.
- **JournalEntryViewController**: This class handles creating and editing surf journal entries. You can see its UI in **Main.storyboard**.
- **JournalEntry:** This class represents a surf journal entry. It is an `NSManagedObject` subclass with six properties for attributes: `date`, `height`, `location`, `period`, `rating` and `wind`. It also includes the CSV export function `csv`. If you're curious about this class's entity definition, head over to **SurfJournalModel.xcdatamodel**.

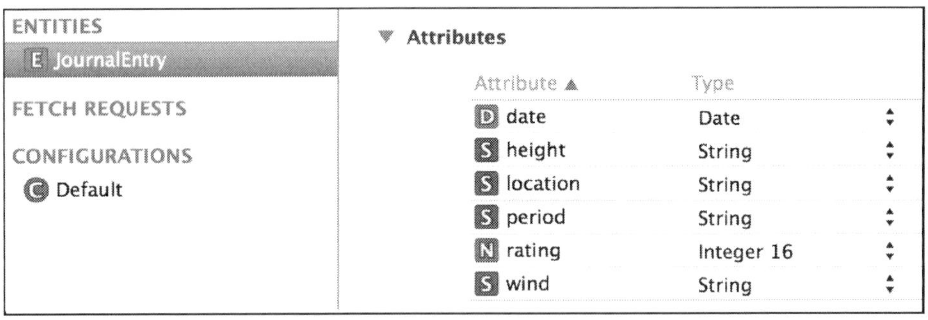

When you first launched the app, it already had a significant amount of data. While the projects in some of the previous chapters import seed data from a JSON file, this sample project comes with a seeded Core Data database. Let's see how it works.

The Core Data stack

Open **CoreDataStack.swift** and find the following code in `init`:

```
// 1
let seededDatabaseURL = bundle
  .URLForResource("SurfJournalDatabase",
    withExtension: "sqlite")

// 2
var fileManagerError:NSError? = nil
let didCopyDatabase = NSFileManager.defaultManager()
  .copyItemAtURL(seededDatabaseURL!, toURL: storeURL,
```

```
    error: &fileManagerError)
// 3
if didCopyDatabase {
```

As you can see, this chapter's version of **CoreDataStack.swift** is a little different. Let's go through the differences step by step:

1. The app bundle comes with a pre-populated Core Data database named **SurfJournalDatabase.sqlite**. To make use of this database, first you have to find it and create a URL reference to it using `URLForResource(_:withExtension:)`.
2. `copyItemAtURL(_:toURL:error:)` attempts to copy the seeded database file to the app's documents directory. If the database file already exists in the documents directory, the copy operation fails. This behavior allows the seeding operation to happen only once, on first launch.
3. On subsequent app launches, the database will already exist and the copy will fail. When the copy operation fails, the variable `didCopyDatabase` will be `false` and the code in the `if`-statement will never execute.

Assume that the app is launching for the first time and therefore `didCopyDatabase` is `true`. Let's see how the rest of the seeding operation works:

```
// 4
fileManagerError = nil
let seededSHMURL = bundle
  .URLForResource("SurfJournalDatabase",
    withExtension: "sqlite-shm")
let shmURL = documentsURL.URLByAppendingPathComponent(
  "SurfJournalDatabase.sqlite-shm")

let didCopySHM = NSFileManager.defaultManager()
  .copyItemAtURL(seededSHMURL!, toURL: shmURL,
    error: &fileManagerError)
if !didCopySHM {
  println("Error seeding Core Data: \(fileManagerError)")
  abort()
}

// 5
fileManagerError = nil
let walURL = documentsURL.URLByAppendingPathComponent(
  "SurfJournalDatabase.sqlite-wal")
let seededWALURL = bundle
  .URLForResource("SurfJournalDatabase",
    withExtension: "sqlite-wal")
```

```
let didCopyWAL = NSFileManager.defaultManager()
  .copyItemAtURL(seededWALURL!, toURL: walURL,
    error: &fileManagerError)
if !didCopyWAL {
  println("Error seeding Core Data: \(fileManagerError)")
  abort()
}
```

To support concurrent reads and writes, SQLite, the persistent store in use by this sample app, utilizes SHM (shared memory file) and WAL (write-ahead logging) files. You don't need to know how these extra files work, but you do need to be aware that they exist and that you need to copy them over when seeding the database. If you fail to copy over these files, the app will work, but it will be missing data.

4. Once the initializer has successfully copied the primary **SurfJournalDatabase.sqlite**, it copies over the support file **SurfJournalDatabase.sqlite-shm**.

5. Finally, the initializer copies over the other support file, **SurfJournalDatabase.sqlite-wal**.

The only reason **SurfJournalDatabase.sqlite**, **SurfJournalDatabase.sqlite-shm** or **SurfJournalDatabase.sqlite-wal** would fail to copy over on first launch is if something really bad happened, such as disk corruption from cosmic radiation. In that case the device, including any apps, would likely also fail. If the app won't work, there's no point in continuing, so the initializer calls `abort`.

> **Note:** We developers often frown upon using `abort`, as it confuses users by causing the app to quit suddenly and without explanation. But this is one example where `abort` is acceptable, since the app needs Core Data to work.
>
> If an app requires Core Data to be useful and Core Data isn't working, there's no point in letting the app continue on, only to fail sometime later in a non-deterministic way. Calling `abort` at least generates a stack trace, which can be helpful when trying to fix the problem.
>
> If your app has support for remote logging or crash reporting, you should log any relevant information that might be helpful for debugging before calling `abort`.

Once the initializer has copied over the pre-populated database and support files, the final step is to add the seeded database store to the persistent store coordinator.

```
// 6
var error: NSError? = nil
let options = [NSInferMappingModelAutomaticallyOption:true,
  NSMigratePersistentStoresAutomaticallyOption:true]
store = psc.addPersistentStoreWithType(NSSQLiteStoreType,
  configuration: nil,
  URL: storeURL,
  options: options,
  error: &error)

// 7
if store == nil {
  println("Error adding persistent store: \(error)")
  abort()
}
```

6. `NSPersistentStoreCoordinator` hands you an `NSPersistentStore` object as a side effect of attaching a persistent store type. You simply have to specify the store type (`NSSQLiteStoreType` in this case), the URL location of the store file and some configuration options.
7. Finally, the initializer checks if the store was successfully created. If it wasn't, the app won't work, so there's no point in continuing; the initializer calls `abort`.

Now that you know something about beginning with a seeded database, let's start learning about multiple managed object contexts by adding a second context with a private queue to the Surf Journal app.

Doing work in the background

If you haven't done so already, tap the Export button at the top-left and then immediately try to scroll the list of surf session journal entries. Notice anything? The export operation will take several seconds and it will prevent the UI from responding to touch events, such as scrolling.

The UI is blocked during the export operation because both the export operation and UI are using the main queue to perform their work. This is the default behavior.

How can you fix this? The traditional way would be to use Grand Central Dispatch to run the export operation on a background queue. However, Core Data managed object contexts are **not** thread-safe. That means you can't just dispatch to a background queue and use the same Core Data stack.

The solution is easy: just add another context for the export operation that uses a private queue rather than the main queue, so the export operation can do its work in the background. This will keep the main queue free for the UI to use.

But before you jump in and fix the problem, you need to understand how the export operation works.

Exporting data

Start by viewing how the app creates the CSV strings for the Core Data entity. Open **JournalEntry.swift** and find `csv()`:

```
func csv() -> String {
  let coalescedHeight = height ?? ""
  let coalescedPeriod = period ?? ""
  let coalescedWind = wind ?? ""
  let coalescedLocation = location ?? ""
  var coalescedRating:String
  if let rating = rating?.intValue {
    coalescedRating = String(rating)
  } else {
    coalescedRating = ""
  }

  return "\(stringForDate()),\(coalescedHeight)," +
    "\(coalescedPeriod),\(coalescedWind)," +
    "\(coalescedLocation),\(coalescedRating)\n"
}
```

As you can see, this `JournalEntry` function returns a comma-separated string of the entity's attributes. Because the `JournalEntry` attributes are allowed to be `nil`, the function uses the `nil` coalescing operator (??) so that it exports an empty string instead of an unhelpful debug message that the attribute is `nil`.

Note: The `nil` coalescing operator (`??`) unwraps an optional if it contains a value; otherwise it returns a default value. For example, the following:

```
let coalescedHeight = height != nil ? height! : ""
```

Can be shortened by using the `nil` coalescing operator:

```
let coalescedHeight = height ?? ""
```

Now that you know how the app creates the CSV strings for an individual journal entry, take a look at how the app saves the CSV file to disk. Switch to **JournalListViewController.swift** and find the following code in `exportCSVFile`:

```
// 1
var fetchRequestError: NSError? = nil
let results = coreDataStack.context.executeFetchRequest(
  self.surfJournalFetchRequest(),
    error: &fetchRequestError)
if results == nil {
  println("ERROR: \(fetchRequestError)")
}

// 2
let exportFilePath =
  NSTemporaryDirectory() + "export.csv"
let exportFileURL =
  NSURL(fileURLWithPath: exportFilePath)!
NSFileManager.defaultManager().createFileAtPath(
  exportFilePath, contents: NSData(), attributes: nil)
```

Let's go through the CSV export code step by step:

1. First, the code retrieves all `JournalEntry` entities by executing a fetch request. The fetch request is the same one used by the fetched results controller and therefore the code uses `surfJournalFetchRequest` to create it, avoiding duplication.

2. The code creates the URL for the exported CSV file by appending the file name ("export.csv") to the output of `NSTemporaryDirectory`. The path returned by `NSTemporaryDirectory` is a unique directory for temporary file storage. This a good place for files that can easily be generated again and don't need to be backed up by iTunes or to iCloud. After creating the export URL, the code calls `createFileAtPath(_:contents:attributes:)` to create the empty file to store

the exported data. If a file already exists at the specified file path, then the code removes it first.

Once the app has the empty file, it can write the CSV data to disk:

```
// 3
var fileHandleError: NSError? = nil
let fileHandle = NSFileHandle(forWritingToURL: exportFileURL,
  error: &fileHandleError)
if let fileHandle = fileHandle {

  // 4
  for object in results! {
    let journalEntry = object as JournalEntry

    fileHandle.seekToEndOfFile()
    let csvData = journalEntry.csv().dataUsingEncoding(
      NSUTF8StringEncoding, allowLossyConversion: false)
    fileHandle.writeData(csvData!)
  }

  // 5
  fileHandle.closeFile()
```

3. First, the app needs to create a file handler for writing, which is simply an object that handles the low-level disk operations necessary for writing data. To create a file handler for writing, the code calls `fileHandleForWritingToURL(_:error:)`.

4. Using a `for-in` statement, the code iterates over all `JournalEntry` entities. During each iteration, the code creates a UTF8-encoded string using `csv` and `dataUsingEncoding(_:allowLossyConversion:)`. It then writes the UTF8 string to disk using `writeData`.

5. Finally, the code closes the export file-writing file handler, since it's no longer needed.

Once the app has written all the data to disk, it shows an alert dialog with the exported file path:

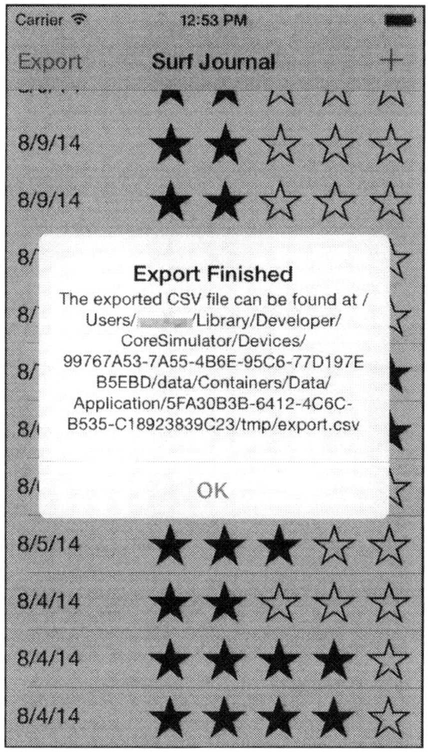

Note: This alert view with the export path is fine for learning purposes, but for a real app, you'll need to provide the user with a way to retrieve the exported CSV file. Attaching the export file to an email is a popular method.

To open the exported CSV file, use Excel, Numbers or your favorite text editor to navigate to and open the file specified in the alert dialog.

If you open the file in Numbers you will see the following:

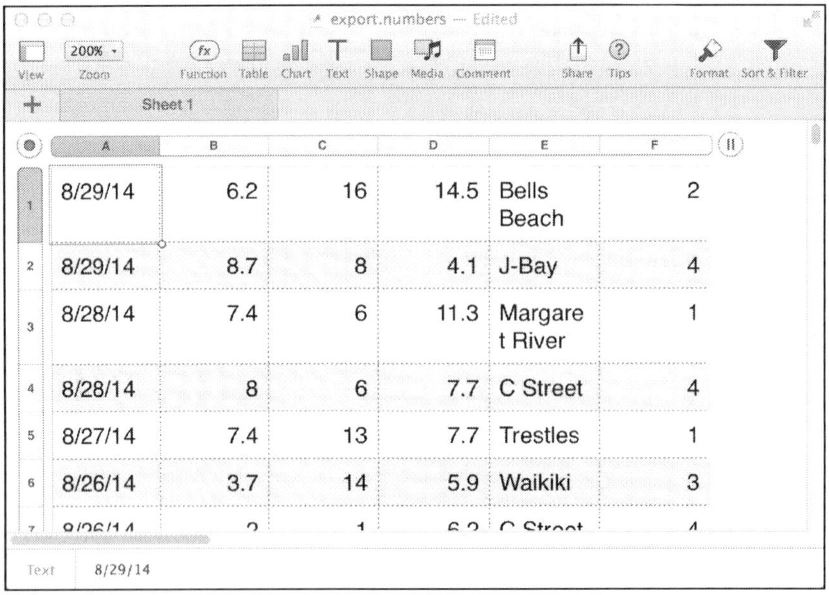

Now that you've seen how the app currently exports data, it's time to make some improvements.

Exporting on a private queue

You want the UI to continue to work while the export is happening. To fix the UI problem, you'll perform the export operation on a private background queue instead of on the main queue.

Open **JournalListViewController.swift** and find the following code in `exportCSVFile`:

```
// 1
var fetchRequestError: NSError? = nil
let results = coreDataStack.context.executeFetchRequest(
  self.surfJournalFetchRequest(),
    error: &fetchRequestError)
if results == nil {
  println("ERROR: \(fetchRequestError)")
}
```

As you saw earlier, this code retrieves all of the journal entries by calling `executeFetchRequest` on the managed object context.

Now replace it with the following:

```
// 1
let privateContext = NSManagedObjectContext(
  concurrencyType: .PrivateQueueConcurrencyType)
privateContext.persistentStoreCoordinator =
  coreDataStack.context.persistentStoreCoordinator

// 2
privateContext.performBlock { () -> Void in

  // 3
  var fetchRequestError:NSError? = nil
  let results = privateContext.executeFetchRequest(
    self.surfJournalFetchRequest(),
      error: &fetchRequestError)
  if results == nil {
    println("ERROR: \(fetchRequestError)")
  }
```

Let's go through the new code, which utilizes a new managed object context, step by step:

1. First, you create a new managed object context called `privateContext` with a concurrency type of `PrivateQueueConcurrencyType`, which specifies that the context will be associated with a private dispatch queue. Once you've created the new context, you assign it the same persistent store coordinator as the main managed object context.

2. Next, you call `performBlock`. This function asynchronously performs the given block on the context's queue. In this case, the queue is private.

3. Just as before, you retrieve all `JournalEntry` entities by executing a fetch request. But this time, you use the private context to execute the fetch request.

Next, find the following code in the same function:

```
self.navigationItem.leftBarButtonItem =
  self.exportBarButtonItem()
println("Export Path: \(exportFilePath)")
self.showExportFinishedAlertView(exportFilePath)

  } else {
      self.navigationItem.leftBarButtonItem =
        self.exportBarButtonItem()
      println("ERROR: \(fileHandleError)")
  }
```

Now replace it with the following:

```
    // 4
    dispatch_async(dispatch_get_main_queue(), { () -> Void in
      self.navigationItem.leftBarButtonItem =
        self.exportBarButtonItem()
      println("Export Path: \(exportFilePath)")
      self.showExportFinishedAlertView(exportFilePath)
    })

  } else {
    dispatch_async(dispatch_get_main_queue(), { () -> Void in
      self.navigationItem.leftBarButtonItem =
        self.exportBarButtonItem()
      println("ERROR: \(fileHandleError)")
    })
  }

} // 5 closing brace for performBlock()
```

4. You should always perform all operations related to the UI, such as showing an alert view when the export operation is finished, on the main queue; otherwise unpredictable things will happen. You use the `dispatch_async` and `dispatch_get_main_queue` to show the final alert view message on the main queue.

5. Finally, the block you opened earlier in step 2 via the `performBlock` call now needs to be closed with a closing curly brace.

> **Note:** There are three concurrency types a managed object context can use:
>
> `ConfinementConcurrencyType` specifies that the context will use the thread confinement pattern and that the developer will be responsible for managing all thread access. You should consider this type deprecated and never use it, as the next two types will cover all use cases.
>
> `PrivateQueueConcurrencyType` specifies that the context will be associated with a private dispatch queue instead of the main queue. This is the type of queue you just used to move the export operation off of the main queue so that it no longer interferes with the UI.

> `MainQueueConcurrencyType`, the default type, specifies that the context will be associated with the main queue. This type is what the main context (`coreDataStack.context`) uses. Any UI operation, such as creating the fetched results controller for the table view, must use a context of this type.

Now that you've moved the export operation to a new context with a private queue, it's time to build and run and see if it works! Give it a go.

You should see exactly what you saw before:

Tap the Export button in the top-left and then immediately try to scroll the list of surf session journal entries. Notice anything different this time? The export operation still takes several seconds to complete, but now the table view continues to scroll during this time. The export operation is no longer blocking the UI.

Cowabunga, dude! Gnarly job making the UI more responsive.

You've just witnessed how creating a new managed object context with a private queue can improve a user's experience with your app. Now let's expand on the use of multiple contexts by examining a child context.

Editing on a scratchpad

Right now, Surf Journal uses the main context (`coreDataStack.context`) when viewing a journal entry or creating a new journal entry. There is nothing wrong with this approach; the starter project works as-is.

But for some apps, such as notes or journal entry apps, you can simplify the app architecture if you think of edits or new entities as a set of changes, like a scratch pad. As the user edits the journal entry, you update the attributes of the managed object. Once the changes are complete, you can either save them or throw them away, depending on the user's desire.

You can think of child managed object contexts the same way: as temporary scratch pads that you can either save, sending the changes to the parent context, or completely throw away.

But what is a child context, technically?

All managed object contexts have a parent store from which you can retrieve and change data in the form of managed objects, such as the `JournalEntry` objects in this project. Typically, the parent store is a persistent store coordinator, which is the case for the main context provided by the `CoreDataStack` class. Alternatively, you can set the parent store for a given context to another managed object context, making it a child context.

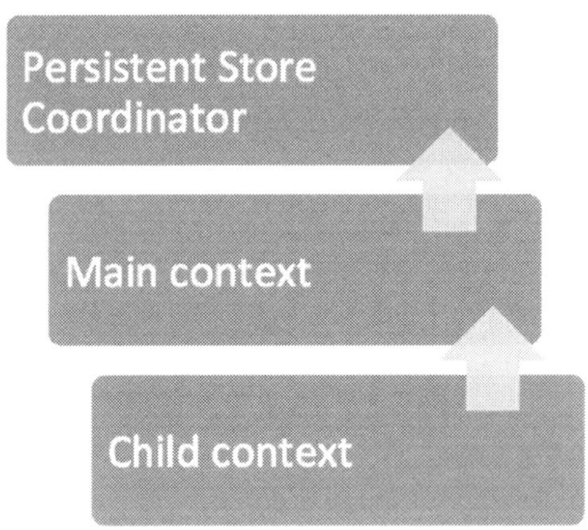

When you save a child context, the changes only go to the parent context. Changes to the parent context are not sent to the persistent store coordinator until the parent context is also saved.

Before you jump in and add a child context, you need to understand how the current viewing and editing operation works.

Viewing and editing

The first part of the operation requires segueing from the main list view to the journal detail view. Open **JournalListViewController.swift** and find `prepareForSegue`:

```
// 1
if segue.identifier == "SegueListToDetail" {

// 2
let indexPath = tableView.indexPathForSelectedRow()
let surfJournalEntry =
  fetchedResultController.objectAtIndexPath(
    indexPath) as JournalEntry

//3
let navigationController = segue.destinationViewController as
  UINavigationController
let detailViewController =
  navigationController.topViewController as
  JournalEntryViewController

//4
detailViewController.journalEntry = surfJournalEntry
detailViewController.context =
  surfJournalEntry.managedObjectContext
detailViewController.delegate = self
```

Let's go through this segue code step by step:

1. There are two segues: "`SegueListToDetail`" and "`SegueListToDetailAdd`". The first, shown in the previous code block, is executed when the user taps on a row in the table view, which she'll do when she wants to view or edit a previous journal entry.

2. To determine which `JournalEntry` entity the user cares about, the code uses `indexPathForSelectedRow` and `objectAtIndexPath`.

3. Now that the app knows what `JournalEntry` the user wants, the app needs to pass it to the `JournalEntryViewController`. The `JournalEntryViewController` is embedded in a navigation controller, so the code uses `topViewController` to retrieve a reference to it.

4. The final step is to set all needed variables on the JournalEntryViewController instance. The surfJournalEntry variable corresponds to the JournalEntry entity retrieved in step 2. The context variable is the managed object context that is to be used for any operation; for now it just uses the main context. The JournalListViewController sets itself as the delegate of the JournalEntryViewController so that it can be informed when the user has completed the edit operation.

Now let's look at "SegueListToDetailAdd". It's very similar to "SegueListToDetail", except that the app creates a new JournalEntry entity instead of retrieving an existing one. The app executes "SegueListToDetailAdd" when the user taps the plus (+) button on the top-right to create a new journal entry.

Now that you know how both segues work, let's look at the JournalEntryViewController protocol. Switch to **JournalEntryViewController.swift** and find the following code at the top of the file:

```
protocol JournalEntryDelegate {
  func didFinishViewController(
    viewController:JournalEntryViewController, didSave:Bool)
}
```

As you can see, the JournalEntryViewController protocol is very short and consists of only didFinishViewController(_:didSave:). This function, which the protocol requires the delegate to implement, indicates that the user is done editing or viewing a journal entry and whether the changes, if there are any, should be saved.

To understand how didFinishViewController(_:didSave:) works, switch back to **JournalListViewController.swift** and find that method:

```
func didFinishViewController(
 viewController:JournalEntryViewController, didSave:Bool) {
  // 1
  if didSave {
    // 2
    var error: NSError? = nil
    let context = viewController.context
    context.performBlock({ () -> Void in
      if context.hasChanges && !context.save(&error) {
        println("Couldn't save: \(error), \(error?.userInfo)")
        abort()
      }
      // 3
      self.coreDataStack.saveContext()
```

```
    })
  }

  // 4
  dismissViewControllerAnimated(true, completion: {})
}
```

Let's go through this delegate method step by step:

1. First, the code checks the `didSave` parameter. It is `true` if the user taps the Save button instead of the Cancel button. If `true`, the app needs to save the user's data.
2. Next, the code saves the `JournalEntryViewController` context inside of a `performBlock` closure. The code sets this context to the main context, which is redundant since there's only one context, but doesn't change the behavior. Once you add a child context to the workflow, the `JournalEntryViewController` context will be different from the main context, making this code necessary. If the save fails, the code prints an error message and aborts the app.
3. The code saves the main context via `saveContext`, defined in **CoreDataStack.swift**, persisting any edits to disk.
4. Finally, the code dismisses the `JournalEntryViewController` using animation.

> **Note:** If a managed object context is of type `MainQueueConcurrencyType`, you don't have to wrap code in `performBlock`, but it doesn't hurt to use it. If you don't know what type the context will be, as is the case in `didFinishViewController(_:didSave:)`, it's safest to use `performBlock` so it will work with both parent and child contexts.

There's a problem with the above implementation—have you spotted it?

When the app adds a new journal entry, it creates a new object and adds it to the managed object context. If the user taps the Cancel button, the app doesn't save the context, but the new object is still present. If the user then adds and saves *another* entry, the cancelled object is still present! You won't see it in the UI unless you've got the patience to scroll all the way to the end, but it will show up at the bottom of the CSV export.

You could solve this problem by deleting the object when the user cancels the view controller. But what if the changes made were more complex, or involved multiple objects, or you had to alter properties of an object as part of the editing workflow?

Canceling could soon get very complicated. It's much easier to use a temporary child context.

Using child contexts for sets of edits

Now that you know how the app currently edits and creates JournalEntry entities, you'll modify the implementation to use a child managed object context as a temporary scratch pad.

It's easy to do—you simply need to modify the segues. Open **JournalListViewController.swift** and find the following code for "SegueListToDetail" in prepareForSegue:

```
detailViewController.journalEntry = surfJournalEntry
detailViewController.context =
  surfJournalEntry.managedObjectContext
detailViewController.delegate = self
```

Now replace that code with the following:

```
// 1
let childContext = NSManagedObjectContext(
  concurrencyType: .MainQueueConcurrencyType)
childContext.parentContext = coreDataStack.context

// 2
let childEntry = childContext.objectWithID(
  surfJournalEntry.objectID) as JournalEntry

// 3
detailViewController.journalEntry = childEntry
detailViewController.context = childContext
detailViewController.delegate = self
```

Let's go through the modified segue code step by step:

1. First, you create a new managed object context called childContext with a MainQueueConcurrencyType. Instead of setting a persistent store coordinator as you normally do when creating a managed object context, you set a parent context. Here, you set the parentContext to the main context.
2. Using the child context's objectWithID function, you retrieve the relevant journal entry. You must use objectWithID to retrieve the journal entry because managed objects are specific to the context that created them. However, objectID values are

not specific to a single context, so you can use them when you need to access objects in multiple contexts.

3. Finally, you set all needed variables on the `JournalEntryViewController` instance. This time, you use the `childEntry` and `childContext` instead of the original `surfJournalEntry` and `surfJournalEntry.managedObjectContext`.

> **Note:** You might be wondering why you need to pass both the managed object and the managed object context to the `detailViewController` since managed objects already have a context variable. You need to pass the context because managed objects only have a weak reference to the context. If you don't pass the context, ARC will remove the context from memory (since nothing else is retaining it) and the app will not behave as expected.

It's time to build and run! Give it a go.

Just like before, the app should behave exactly the same. In this case, no visible changes to the app are a good thing. The user can still tap on a row to view and edit a surf session journal entry.

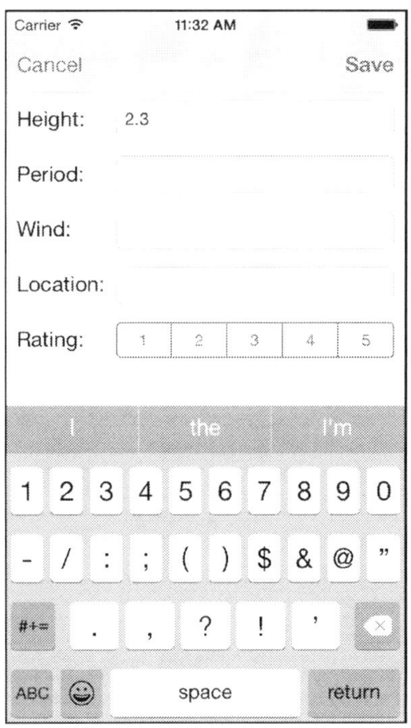

But behind the scenes, by using a child context as a container for edits to a journal entry, you've reduced the complexity of your app's architecture. With the edits on a separate context, cancelling or saving managed object changes is trivial.

Nice work, dude! You're no longer a kook when it comes to multiple managed object contexts. Bodacious!

Where to go from here?

If you followed this chapter all the way through, you've turned an app with a single managed object context into an app with multiple contexts. You'll find the final project for this chapter in the **SurfJournal-Final** folder.

First, you improved UI responsiveness by performing the export operation on a managed object context with a private queue.

Next, you improved the app's architecture by creating a child context and using it like a scratch pad.

You also learned how to talk like a surfer. That's a good day's work!

Challenge

With your newfound knowledge, try to update `"SegueListToDetailAdd"` so that it also utilizes a child context when adding a new journal entry.

Just like before, you'll need to create a child context that has the main context as its parent. You'll also need to remember to create the new entry on the correct context.

If you get stuck, check out the project with the challenge solution in the **SurfJournal-Challenge** folder.

Conclusion

We hope this book has helped you get up to speed with Core Data and Swift! You're well on your way to developing your own high-performance apps with well-designed models and unit tests.

As you've seen, you can use Core Data to model all kinds of data—from names and addresses to images and the relationships in between. We encourage you to find where Core Data and its object graph-based persistence can work for you and give it a try.

If you have any questions or comments as you continue to use Core Data, please stop by our forums at http://www.raywenderlich.com/forums.

Thank you again for purchasing this book. Your continued support is what makes the tutorials, books, videos and other things we do at raywenderlich.com possible—we truly appreciate it!

Wishing you speed, stability and smooth migrations in all your Core Data adventures,

– Pietro, Saul, Aaron, Matthew, Richard, Bradley and Greg

The *Core Data by Tutorials* team

37056201R00163

Made in the USA
Charleston, SC
27 December 2014